Blacks
in
Classical Music

BLACKS
IN
CLASSICAL MUSIC

*A Bibliographical Guide to Composers,
Performers, and Ensembles*

Compiled by
John Gray

Music Reference Collection, Number 15

Greenwood Press
New York • Westport, Connecticut • London

Library of Congress Cataloging-in-Publication Data

Gray, John, 1962-
Blacks in classical music : a bibliographical guide to composers,
performers, and ensembles / compiled by John Gray.
p. cm. — (Music reference collection, ISSN 0736-7740 ; no.
15)
Includes indexes.
ISBN 0-313-26056-7 (lib. bdg. : alk. paper)
1. Musicians, Black—Bibliography. 2. Afro-American musicians—
Bibliography. I. Title. II. Series.
ML128.B45G7 1988
016.78'043'08996—dc19 87-37567

British Library Cataloguing in Publication Data is available.

Library of Congress Catalog Card Number: 87-37567
ISBN: 0-313-26056-7
ISSN: 0736-7740

First published in 1988

Greenwood Press, Inc.
88 Post Road West, Westport, Connecticut 06881

Printed in the United States of America

∞™

The paper used in this book complies with the
Permanent Paper Standard issued by the National
Information Standards Organization (Z39.48-1984).

10 9 8 7 6 5 4 3 2 1

Contents

Acknowledgments

The current work owes its existence to three major factors:
(1) the acquisition of that miracle of modern technology,
the personal computer; (2) the continued support and
forbearance of my mother; and (3) a lengthy letter from
black music scholar, writer, and editor Samuel A. Floyd,
whose criticisms and suggestions concerning an earlier,
preliminary draft of this work planted the necessary seed
for its realization. To these three I now pay tribute. In
addition, I would also like to pay homage to all those
artists, sung and unsung, who have continued to persevere,
often despite ridiculous odds, in perpetuating their art and
demanding a place for themselves in the concert halls and
cultural forums of the world. It is to them that this work
is dedicated.

Introduction

This work is the first fruit of what I hope to be a series of
well-organized, comprehensive, and idiom-specific bibliographies in black music.

Directed at both the student and scholar, this work
attempts to fill one of black music research's major gaps,
that is, the need for a reference guide to the full range of
black activity in classical music. Through its chapters on
composers, symphony and concert artists, conductors, symphony
orchestras, concert and opera singers and opera companies,
Blacks in Classical Music strives to provide just that. In
addition, it trys to build on the foundations laid by
researcher/scholars Eileen Southern and Dominique-Rene de
Lerma in their efforts to bring the black musical legacy to
new levels of prominence and accessibility. I hope that the
information contained herein will provide a stimulus to new
work similar to the one begun by these two pioneers.

For users new to the subject I suggest consulting some of
the works cited at the beginning of the book's General
Section, particularly those by Raoul Abdul, Tilford Brooks,
Maud Cuney Hare, Hildred Roach, and Eileen Southern. These
works will provide both the general and background
information necessary to begin more focused studies. After
this, more advanced researchers will want to check the Index
of Artists at the back of this volume. There they will find a
complete listing of references for the more than three hundred
artists and ensembles referred to in this work. This index
should act as a guide to the bibliography's riches.

A NOTE ON METHODOLOGY

I attempted to be as inclusive in my coverage as possible,
with my starting point being the list of names provided in
James A. Standifer and Barbara Reeder's Source Book of
African and Afro-American Materials for Music Educators
(Washington, D.C., 1972). Thus, references span from the mid-
1700s to the present, and range geographically from Europe and

Africa to the United States, Latin America and the Caribbean. My criteria for inclusion was simple: First, the artist under consideration must have been identified at some point as a person of color and, second, that the individual has been, or is now, active as a performer or writer of Western or Western-derived "art music." The one exception to these rules is the inclusion of composer Alejandro Garcia Caturla whose contribution to the integration of Afro-Cuban elements into Cuban classical music seems to me to override his white parentage.

In order to achieve this comprehensiveness I performed a manual search of all standard finding sources along with all pertinent bibliographies, biographical dictionaries, and even the bibliographies of most of the book length studies listed in this work. (See the Reference Works chapter for a complete listing of items checked). In addition, where citations were incomplete I tried to view the works myself so as to provide as complete bibliographical information as possible. With the exception of the Music Index, all indexes were searched up to their latest issue as of September 1987. In the case of the Music Index, due to the fact that there is no cumulative annual volume available after the 1979-1980 edition, I decided that a manual search of the monthly issues beyond that date was impractical. However, as future volumes of this and other indexes are compiled I intend to add all relevant citations to updated editions of this bibliography. I would also like to encourage all interested students, scholars, researchers, and even relatives of artists included to help make future editions more complete by sending me a record of any items that I may have omitted.

In this first edition of the bibliography I decided to include comprehensive listings of concert reviews for all but six of the concert and opera singers covered. For these six-- superstars Martina Arroyo, Kathleen Battle, Grace Bumbry, Jessye Norman, George Shirley, and Shirley Verrett--I collected only a portion (primarily from the early years of their careers) of a much larger body of reviews to be found under the names of the individual singers in the yearly volumes of the Music Index. Readers wishing a more complete picture of this material should check that index. In the Individual Vocalists section another exception was also made: Due to the publication of recent comprehensive bibliographies on both Marian Anderson and Paul Robeson, I decided to limit my entries on each of these artists to a few major works. Those interested in further information on either artist should consult the bibliographies to be found under their names. With regard to the nationality of individual artists I have chosen to note the country of birth only of non-American born artists. For birth and death dates I attempted to be as up-to-date and complete as possible, relying in large part on the landmark scholarship of Eileen Southern's Biographical Dictionary of Afro- American and African Musicians (Westport, 1982) and the annual obituary listings to be found in fall issues of The Black Perspective in Music.

Blacks
in
Classical Music

I

General Section

1
General Section

Abdul, Raoul. Blacks in Classical Music: A Personal History. New York: Dodd, Mead & Co., 1977. 253pp.

_____. Famous Black Entertainers of Today. New York: Dodd, Mead and Co., 1974.

Bardolph, Richard. The Negro Vanguard. New York: Rinehart & Co., 1959, pp. 156-166.

Brawley, Benjamin. The Negro Genius. New York: Biblo & Tannen, 1969. (Reprint of 1937 ed.)

Brooks, Tilford. America's Black Musical Heritage. Englewood, NJ: Prentice-Hall, 1984.

Butcher, Margaret Just. The Negro in American Culture. New York: Mentor Books, 1957.

De Lerma, Dominique-Rene. Black Concert and Recital Music: A Provisional Repertoire List. Beverly Hills, CA: Theodore Front Musical Literature, 1975.

_____, ed. Black Music in Our Culture. Kent: Kent State University Press, 1970.

_____, ed. Classical Black Heritage. Detroit, MI: Classical Black Heritage, 1976.

Dumerve, Constantin. Histoire de la Musique en Haiti. Port-au-Prince, Haiti: Imprimerie des Antilles, 1968.

Gordon, E. Harrison. Black Classical Musicians of the Twentieth Century. New York: MSS Information Corporation, 1977. 146pp.

Hare, Maud Cuney. Negro Musicians and Their Music. New York: Da Capo Press, 1974. (Reprint of 1936 ed.)

Jackson, Clyde Owen. The Songs of Our Years: A Study of Negro Folk Music. New York: Exposition Press, 1968. 54pp.

Locke, Alain. The Negro and His Music. Port Washington, NY: Kennikat Press, 1968, pp. 36-42, 118-128.

Lovingood, Penman. Famous Modern Negro Musicians. 2nd ed. New York: Da Capo Press, 1978. 68pp. (Reprint of 1921 ed.)

Nelson, Rose K., and Dorothy L. Cole. "Concert Music." In The Negro's Contribution to Music in America. New York: Service Bureau for Intercultural Education, 1941, pp. 21-23.

Perry, Edward G. "Negro Creative Musicians." In Negro, comp. Nancy Cunard. Edited and abridged by Hugh Ford. New York: Frederick Ungar Publishing Co., 1984, pp. 220-223. (Orig. 1934)

Roach, Hildred. Black American Music: Past and Present. Miami: Krieger Publishing Co., 1985. 2 Vols. (Orig. 1971)

Southern, Eileen. The Music of Black Americans: A History. 2nd ed. New York: W.W. Norton, 1983.

Spearman, Rawn W., and Carlesta Henderson. "The Black Art Song: An Interdisciplinary Encounter." In 1980 Conference on Black Music Research; Papers. Nashville: Fisk University, 1981, pp. 107-114.

Trotter, James M. Music and Some Highly Musical People. Chicago: Afro-Am Press, 1969. (Reprint of 1878 ed.)

Dissertations

Adkins, Aldrich Wendell. "The Development of Black Art Songs." Dissertation (D.M.A.) University of Texas, 1971. 161pp.

Harris, Robert A. "Serious Music and the Negro Musician, 1900-1924: An Oral History." Thesis, Wayne State University, 1962. 106pp. [Held by the Detroit Public Library, E. Azalia Hackley Collection.]

Journals and Newsletters

AAMOA Reports (formerly AAMOA News), Vol. 1, No. 1- , June 1969- . Newsletter of the Afro-American Music Opportunities Association.

Black Music Research Journal, Vol. 1- , 1980- . (Center for Black Music Research, Columbia College, 600 South Michigan Avenue, Chicago, Illinois 60605). Editor: Samuel A. Floyd, Jr. Annual.

Black Music Research Newsletter, Vol. 1- , 1977- . (Same address as above).

The Black Perspective in Music, Vol. 1, No. 1, Spring 1973- .
(Foundation for Research in the Afro-American Creative Arts,
Inc., Drawer I, Cambria Heights, NY 11411). Editor: Dr.
Eileen Southern. Semi-Annual.

Lyric; A Review of Serious Music (later years have the
subtitle "A Magazine of the Fine Arts"), Vol. 1, No. 1,
September 1958- . (Lyric Publishing Company, 7826 Crenshaw
Blvd., Los Angeles, CA 90043). Monthly. [Held by the Music
Research Division of the Performing Arts Research Center at
Lincoln Center and the Library of Congress.]

The Negro Music Journal, Vol. 1, No. 1 - Vol. 2, No. 15
(1902-1903). [Reprinted by Negro Universities Press,
Westport, CT, 1970.]

Tones and Overtones. Montgomery: Department of Music,
Alabama State University, 1954-, Vol. 1-. Issued
irregularly. Editor: John Duncan.

Articles

Allen, William Duncan. "Musings of a Music Columnist."
Black Perspective in Music, Vol. 1, No. 2 (Fall 1973):
107-114.

Borroff, Edith. "Black Musicians in the United States."
American Music Teacher (November-December 1972): 30-31, 41.

"Classical Blacks." Sepia (March 1982): 5.

De Lerma, Dominique-Rene. "Black Concert and Recital Music:
A Glimpse of Afro-Caribbean Music in the Early 17th Century."
Black Music Research Newsletter, Vol. 4, No. 2 (Fall 1980):
2-3.

Euba, Akin. "Criteria for the Evaluation of New African Art
Music." Transition, Vol. 9, No. 49 (July-September 1975):
46-50.

_____. "Traditional Elements as the Basis of New African
Art Music." African Urban Notes, Vol. 5, No. 4 (1970):
52-62.

Henahan, Donal. "Does a Cultural Apartheid Dominate the
Arts?" New York Times (August 28 1977): Sec. II, p. 7.
Article on discrimination against blacks in the fields of
music and opera.

Henderson, W. "Negro Musicians." Musical News, Vol. 67
(August 1924).

Hentoff, Nat. "Classical Color Line?" Down Beat (March 7
1952): 1.

Holt, Nora. "The Chronological History of the NANM." The
Black Perspective in Music, Vol. 2, No. 2 (Fall 1974):
234-235. History of the National Association of Negro
Musicians.

"In Retrospect: Black Music Concerts in Carnegie Hall, 1912-1915." The Black Perspective in Music, Vol. 6, No. 1 (Spring 1978): 71-88.

Kirby, Percival R. "The Use of European Musical Techniques by the Non-European Peoples of Southern Africa." Journal of the International Folk Music Council, Vol. 11 (1959): 37-40.

Moe, Orin. "A Question of Value: Black Concert Music and Criticism." Black Music Research Journal (1986): 57-66.

Molleson, John. "The Negro in Music." Musical America (December 1963): 24-25, 267.

"Negro History Week to Feature Musicians and Their Music." Negro History Bulletin, Vol. 2, No. 5 (February 1939). Special issue including biographical sketches of a number of black composers and singers.

"Negroes in Musical Careers." America (May 12 1956): 152.

Novak, Benjamin. "Opening Doors in Music." Negro History Bulletin (January 1971): 10-14.

Russcol, Herbert. "Can The Negro Overcome the Classical Music Establishment?" High Fidelity (August 1968): 42-46. (See also responses in November 1968 issue, pp. 6+.)

Salazar, Adolfo. "El Movimento Africanista en la Musica de Arte Cubana." Estudios Cubanos, Vol. 2 (1938): 3-18.

Schomburg, Arthur A. "West Indian Composers and Musicians." Opportunity, Vol. 4 (1926): 353-356, 363.

Stevenson, Robert. "The Afro-American Legacy to 1800." The Musical Quarterly, Vol. 54, No. 4 (October 1968): 475-502.

Wilson, Warren George. "Black Classical Musicians: Their Struggle to the Top." Essence (September 1974): 51, 91, 94, 97.

Wright, Josephine R. B. "Black Women in Classical Music - 1850-1930." Women's Studies Quarterly (Fall 1984).

Wyatt, Lucius R. "The State and Future Needs of Research in Black Concert and Recital Music." Black Music Research Journal (1980): 80-94.

Media Materials

Black Composers and Performers Discuss Black Music. Produced under the auspices of the Black Music Seminar, Summer 1968, Dominique-Rene de Lerma, director. WNET-TV. 45 min., b&w, 1969. Black musicians (T. J. Anderson, David Baker, Natalie Hinderas, Hale Smith and Olly Wilson) discuss the problems of defining "black music."

Conversations from Wingspread: Blacks and Classical Music
(Radio program).   Racine, Wis.: Johnson Foundation, 1975.
Duration: 28'17" min.   [Sound recording held by the
Schomburg Collection, NYPL, NYC -- Sc Audio C-353].   Program
documenting a meeting sponsored by the Afro-American Music
Opportunities Association, Inc., on the involvement of the
black musician in classical music.   It features a history of
black influence in classical music dating from the 18th
century to modern times, profiles contemporary Afro-American
composers and their styles, details performances over the
years of black symphonic composers, the problems of gaining
acceptance of black classical music, the need for making
this music more widely available, foreign interest in black
classical music, recordings of this music, and options
available to the black performer.   Moderator: Dan Price.
Participants: Paul Freeman, George Walker.

2
Composers

GENERAL

Books

Afro-America Sings. Detroit, MI: Detroit Public Schools, 1971. Contains brief biographies of composers E. Rogie Clark, Charles D. Coleman, S. Coleridge-Taylor, R. N. Dett, Ulysses Kay, and William Grant Still.

Anderson, T. J. "Black Composers and the Avant-Garde." In Readings in Black American Music, ed. Eileen Southern. 2nd ed. New York: Norton, 1983, pp. 318-322. (Orig. published in Black Music in Our Culture, ed. Dominique-Rene de Lerma. Kent: Kent State University Press, 1970.)

Brown, Marian Tally. Classical Black Heritage presents Black Composers Series (Columbia Records) volumes 1, 2, 3, 4; Instructional Manual. Detroit, MI: Music for Education and Cultural Appreciation, 1976. 21pp. [See Discography section for reviews of the Black Composers Series lps.]

Carter, Madison H. An Annotated Catalog of Composers of African Ancestry. New York: Vantage Books, 1986.

Celebration of Black Composers. New York: AFRAM Associates, 1979. 44pp. [Held by the Schomburg Collection, NYPL, NYC -- Sc Micro R-3668]. Reprint of newspaper articles.

Cohen, Aaron I. International Encyclopedia of Women Composers. New York: R. R. Bowker, 1981. Contains short profiles of Lettie M. Beckon, M. Bonds, S. G. DuBois, L. Evanti, E. A. Hackley, Helen Hagan, M. Harris, T. Leon, L. McLin, D. R. Moore, U. S. Moore, J. Perry, E. Pittman, F. B. Price, P. D. Schuyler.

De Lerma, Dominique-Rene. A Name List of Black Composers. Minneapolis, MN: AAMOA Press, 1973. 76pp. (AAMOA Resource Papers).

_____, ed. <u>Symposium of Symphonic Music by Black
Composers, Baltimore</u>. Minneapolis, MN: The AAMOA Press,
1973.

Green, Mildred Denby. <u>Black Women Composers: A Genesis</u>.
New York: Twayne Publishers, 1983.

Huskisson, Yvonne. <u>The Bantu Composers of Southern Africa</u>.
Johannesburg, South Africa: South African Broadcasting
Corporation, 1969. 335pp.

Suthern, Orrin Clayton. <u>The Case of the Negro Composer</u>.
Lincoln University: American Studies Institute, Lincoln
University, ca. 1964. 24pp.

Dissertations, Theses and Unpublished Papers

Braithwaite, Coleridge. "A Survey of the Lives and Creative
Activities of Some Negro Composers." Dissertation (Ed.D.)
Columbia University, Teachers College, 1952.

Brooks, Tilford U. "A Historical Study of Black Music and
Selected Twentieth Century Black Composers and Their Role in
American Society: A Source Book for Teachers." Dissertation
(Ed.D.) Washington University, 1972. 795pp.

Caldwell, Hansonia Laverne. "Black Idioms in Opera as
Manifested in the Works of Six Afro-American Composers."
Dissertation (Ph.D., Musicology) University of Southern
California, 1974. 285pp.

_____. "The Plight of the Black Composer of Opera
(1890-1970)." Paper presented at ASUC meeting, November 15,
1974, Albuquerque, New Mexico.

Davidson, Celia Elizabeth. "Operas by Afro-American
Composers: A Critical Survey and Analysis of Selected
Works." Dissertation (Ph.D., Theory) Catholic University,
1980. 526pp.

Evans, Arthur L. "The Development of the Negro Spiritual as
Choral Art Music by Afro-American Composers with an
Annotated Guide to the Performance of Selected Spirituals."
Dissertation (Ph.D.) University of Miami, 1972.

Gardner, Effie Tyler. "An Analysis of the Technique and
Style of Selected Black American Composers of Contemporary
Choral Music." Dissertation (Ph.D.) Michigan State
University, 1979. 440pp.

Harris, Carl Gordon. "A Study of Characteristic Stylistic
Trends Found in the Choral Works of a Selected Group of
Afro-American Composers and Arrangers." Dissertation
(D.M.A., Performance) University of Missouri, Kansas City,
1973. 178pp.

Hildreth, John. "Keyboard Works of Selected Black
Composers." Dissertation (Ph.D.) Northwestern University,
1978. 419pp.

Horne, Aaron. "Twentieth-Century Solo and Ensemble Music for Woodwinds by Black Composers." Dissertation (D.M.A., Performance) University of Iowa, 1976. 121pp.

Ryder, Georgia A. "Melodic and Rhythmic Elements of American Negro Folk Songs as Employed in Cantatas by Selected American Composers Between 1932 and 1967." Dissertation (Ph.D.) New York University, 1970.

Tocus, Clarence Spencer. "The Negro Idiom in American Musical Composition." Thesis (M.M.) University of Southern California, 1941.

Wilson, Dora. "Selected Piano Compositions of Contemporary Black Composers in America." Thesis, Washington University, 1970.

Wyatt, Lucius R. "The Mid-Twentieth Century Orchestral Variation, 1953-1963: An Analysis and Comparison of Selected Works by Major Composers." Dissertations (Ph.D., Music) Eastman School of Music, 1974. 488pp.

Articles

Arvey, Verna. "Is There a Place For Negroes in Classical Music?" Upbeat (January 1939).

_____. "Outstanding Achievements of Negro Composers." Musical America, Vol. 60, No. 3 (March 1942): 120, 171.

_____. "Symphonies in Black." Music Journal, Vol. 32, No. 4 (April 1974): 27-28, 32-36.

Carter, Warrick L. "Black Composers: Their Contribution to Serious Music." Orchestral News (Cleveland, OH), Vol. 11, No. 3 (June 1972): 6, 10.

"Chance for Colored Composers." The Cadenza (September 1902): 14.

Clark, Edgar R. "The Negro Composer: A Mid-Century Review." Negro History Bulletin (March 1954): 132-133.

Cunningham, C. "How Black is Black? Symposium and Performance Sessions in Houston." High Fidelity (January 1975): 24-26.

Current, Gloster B. "Celebration of Black Composers: Black Music at the Philharmonic." The Crisis, Vol. 85, No. 1 (January 1978): 7-13.

De Lerma, Dominique-Rene. "Black Women Composers." Black Arts Review, Vol. 2, No. 2 (July-August 1979): 8.

Duncan, John. "Negro Composers of Opera." Negro History Bulletin, Vol. 29 (January 1966): 79-80.

Ericson, Raymond. "Collection." New York Times (November 21 1971): Sec. 2, p. 20. On the establishing of a collection of over a 100 works by 19th century black composers Joseph White, Lucien and Sidney Lambert, and Edmund Dede at Brooklyn College's Institute for Studies in American Music. [See Research Centers section for more information.]

Goines, Leonard. "Contemporary Black Composers." Allegro (July-August 1973): 8.

Harris, Carl G. "Three Schools of Black Choral Composers and Arrangers 1900-1970." The Choral Journal (April 1974): 11-18.

Herrema, Robert D. "Choral Music by Black Composers." Choral Journal, Vol. 10, No. 4 (January 1970): 15-17.

Kolodin, Irving. "The Racial Bias in Music (Serious)." Saturday Review (December 26 1970): 43. Review of Natalie Hinderas LP of music by black composers.

Saal, H. "Black Composers." Newsweek (April 15 1974): 82. [Ulysses Kay, Olly Wilson, Chevalier de Saint-Georges]

"Saluting Negro Composers." Tones and Overtones [Montgomery, Ala.] (Spring 1954). Special black composers issue.

Society of Black Composers. Newsletter (New York). [Held by the Schomburg Collection, NYPL, NYC -- Sc Ser. -N .S653].

Southern, Eileen. "America's Black Composers of Classical Music." Music Educators Journal (November 1975): 46-59.

Still, William Grant. "Are Negro Composers Handicapped?" Baton (March 1937).

_____, and Verna Arvey. "Serious Music: New Field for the Negro." Variety (January 1 1955).

Wilson, Olly. "The Black American Composer." The Black Perspective in Music, Vol. 1, No. 1 (Spring 1973): 33-36. [Reprinted in Readings in Black American Music, ed. Eileen Southern. 2nd ed. New York: Norton, 1983, pp. 327-332.]

Yuhasz, Marie Joy. "Black Composers and Their Piano Music." American Music Teacher, Vol. 19, No. 4 (February-March 1970): 24-26; Vol. 19, No. 5 (April-May 1970): 28-29, 46. [T. J. Anderson, Margaret Bonds, R. Nathaniel Dett, Ulysses Kay, Florence B. Price, W. G. Still, Howard Swanson]

Newspaper Articles

"Blacks." New York Times (April 26, 1970): Sec. 2, p. 22. Letters in response to Harold C. Schonberg "Black Swan" article of April 12 1970 (see below).

Kerner, Leighton. "The Whiter Half of a Black Heritage."
Village Voice (September 1977): 71-72. Review of Black
composers concert.

Moore, Carman. "Does a Black Mozart - Or Stravinsky - Wait
in the Wings?" New York Times (September 7, 1969): Sec. 2,
pp. 23, 28. General piece on black music and Society of
Black Composers.

"Of Black Art Music." New York Times (November 2, 1969):
Sec. 2, p. 34. Letters in response to Carman Moore article
of Sept. 7, 1969 (see above).

Schonberg, Harold C. "The Black Swan That Sang for
Nobility." New York Times (April 12, 1970): Sec. 2, p. 15.
Piece on Paul Glass study of black composers and
instrumentalists in 19th century U.S.

INDIVIDUAL COMPOSERS

LESLIE ADAMS (1932-   )

Fain, Kenneth. "Artists and Their Art: Composers."
Cultural Post/National Endowment for the Arts (May-June
1979).

Finn, Robert. "Slave Rebellion Before Civil War Stirs Work
on Opera." Cleveland Plain Dealer (January 1, 1983).

Green-Crocheron, Karen. "Meet Composer Leslie Adams."
Galore Magazine [Cleveland, OH] (May 1982).

T. J. ANDERSON (1928-   )

Anderson, T. J. "Black Composers and the Avant-Garde." In
Readings in Black American Music, ed. Eileen Southern. 2nd
ed. New York: Norton, 1983, pp. 318-322. (Orig. published
in Black Music in Our Culture, ed. Dominique-Rene de Lerma.
Kent: Kent State University Press, 1970.)

Southern, Eileen. "Anderson, T(homas) J(efferson)." In The
New Grove Dictionary of Music and Musicians, Vol. 1, pp.
400-401.

_____. "Anderson, T(homas) J(efferson)." In The New
Grove Dictionary of American Music, Vol. 1, pp. 49-50.

_____. Biographical Dictionary of Afro-American and
African Musicians. Westport,CT: Greenwood Press, 1982, pp.
14-15.

"Thomas J. Anderson." In The Black Composer Speaks, eds.
David N. Baker, Lida M. Belt, and Herman H. Hudson.
Metuchen, NJ: Scarecrow Press, 1978, pp. 1-14.

Who's Who Among Black Americans (1975-76).

Dissertations

Oliver, Christine E.   "Selected Orchestral Works of Thomas
J. Anderson, Arthur Cunningham, Talib Rasul Hakim, and Olly
Wilson: A Descriptive Study." Dissertation (Ph.D.) Florida
State University, 1978.

Thompson, Bruce.   "Musical Style and Compositional
Techniques in Selected Works of T. J. Anderson."
Dissertation (Ph.D.) Indiana University, 1978.   228pp.

Articles

Anderson, T. J.   "Educating the Creative Musician."   ISME
Yearbook (Mainz, W. Germany), No. 4 (1977): 27-30.

Chicago Defender Accent (September 30 1978): 12.

Hunt, J.   "Conversation with Thomas J. Anderson: Blacks and
the Classics." The Black Perspective in Music, Vol. 1, No.
2 (Fall 1973): 156-165.

Pittsburgh Courier (September 30 1978): 7.

Thompson, Bruce.   "T. J. Anderson: Composer." The Sinfonian
Newsletter (February 1975): 4+.

Trythall, Gilbert.   "T. J. Anderson." BMI: The Many Worlds
of Music (April 1969): 17.

RUSSELL ATKINS (1926-   )

Free Lance, Vol. 14 (1970).   Special Russell Atkins issue.

Southern, Eileen.   Biographical Dictionary of Afro-American
and African Musicians.   Westport, CT: Greenwood Press, 1982,
p. 21.

Stuckenschmidt, H. H.   "Contemporary Techniques in
Twentieth-Century Music." The Musical Quarterly, Vol. 49
(January 1963): 11.

DAVID BAKER (1931-   )

"David Nathaniel Baker."   In The Black Composer Speaks, eds.
David N. Baker, Lida M. Belt, and Herman C. Hudson.
Metuchen, NJ: Scarecrow Press, 1978, pp. 15-69.

Moore, Carman.   "Baker, David (Nathaniel)."   In The New
Grove Dictionary of American Music, Vol. 1, p. 114.

Negro Almanac, pp. 851-852.

Southern, Eileen.   Biographical Dictionary of Afro-American
and African Musicians.   Westport, CT: Greenwood Press, 1982,
p. 23.

Thomas, Andre Jerome. "A Study of the Selected Masses of
Twentieth-Century Black Composers: Margaret Bonds, Robert
Ray, George Walker, and David Baker." Dissertation (D.M.A.)
University of Illinois at Urbana-Champaign, 1983. 214pp.

Articles

Bourne, Mike. "Defining Black Music: An Interview with
David Baker." Down Beat, Vol. 36 (September 18, 1969):
14-15.

Courier-Journal Magazine (February 10 1974): 29+.

"Professor Plays Jazz." Ebony (May 1970): 104-111.

EDWARD BOATNER (1898-1981)

Hare, Maud Cuney. Negro Musicians and Their Music.
Washington, D.C.: Associated Press, 1936, p. 347.

Southern, Eileen. Biographical Dictionary of Afro-American
and African Musicians. Westport, CT: Greenwood Press, 1982,
p. 39.

Tischler, Alice. "Edward Boatner." In Fifteen Black
American Composers: A Bibliography of Their Works. Detroit,
MI: Information Coordinators, 1981, pp. 15-35.

Articles

Chicago Defender (July 16 1927).

Chicago Defender (August 30 1930).

Chicago Defender (December 30 1933).

Chicago Defender Accent (January 27 1979): 1.

New York Times (September 30 1971): 49.

Obituary. The Black Perspective in Music, Vol. 9, No. 2
(Fall 1981): 239.

MARGARET BONDS (1913-1972)

Abdul, Raoul. "Black Women in Music." In Blacks in
Classical Music. New York: Dodd, Mead & Co., 1977, pp.
53-55.

Ammer, Christine. Unsung: A History of Women in American
Music. Westport, CT: Greenwood Press, 1980, pp. 153-156.

Bonds, Margaret. "A Reminiscence." In The Negro in Music
and Art, ed. Lindsay Patterson. New York: Publishers
Company, Inc., 1968, pp. 190-193.

Green, Mildred Denby. "A Study of the Lives and Works of Five Black Women Composers in America." Dissertation (Ph.D.) University of Oklahoma, 1975.

_____. "Margaret Bonds." In Black Women Composers: A Genesis. Boston: Twayne Publishers, 1983, pp. 47-70.

Hare, Maud Cuney. Negro Musicians and Their Music. Washington, D.C.: Associated Publishers, 1936, pp. 263-264.

Jackson, Barbara Garvey. "Bonds, Margaret (Allison)." In The New Grove Dictionary of American Music, Vol. 1, pp. 255-256.

Southern, Eileen. Biographical Dictionary of Afro-American and African Musicians. Westport, CT: Greenwood Press, 1982, pp. 40-41.

Thomas, Andre Jerome. "A Study of the Selected Masses of Twentieth-Century Black Composers: Margaret Bonds, Robert Ray, George Walker, and David Baker." Dissertation (D.M.A.) University of Illinois at Urbana-Champaign, 1983. 214pp.

Tischler, Alice. "Margaret Allison Bonds." In Fifteen Black American Composers: A Bibliography of Their Works. Detroit, MI: Information Coordinators, 1981, pp. 37-57.

Articles

Chicago Defender (October 15 1932).

Chicago Defender (December 10 1938).

Chicago Defender (November 4 1939).

"Margaret Bonds." Musical America (February 1952): 218.

New York Age (May 6 1944).

New York Amsterdam News (August 5 1944).

Obituaries

Black Perspective in Music, Vol. 1, No. 2 (Fall 1973): 197.

Chicago Defender (January 13 1973): 20.

Jet (May 18 1972): 62.

Tuesday-at-Home (December 1973): 4.

Variety (May 10 1972): 86.

J. HAROLD BROWN (1902-   )

Buckner, Reginald. "A History of Music Education in the Black Community of Kansas City, Kansas, 1905-1954." Dissertation (Ph.D.) University of Minnesota, 1974.

Hare, Maud Cuney. <u>Negro Musicians and Their Music</u>.
Washington, D.C.: Associated Publishers, 1936, pp. 262-263,
342.

Southern, Eileen. <u>Biographical Dictionary of Afro-American</u>
<u>and African Musicians</u>. Westport, CT: Greenwood Press, 1982,
pp. 50-51.

HARRY T. BURLEIGH (1866-1949)

Adams, Russell L. <u>Great Negroes, Past and Present</u>. 3rd ed.
Chicago: Afro-Am Publishing Co., 1969, p. 176.

Allison, Roland. "Burleigh, Harry [Henry] T(hacker)." In
<u>The New Grove Dictionary of American Music</u>, Vol. 1, p. 327.

Bullock, Ralph W. <u>In Spite of Handicaps</u>. New York:
Association Press, 1927, pp. 35-42.

"Burleigh, Harry Thacker." <u>Dictionary Catalogue of the</u>
<u>Schomburg Collection</u>, Vol. 2, pp. 1121-1124. Contains an
extensive list of Burleigh scores held by the Schomburg.

Fax, Elton C. "Burleigh, Harry T[hacker]." In <u>Dictionary</u>
<u>of American Negro Biography</u>, eds. Rayford W. Logan and
Michael R. Winston. New York: W.W. Norton, 1982, pp. 79-80.

Hammond, Lily. <u>In the Vanguard of a Race</u>. New York:
Council of Women for Home Missions, and Missionary Education
Movement of the United States and Canada, 1922.

Hare, Maud Cuney. <u>Negro Musicians and Their Music</u>.
Washington, D.C.: Associated Publishers, 1936, pp. 239,
261-262, 275-276, 323-329.

Johnson, James Weldon. <u>Along This Way: The Autobiography of</u>
<u>James Weldon Johnson</u>. New York: Viking Press, 1933, pp.
172-174.

Lovingood, Penman. <u>Famous Modern Negro Musicians</u>. New
York: Da Capo Press, 1978. (Reprint of 1921 ed.)

Robinson, Wilhelmena S. <u>Historical Afro-American</u>
<u>Biographies</u> (International Library of Afro-American Life and
History). Washington, D.C.: Associated Publishers, 1976,
pp. 57-58.

Southern, Eileen. <u>Biographical Dictionary of Afro-American</u>
<u>and African Musicians</u>. Westport, CT: Greenwood Press, 1982,
pp. 55-57.

_____. "Burleigh, Harry [Henry] T(hacker)." In <u>The New</u>
<u>Grove Dictionary of Music and Musicians</u>, Vol. 3, pp. 421-422.

_____. "Burleigh, Henry Thacker." <u>Dictionary of</u>
<u>American Biography</u>, Supplement 4, pp. 125-126.

Toppin, Edgar A.   A Biographical History of Blacks in America since 1528. New York: David McKay, 1971, p. 262.

Dissertations

Allison, Roland Lewis. "Classification of the Vocal Works of Harry T. Burleigh (1866-1949) and Some Suggestions for Their Use in Teaching Diction In Singing." Dissertation (Ph.D.) Indiana University, 1966. 2 Vols.

Articles

"American Negro Whose Music Stirs the Blood of Warring Italy." Current Opinion (August 1916): 100-101.

Arvey, Verna. "Afro-American Music Memo." Music Journal, Vol. 27 (November 1969): 68-69.

"Burleigh, Harry T." Current Biography 1941, pp. 120-121.

"Don't Be Weary, Traveler: For SATB." Musical Courier (March 1 1957): 38.

"Harry Thacker Burleigh: Standard Bearer of Negro Music." Our World, Vol. 1, No. 1 (April 1946): 15.

"He Got J. P. Morgan's Vote." Negro Digest (April 1944): 15-16. [Condensed from Time (February 14 1944) article.]

H.K.M. "'Deep River' Popularizes a Composer: The Rise And Progress of Harry T. Burleigh Through His Negro Melodies into the Large Vogue of Song Recitals." In The Black Perspective in Music, Vol. 2, No. 1 (Spring 1974): 75-79. [Reprinted from Boston Evening Transcript (March 10 1917)].

"H. T. Burleigh: Composer by Divine Right." Musical America, Vol. 23, No. 26 (April 29 1916).

Janifer, Ellsworth. "H. T. Burleigh Ten Years Later." Phylon, Vol. 21 (Summer 1960): 144-154.

Lee, Henry. "Swing Low, Sweet Chariot." The Black Perspective in Music, Vol. 2, No. 1 (Spring 1974): 84-86. [Reprinted from Coronet (July 1947)].

Murray, Charlotte W. "The Story of Harry T. Burleigh." The Papers of The Hymn Society, Vol. 17, No. 4 (October 1966): 101-111.

"Negro Composer Nominated for ASCAP Board." PM [New York] (August 6 1941): 20.

Negro History Bulletin (February 1939): 35-36. Biographical sketch.

New York Age (October 29, 1938): 7.

New York Herald Tribune (May 22, 1933): 13.

New York Herald Tribune (March 26, 1934): 7.

New York Herald Tribune (August 7, 1941): 10.

New York World (October 25, 1924).

"Spiritualist." Time (May 29 1939): 49.

Tobias, C. H.   "Some Outstanding Negro Christians."
Missionary Review of the World (June 1936): 297.

Walton, Lester A.   "Harry T. Burleigh Honored To-Day at St.
George's."   The Black Perspective in Music, Vol. 2, No. 1
(Spring 1974): 80-83.   [Reprinted from Schomburg Collection
Clippings File (March 30 1924)].

Obituaries

American Organist (October 1949): 357.

Billboard (September 24 1949): 50.

Current Biography 1949.

Diapason (October 1 1949): 2.

Down Beat (October 21 1949): 10, 19.

Etude (November 1949): 56.

Musical America (October 1949): 26.

Newsweek (September 26 1949): 64.

New York Times (September 13 1949): 29.

Time (September 19 1949): 79.

Variety (September 14 1949): 63.

Wilson Library Bulletin (November 1949): 200.

Woodson, Carter G.   "Harry Thacker Burleigh."   Journal of
Negro History (January 1950): 104-105.

ALEJANDRO GARCIA CATURLA (1906-1940) - Cuba

Asche, Charles Byron.   "Cuban Folklore Traditions and
Twentieth Century Idioms in the Piano Music of Amadeo Roldan
and Alejandro Carcia Caturla."   Dissertation (D.M.A.)
University of Texas at Austin, 1983.   101pp.

Garcia Caturla, Alejandro.   "The Development of Cuban
Music." In American Composers on American Music, ed. Henry
Cowell.   Stanford: Stanford University Press, 1933, pp.
173-174.   (Repr. New York: Frederick Ungar Publishing Co.,
1961.)

"Garcia Caturla, Alejandro." In Encyclopedia of Latin
America, ed. Helen Delpar. New York: McGraw-Hill, 1974, p.
247.

Vega, Aurelio de la.   "Caturla, Alejandro Garcia." In The
New Grove Dictionary of Music and Musicians, Vol. 4, p.15.

Articles

Boletin Musical (April 1945): 3.

Carpentier, Alejo.   "Alejandro Garcia Caturla." Composers
of the Americas: Biographical Data and Catalogs of Their
Works, Vol. 3 (1957): 83-95.

"Chronological Catalogue of Works by the Cuban Composer,
Alejandro Garcia Caturla." Boletin de Musica y Artes
Visuales. Union Panamericana (Washington, D.C.), No. 74/76
(April-June 1956): 25-30.

Cowell, Henry.   "Roldan and Caturla of Cuba." Modern Music,
Vol. 18, No. 2 (January-February 1941): 98-99.

Garcia Caturla, Alejandro.   "Posibilidades Sinfonicas de le
Musica Afrocubana." Musicalia (La Habana), Vol. 2, No. 7
(July-August 1929): 15-17.

Nodal-Consuegra, Roberto.   "La Figura de Alejandro Garcia
Caturla en la Musica Cubana." Exilio (New York), Vol. 5,
No. 2 (Summer 1971): 125-132.

Salazar, Adolfo.   "La Obra Musical de Alejandro Caturla."
Revista Cubana, Vol. 11, No. 31 (January 1938): 5-43.

Obituaries

Munoz de Quevado, Maria.   "Alejandro Garcia Caturla."
Boletin Latinoamericano de Musical (Bogota), ano 5, tomo 5
(October 1941): 611-616.

_____.   "Maestro Alejandro Garcia Caturla." Estudios
Afrocubanos, Vol. 4, No. 1/4 (1940): 58-64.

Musical Record (June 1941): 9.

Musicalia, Vol. 2, No. 2 (January-February 1941): 8-14.

Slonimsky, Nicolas.   "Caturla of Cuba." Modern Music, Vol.
17, No. 2 (1940): 76-80.

EDGAR ROGIE CLARK (1913-1978)

Clark, Edgar Rogie. Moment Musical: Ten Selected Newspaper
Articles. Fort Valley, GA: Fort Valley State College,
Department of Music, 1940.

Southern, Eileen. Biographical Dictionary of Afro-American
and African Musicians. Westport, CT: Greenwood Press, 1982,
pp. 71-72.

Tischler, Alice. "Edgar Rogie Clark." In Fifteen Black
American Composers: A Bibliography of Their Works. Detroit,
MI: Information Coordinators, 1981, pp. 59-76.

Who's Who in Colored America, 1950.

Articles

"Faith of an American." Survey (July 1951): 313.

New York Amsterdam News (June 29 1944).

Obituary. The Black Perspective in Music, Vol. 6, No. 2
(Fall 1978): 240.

SAMUEL COLERIDGE-TAYLOR (1875-1912) - England

Abdul, Raoul. "Coleridge-Taylor: 100 Years Later." In
Blacks in Classical Music. New York: Dodd, Mead & Co.,
1977, pp. 26-28.

Adams, Russell L. Great Negroes, Past and Present.
Chicago: Afro-Am Publishing Co., 1969, p. 173.

Banfield, Stephen. "Coleridge-Taylor, Samuel." In The New
Grove Dictionary of Music and Musicians, Vol. 4, pp. 528-530.

Child, Harold Hannyngton. "Coleridge-Taylor, Samuel." In
The Dictionary of National Biography. Twentieth Century
1912-1921, eds. H. W. C. Davis and J. R. H. Weaver. London:
Oxford Unversity Press, 1927, pp. 122-123.

Clelland, Frank Wesley. "Samuel Coleridge-Taylor." In
Rising Above Color, ed. Philip H. Lotz. Freeport, NY: Books
for Libraries, 1972, pp. 38-49. (Reprint of 1943 ed.)

Coleridge-Taylor, Avril Gwendolyn. The Heritage of Samuel
Coleridge-Taylor. London: Dobson, 1979. 160pp.

Coleridge-Taylor, Jessie. A Memory Sketch; or, Personal
Reminiscences of My Husband, Genius and Musician, Samuel
Coleridge-Taylor, 1875-1912. New York: Bognor Regis; and
London: J. Crowther Ltd., 1943. 76pp.

Coleridge-Taylor, Samuel. Twenty-four Negro melodies.
Transcribed for the piano with preface by Booker T.
Washington. Boston: Oliver Ditson, 1905.

"Coleridge-Taylor, Samuel." Dictionary Catalogue of the
Schomburg Collection, Vol. 3, pp. 1476-1482. Extensive
catalogue of Coleridge-Taylor scores and their location in
the Schomburg Collection.

DuBois, W. E. B. Darkwater: Voices from within the Veil.
New York: AMS Press, 1969, pp. 193-202. (Reprint of 1920
ed.)

Ewen, David. "Samuel Coleridge-Taylor 1875-1912." In
Composers Since 1900. New York: H.W. Wilson Co., 1969, pp.
132-134.

Fleming, Beatrice J., and Marion J. Pryde. "Samuel
Coleridge-Taylor." In Distinguished Negroes Abroad.
Washington, D.C.: Associated Publishers, 1946, pp. 130-138.

Foss, Hubert. "Samuel Coleridge-Taylor: A Calm Life." In
The Music Masters, Vol. 4. The Twentieth Century, ed. by
A.L. Bacharach. Harmondsworth, Middlesex: Penguin Books,
1957, pp. 71-77.

Hare, Maud Cuney. Negro Musicians and Their Music.
Washington, D.C.: Associated Publishers, 1936, pp. 244-247,
308-314.

Haynes, Elizabeth R. "Samuel Coleridge-Taylor." In Unsung
Heroes. New York: DuBois & Dill, 1921, pp. 127-149.

Hennessy, Maurice. Our Pioneers. Lagos, Nigeria: Crownbird
Publishers, 1951.

Lovingood, Penman. Famous Modern Negro Musicians. New
York: Da Capo Press, 1978. (Reprint of 1921 ed.)

Nettel, R. Music in the Five Towns 1840-1914: A Study of
the Social Influence of Music in an Industrial District.
London: Oxford University Press, 1944, pp. 42-43, 46, 50, 87.

Robinson, Wilhelmena S. Historical Afro-American
Biographies (International Library of Afro-American Life and
History). Washington, D.C.: Associated Publishers, 1976, p.
65.

Rogers, J. A. "Samuel Coleridge-Taylor: England's 'Greatest
Musical Sensation' (1875-1912)." In World's Great Men of
Color. Vol. II. New York: Macmillan, 1972, pp. 146-153.
(Orig. 1947)

Sayers, William C. Berwick. Samuel Coleridge-Taylor,
Musician: His Life and Letters. Arlington Heights, IL:
Metro Books, 1969. (Reprint of 1915 ed.)

Scobie, Edward. Black Brittania: A History of Blacks in
Britain. Chicago: Johnson Publishing Co., 1972, pp. 134-135.

Southern, Eileen. Biographical Dictionary of Afro-American
and African Musicians. Westport, CT: Greenwood Press, 1982,
pp. 78-79.

Tortolano, William. Samuel Coleridge-Taylor: Anglo-Black
Composer, 1875-1912. Metuchen, NJ: Scarecrow Press, 1977.

White, Clarence Cameron. "Samuel Coleridge Taylor." Reel
4, No. 8 of Clarence Cameron White's Paper's. [Held by the
Schomburg Collection, NYPL, NYC - Sc Micro R-2474 reel 4]

Dissertations

Batchman, John C. "Samuel Coleridge-Taylor: An Analysis of
Selected Piano Works and an Examination of His Influence on
Black American Musicians." Dissertation (Ed.D.) Washington
University, 1977. 500pp.

Braithwaite, Coleridge Alexander. "The Achievements and
Contributions to the History of Music by Samuel
Coleridge-Taylor, Colored English Musician." Thesis (B.A.)
Harvard University, 1939. 150pp.

Carter, Nathan M. "Samuel Coleridge-Taylor: His Life and
Works." Dissertation (D.M.A.) Peabody Institute, 1984.
392pp.

Phillips, Theodore DeWitt. "The Life and Musical
Compositions of Samuel Coleridge-Taylor." Thesis (M.Mus.)
Oberlin College, 1935. 119pp.

Articles

Antcliffe, Herbert. "Some Notes on Coleridge-Taylor."
Musical Quarterly, Vol. 8 (April 1922): 180-192.

Coleridge-Taylor, Avril. "The Music of Coleridge-Taylor."
Sound (April 1947).

_____. "My Father and His Music." Fanfare [Birmingham,
Eng] (1948).

_____. "Samuel Coleridge-Taylor." Music and Musicians
[London] (August 1975): 6-7.

"Coleridge-Taylor's 'Hiawatha.'" The Vocalist, No. 1
(1902): 70.

"The Composer and the Organ Grinder." Musical Box Society
International, Vol. 22, No. 3 (1976): 240. [Reprinted from
Etude (April 1916)].

Dashwood, Gwendolyn Coleridge-Taylor. "Samuel
Coleridge-Taylor: Reminiscences." The Crisis (February 19
1925): 158-161.

Gaul, Harvey B. "Samuel Coleridge-Taylor, An Afro-British
Composer." Musician (August 1917): 577.

Green, Jeffrey P. "A Note on Coleridge-Taylor's Origins."
Musical Times (August 1985): 461.

_____. "Perceptions of Samuel Coleridge-Taylor on His
Death." New Community (Summer 1985): 321-325.

_____. "Samuel Coleridge-Taylor: A Postscript." The Black Perspective in Music, Vol. 14, No. 3 (Fall 1986): 259-266.

"Here and There." (Centenary) Gramophone, Vol. 53 (August 1975): 307.

Hill, Roy. "Conversation with...Fannie Douglass: Reminiscences of Yesteryear." The Black Perspective in Music, Vol. 2, No. 1 (Spring 1974): 57-58.

Janifer, Ellsworth. "Samuel Coleridge-Taylor in Washington." Phylon (Summer 1967): 185-196.

Kramer, A. W. "Impressions of Coleridge-Taylor's New Violin Concerto." Musician (March 1914): 201.

McGilchrist, Paul, and Jeffrey Green. "Some Recent Findings on Samuel Coleridge-Taylor." The Black Perspective in Music (Fall 1985): 151-178.

"Mr. Coleridge-Taylor." The Musical Times (London), Vol. 1 (March 1909): 153.

"Samuel Coleridge-Taylor." The Canon, Vol. 10 (July 1957): 399.

Simms, L. M. "Samuel Coleridge-Taylor, Black Composer." The Crisis (November 1971): 291-292.

Sprigge, S. S. "Copyright and the Case of Coleridge Taylor." English Review [London] (February 1913): 446-453.

Storer, H. J. "S. Coleridge Taylor. A Sketch." The Negro Music Journal, Vol. 1, No. 1 (September 1902): 3-4. (Reprinted from The Musical Record and Review).

Terrell, Mary Church. "The Great Anglo-African Composer." The Voice of the Negro (January 1905): 667.

_____. "Samuel Coleridge-Taylor: The Anglo-African Composer." Independent (November 24 1904): 1191-1195.

Tortolano, William. "Samuel Coleridge-Taylor." Music/The AGO and RCCO Magazine (August 1975): 25-27.

Tuesday (October 1968): 30-31+.

Young, Percy. "Samuel Coleridge-Taylor, 1875-1912." The Musical Times (London), Vol. 116 (August 1975): 703.

Obituaries

"Higher Music of Negroes." Literary Digest (October 5 1912): 505.

The Monthly Musical Record, Vol. 43 (1912): 253.

New York Times (September 2 1912): 9.

Parry, H. "Samuel Coleridge-Taylor: A Tribute." The
Musical Times (London), Vol. 53 (October 1912): 637.

ROQUE CORDERO (1917-   ) - Panama

Chase, Gilbert. "Cordero, Roque." In The New Grove
Dictionary of Music and Musicians, Vol. 4, pp. 766-767.

_____. "Cordero, Roque." In The New Grove Dictionary of
American Music, Vol. 1, p. 510.

Orrego-Salas, Juan A. "Cordero, Roque." In Encyclopedia of
Latin America, ed. Helen Delpar. New York: McGraw-Hill,
1974, p. 171.

Southern, Eileen. Biographical Dictionary of Afro-American
and African Musicians. Westport, CT: Greenwood Press, 1982,
pp. 84-85.

Dissertations

Brawand, John Edward. "The Violin Works of Roque Cordero."
Dissertation (Ph.D.) University of Texas, Austin, 1985.
125pp.

Dobay, Thomas Raymond de. "A Stylistic Analysis of Selected
Short Works by Roque Cordero." Thesis (M.M., Theory)
Indiana University, 1971. 89pp.

Engle, Susan Stancil. "A Harmonic Analysis and Comparison
of Selected Twelve-Tone Compositions of Krenek and
Cordero." Thesis (M.M.) Indiana University, 1969. 145pp.

Ennett, Dorothy. "An Analysis and Comparison of Selected
Piano Sonatas by Three Contemporary Black Composers: George
Walker, Howard Swanson, and Roque Cordero." Dissertation
(Ph.D., Education) New York University, 1973.

Gooch, Priscilla Filos. "The Piano in the Works of Roque
Cordero." Doctoral Document (D.M.) Indiana University,
1974. 87pp.

Hegemann, Sarah C. "The Latin American Piano Sonata in the
Twentieth Century." Document (D.M.) Indiana University,
1975. 142pp.

Jakey, Lauren R. "An Analysis of Six Latin American Works
for Violin and Piano Composed Since 1945." Document (D.M.)
Indiana University, 1971. 176pp.

Nichols, David C. "The String Quartet in Contemporary Latin
American Music: A Study of Nationalisation and Cosmopolitan
Influences." Thesis (M.M.) Indiana University, 1965. 239pp.

Articles

"Among Latin American Composers - Leaders." Pan Pipes, Vol. 62, No. 3 (1970): 2-5.

Chase, Gilbert.   "Composed by Cordero." Americas, Vol. 10 (July 1958): 7.

_____. "Creative Trends in Latin American Music." Tempo, No. 48 (1958): 28.

Chicago Defender Accent (September 30 1978): 4.

Cordero, Roque. "Nacionalismo versus Dodecafonismo." Revista Musical Chilena (September-October 1959): 28-38.

Kyle, M. K. "AmerAllegro." Pan Pipes, Vol. 60, No. 2 (1968): 66.

_____. "AmerAllegro." Pan Pipes, Vol. 61, No. 2 (1969): 48-49.

_____. "AmerAllegro." Pan Pipes, Vol. 62, No. 2 (1970): 56.

_____. "AmerAllegro." Pan Pipes, Vol. 64, No. 2 (1972): 49-50.

_____. "AmerAllegro." Pan Pipes, Vol. 65, No. 2 (1973): 47.

_____. "AmerAllegro." Pan Pipes, Vol. 66, No. 2 (1974): 46.

_____. "AmerAllegro." Pan Pipes, Vol. 69, No. 2 (1977): 38.

_____. "AmerAllegro." Pan Pipes, Vol. 70, No. 2 (1978): 37.

_____. "AmerAllegro." Pan Pipes, Vol. 71, No. 2 (1979): 29.

Orrego Salas, J. "The Young Generation of Latin American Composers: Backgrounds and Perspectives." Inter-American Music Bulletin, No. 38 (November 1963): 8-9.

"Roque Cordero." Composers of the Americas, Vol. 8 (1962): 59-64.

Sider, R. R. "Roque Cordero: The Composer and His Style Seen in Three Representative Works." Interamerican Music Bulletin, No. 61 (September 1967): 1-17.

_____. "Central America and Its Composers." Interamerican Music Bulletin, Vol. 77 (May 1970): 12-14.

Stevens, Halsey. Notes, Vol. 30, No. 1 (September 1973): 155. Review of Cordero's "Segunda Sinfonia."

Vega, Aurelio de la. "Latin American Composers in the
United States." Latin American Music Review, Vol. 1, No. 2
(1980): 167-168.

ARTHUR CUNNINGHAM (1928-   )

Abdul, Raoul. "Recordings: Black Piano Music." In Blacks
in Classical Music. New York: Dodd, Mead & Co., 1977, p. 63.

Caldwell, Hansonia Laverne. "Black Idioms in Opera as
Manifested in the Works of Six Afro-American Composers."
Dissertation (Ph.D.) University of Southern California,
1974. Includes a discussion of Cunningham's His Natural
Grace.

Oliver, Christine E. "Selected Orchestral Works of Thomas
J. Anderson, Arthur Cunningham, Talib Rasul Hakim, and Olly
Wilson: A Descriptive Study." Dissertation (Ph.D.) Florida
State University, 1978.

Southern, Eileen. Biographical Dictionary of Afro-American
and African Musicians. Westport, CT: Greenwood Press, 1982,
p. 90.

_____. "Cunningham, Arthur." In The New Grove
Dictionary of Music and Musicians, Vol. 5, p. 97.

_____. "Cunningham, Arthur." In The New Grove
Dictionary of American Music, Vol. 1, p. 555.

Tischler, Alice. "Arthur Cunningham." In Fifteen Black
American Composers: A Bibliography of Their Works. Detroit,
MI: Information Coordinators, 1981, pp. 79-105.

NOEL DA COSTA (1930-   ) - Nigeria

Abdul, Raoul. "Folk Music in Symphonic Garb." In Blacks in
Classical Music. New York: Dodd, Mead & Co., 1977, pp.
45-47.

McDaniel, L. "Out of the Black Church." American Organist,
Vol. 13, No. 5 (1979): 34-38.

Moore, Carman. "Da Costa, Noel (George)." In The New Grove
Dictionary of American Music, Vol. 1, p. 560.

"Noel G. Da Costa." The Black Composer Speaks, ed. David N.
Baker, Lida N. Belt, and Herman C. Hudson. Metuchen, NJ:
Scarecrow Press, 1978, pp. 70-92.

Southern, Eileen. Biographical Dictionary of Afro-American
and African Musicians. Westport, CT: Greenwood Press, 1982,
p. 91.

ANTHONY DAVIS (1951-)

Mandel, Howard.   "Caught: X (The Life and Times of Malcolm
X) New York City Opera/New York." Down Beat (January 1987):
50.

Rowes, B.   "For Composer Anthony Davis, X Marks the Premiere
of What May Be the First Major Black Opera." People, Vol.
26 (October 6 1986): 129-130.

Seligman, G.   "The Road to X." Opera News, Vol. 51
(September 1986): 28-30.

"X." New Yorker, Vol. 61 (October 28 1985): 83+.   On the
Philadelphia production of X.

Newspapers Articles

Blair, Gwenda.   "Evening the Score." Daily News Magazine
(September 28, 1986): 20-24.   Interviews with Anthony,
Christopher and Thulani Davis on their operatic
collaboration "X", about the late civil rights leader
Malcolm X.

Kerner, Leighton.   "Malcolm X, His Opera." Village Voice
(October 29 1985): 82.

_____.   "The Overhaul of X." Village Voice (October 21
1986): 78.

Piccarella, John.   "Malcolm in Midtown: The Terrain of
Recent Black American History Shifts Beneath X's Operatic
Conventions." Village Voice (October 21 1986): 77-78.

Rockwell, John.   "Malcolm X - Hero To Some, Racist to Others
- Is Now the Stuff of Opera." New York Times (September 28,
1986): Sec. 2, pp. 1, 21.

_____.   Review of Philadelphia pre-debut production of
"X". New York Times (October 11 1985): Sec. III, p. 3.

Schneider, Steve.   "Cable TV Notes - Series Explores
Contemporary Composers and Choreographers." New York Times
(September 21 1986): Sec. 2.   Short notice on video profile
of Anthony Davis's opera "X" (The Life and Times of Malcolm
X).

Videos

Works and Process at the Guggenheim: "X." WNET-TV, 30 min.,
1987.   Performance excerpts and discussion with the
composer, Anthony Davis; the librettist, Thulani Davis, and
his brother Christopher, creator of the story.   Moderator,
Christopher Keene.

WILLIAM LEVI DAWSON (1899-   )

Abdul, Raoul. "Spotlight on Black Composers." In Blacks in Classical Music. New York: Dodd, Mead & Co., 1977, pp. 58-59.

Adams, Russell L. Great Negroes, Past and Present. 3rd ed. Chicago: Afro-Am Publishing Co., 1969, p. 181.

Hare, Maud Cuney. Negro Musicians and Their Music. Washington, D.C.: Associated Publishers, 1936, pp. 263, 343-344.

Reis, Claire. Composers in America: Biographical Sketches of Contemporary Composers with a Record of Their Works. New York: The Macmillan Co., 1947, p. 93.

Robinson, Wilhelmena S. Historical Afro-American Biographies (International Library of Afro-American Life and History). Washington, D.C.: Associated Publishers, 1976, pp. 180-181.

Southern, Eileen. Biographical Dictionary of Afro-American and African Musicians. Westport, CT: Greenwood Press, 1982, pp. 98-99.

_____. "Dawson, William Levi." In The New Grove Dictionary of Music and Musicians, Vol. 5, p. 286.

_____. "Dawson, William Levi." In The New Grove Dictionary of American Music, Vol. 1, p. 590.

Spady, James G., ed. William Dawson: A Umum Tribute and a Marvelous Journey. Philadelphia, PA: Creative Artists' Workshop, 1981. 60pp.

Tischler, Alice. "William Levi Dawson." In Fifteen Black American Composers: A Bibliography of Their Works. Detroit, MI: Information Coordinators, 1981, pp. 107-123.

Dissertations

Malone, M. H. "William Levi Dawson: American Music Educator." Dissertation (Ph.D.) Florida State University, 1981.

Articles

Afro-American Magazine (May 6 1975): 1.

Atlanta University Bulletin (March 1974): 17-19.

Chicago Defender Accent (June 15 1974): 5.

Dawson, William L. "Interpretation of the Religious Folk-Songs of the American Negro." Etude (March 1955): 11+.

"The First Negro Symphony." Literary Digest (March 4 1933).

Fuller, C. "Black Composer Dawson's Works Honored."
Biography News (March 1974): 263.

"Hail Mary!" Cincinnati Symphony Program Notes (December 17
1954): 17.

Jet (April 2 1970): 16-21.

Missouri Journal of Research in Music Education, Vol. 4, No.
3 (1979): 104-105. An analysis of the Negro Folk Symphony.

"Negro Composer: Philadelphia Orchestra Plays Dawson's
Symphony." News-Week (November 24 1934): 27.

"Negro Folk Symphony is Performed Amid Cheers." Literary
Digest (December 1 1934): 24.

"Schools. Music and Artists, Vol. 4, No. 4 (1971): 40.

EDMUND DEDE (1827-1903)

Christian, Marcus B. "Dede, Edmund." In Dictionary of
American Negro Biography, eds. Rayford W. Logan and Michael
R. Winston. New York: W.W. Norton, 1982, pp. 168-169.

Desdunes, Rodolphe. Our People and Our History. Trans. by
Dorothea Olga McCants. Baton Rouge: Louisiana State
University Press, 1973. [Originally published as Nos Hommes
et Notre Histoire. Montreal, 1911.]

Hare, Maud Cuney. Negro Musicians and Their Music.
Washington, D.C.: Associated Publishers, 1936, pp. 237-238.

Southern, Eileen. Biographical Dictionary of Afro-American
and African Musicians. Westport, CT: Greenwood Press, 1982,
p. 101.

Trotter, James M. Music and Some Highly Musical People.
Chicago: Afro-Am Press, 1969, pp. 340-341. (Orig. 1878)

R. NATHANIEL DETT (1882-1943)

Abdul, Raoul. "Recordings: Black Piano Music." In Blacks
in Classical Music. New York: Dodd, Mead & Co., 1977, pp.
61-62.

Adams, Russell L. Great Negroes, Past and Present.
Chicago: Afro-Am Publishing Co., 1969, p. 177.

Dett, R. Nathaniel. The Collected Piano Works.
Introductions by Dominique-Rene de Lerma and Vivian
McBrier. Evanston, IL: Summy-Birchard, 1973. 195pp.

Fisher, Walter. "Dett, Robert Nathaniel." In Dictionary of
American Biography, Supplement 3, pp. 224-226.

Hare, Maud Cuney. Negro Musicians and Their Music.
Washington, D.C.: Associated Publishers, 1936, pp. 249, 262,
336-339.

Lovingood, Penman. Famous Modern Negro Musicians. New
York: Da Capo Press, 1978. (Reprint of 1921 ed.)

McBrier, Vivian F. "Dett, R[obert] Nathaniel." In
Dictionary of American Negro Biography, eds. by Rayford W.
Logan and Michael R. Winston. New York: W.W. Norton, 1982,
pp. 175-176.

_____. R. Nathaniel Dett: His Life and Works, 1882-1943.
Washington, D.C.: Associated Publishers, 1977. 152pp.

Reis, Claire. Composers in America: Biographical Sketches
of Contemporary Composers with a Record of Their Works. New
York: The Macmillan Co., 1947, p. 98.

Robinson, Wilhelmena S. Historical Afro-American
Biographies (International Library of Afro-American Life and
History). Washington, D.C.: Associated Publishers, 1976,
pp. 182-183.

Southern, Eileen. Biographical Dictionary of Afro-American
and African Musicians. Westport, CT: Greenwood Press, 1982,
pp. 104-105.

_____. "Dett, R(obert) Nathaniel." In The New Grove
Dictionary of Music and Musicians, Vol. 5, pp. 404-405.

_____. "Dett, R(obert) Nathaniel." In The New Grove
Dictionary of American Music, Vol. 1, pp. 610-611.

Who's Who in Colored America, 1941-1944.

Dissertations

Jackson, Raymond. "The Piano Music of Twentieth-Century
Black Americans as Illustrated Mainly in the Works of Three
Composers [Dett, Swanson, and Walker]." Dissertation
(Ph.D.) Juilliard School of Music, 1973.

Miles, Debra Ann. "An Analysis of Robert Nathaniel Dett's
'In The Bottoms'." Dissertation (M.M.) North Texas State
University, 1983. 81pp.

Wilson, J. Harrison. "A Study and Performance of The
Ordering of Moses by Robert Nathaniel Dett." Dissertation
(Ph.D.) University of Southern California, 1970.

Articles

"Composer Dett." Time (October 17 1938): 45.

Current, G. B. "National Association of Negro Musicians,
Inc. salutes R. Nathaniel Dett's 100th Birthday." The
Crisis (February 1983): 18-20.

De Lerma, Dominique-Rene. "Dett and Engel: A Question of Cultural Pride." The Black Perspective in Music, Vol. 1, No. 1 (Spring 1973): 70-72. [Reprinted from Your Musical Cue (November 1970)].

Dett, R. Nathaniel. "From Bell Stand to Throne Room." The Black Perspective in Music, Vol. 1, No. 1 (Spring 1973): 73-81. [Reprinted from Etude (February 1934)].

_____. "The Emancipation of Negro Music." The Southern Workman, Vol. 47 (April 1918): 172-176.

_____. "Musical Standards." Etude, Vol. 15, No. 323 (1920).

Downes, Olin, D. L. Bicknell, and F. Yeiser. "Dr. Dett's Outstanding Contribution for 1937: His Oratorio 'The Ordering of Moses.'" Southern Workman (October 1937): 303-310.

Maynor, Dorothy. "Remarks." (Honoring the memory of R. Nathaniel Dett). National Music Council Bulletin, Vol. 36, No. 2 (1977): 7-8.

Negro History Bulletin (February 1939): 36. Biographical sketch.

Pope, Marguerite. "A Brief Biography of Dr. Robert Nathaniel Dett." The Hampton Bulletin (Hampton, VA), Vol. 42, No. 1 (October 1945).

Spencer, Jon Michael. "R. Nathaniel Dett's Views on the Preservation of Black Music." The Black Perspective in Music (Fall 1982): 133-148.

Stanley, May. "R. N. Dett, Of Hampton Institute Helping to Lay Foundation for Negro Music of Future." The Black Perspective in Music, Vol. 1, No. 1 (Spring 1973): 64-69. [Reprinted from Musical America (July 1918)].

Obituaries

Current Biography 1943.

Etude (November 1943): 697+.

Journal of Negro History (October 1943): 507-509.

New York Amsterdam News (October 9 1943).

New York Times (October 4 1943): 17.

ROGER DICKERSON (1934-   )

McGinty, Doris Evans. "Dickerson, Roger." In The New Grove Dictionary of American Music, Vol. 1, p. 615.

Southern, Eileen. Biographical Dictionary of Afro-American
and African Musicians. Westport, CT: Greenwood Press, 1982,
p. 106.

Tischler, Alice. "Roger Dickerson." In Fifteen Black
American Composers: A Bibliography of Their Works. Detroit,
MI: Information Coordinators, 1981, pp. 125-133.

Articles

Gagnard, Frank. "On the Scene: A Premiere, A Farewell."
New Orleans Times-Picayune (March 20 1975): Sec. 7, p. 2.
Review of Dickerson's "Orpheus an' His Slide Trombone."

_____. "On the Scene: A New Concerto, Miles of
Bruckner." New Orleans Times-Picayune (January 20 1977):
Sec. 3, p. 9. Review of "New Orleans Concerto."

Videos

PBS documentary on Roger Dickerson. 60 min.

JOHN DUNCAN (1913-1975)

Obituary. The Black Perspective in Music, Vol. 4, No. 3
(Fall 1976): 345.

Southern, Eileen. Biographical Dictionary of Afro-American
and African Musicians. Westport, CT: Greenwood Press, 1982,
pp. 117-118.

Spence, Martha Ellen Blanding. "Selected Song Cycles of
Three Contemporary Black American Composers: William Grant
Still, John Duncan and Hale Smith." Dissertation (D.M.A.)
University of Southern Mississippi, 1977. 143pp.

JUSTIN ELIE (1883-1931) - Haiti

New York Age (November 27 1920).

Southern, Eileen. Biographical Dictionary of Afro-American
and African Musicians. Westport, CT: Greenwood Press, 1982,
p. 124.

AKIN EUBA (1935-   ) - Nigeria

Southern, Eileen. Biographical Dictionary of Afro-American
and African Musicians. Westport, CT: Greenwood Press, 1982,
p. 128.

Uzoigwe, Joshua. "Akin Euba: An Introduction to the Life
and Music of a Nigerian Composer." Thesis (M.A.) Queen's
University at Belfast, Ireland, 1978.

MARK FAX (1911-1974)

Caldwell, Hansonia Laverne.   "Black Idioms in Opera as Manifested in the Works of Six Afro-American Composers." Dissertation (Ph.D.) University of Southern California, 1974.   Includes a discussion of Fax's opera Till Victory is Won.

Jones, Velma.   "The Life and Works of Mark Oakland Fax." Thesis (M.A.) Morgan State University, 1978.

Southern, Eileen.   Biographical Dictionary of Afro-American and African Musicians.   Westport, CT: Greenwood Press, 1982, p. 131.

Articles

Baltimore Afro-American (July 22 1978).

Obituary.   The Black Perspective in Music, Vol. 2, No. 2 (Fall 1974): 225.

Obituary.   Jet (February 7 1974): 45.

PRIMOUS FOUNTAIN (1949-   )

Abdul, Raoul.   "Primous Fountain and the Amaks."   In Blacks in Classical Music.   New York: Dodd, Mead & Co., 1977, pp. 48-49.

McGinty, Doris Evans.   "Fountain, Primous, III."   In The New Grove Dictionary of American Music, Vol. 2, p. 159.

Southern, Eileen.   Biographical Dictionary of Afro-American and African Musicians.   Westport, CT: Greenwood Press, 1982, p. 137.

Articles

"Black Composer is Named J.S. Guggenheim Fellow."   Jet (July 11 1974): 24.

Chicago Defender Accent (September 30 1978).

Chicago Tribune (March 8 1970): Sec. 1, p. 5.

Clemons, J. G.   "Classical Composer Primous Fountain, 3d." Black Enterprise (July 1980): 35.

"Noted Black Composer Wins $10,000 Fellowship."   Jet, Vol. 66 (July 28 1984): 24.

HARRY LAWRENCE FREEMAN (1869-1954)

Abdul, Raoul.   "Operas by Black Composers."   In Blacks in Classical Music.   New York: Dodd, Mead & Co., 1977, p. 123.

De Lerma, Dominique-Rene. "Freeman, Harry Lawrence." In
Dictionary of American Negro Biography, eds. Rayford W.
Logan and Michael R. Winston. New York: Norton, 1982, pp.
244-245.

Hare, Maud Cuney. Negro Musicians and Their Music.
Washington, D.C.: Associated Publishers, 1936, pp. 262, 342.

Hipsher, Edward E. "Harry Lawrence Freeman." In American
Opera and Its Composers. New York: Da Capo Press, 1978, pp.
189-195. (Reprint of 1927 ed.)

Osburn, Mary Hubbell. Ohio Composers and Musical Authors.
Colombus, OH: F. J. Heer Printing Co., 1942, pp. 76-77.

Southern, Eileen. Biographical Dictionary of Afro-American
and African Musicians. Westport, CT: Greenwood Press, 1982,
p. 138.

_____. "Freeman, Harry Lawrence." In The New Grove
Dictionary of Music and Musicians, Vol. 6, p. 815.

_____. "Freeman, Harry Lawrence." In The New Grove
Dictionary of American Music, Vol. 2, p. 167.

Articles

Brawley, Benjamin. "Composer of Fourteen Operas: H. L.
Freeman." Southern Workman, Vol. 62 (July 1933): 311-315.

Ellsworth, R. "The 1,950 Operas America Forgot." Hi
Fi/Stereo Review, Vol. 13 (October 1964): 96.

Indianapolis Freeman (October 12 1907).

Indianapolis Freeman (July 15 1911).

Indianapolis Freeman (May 8 1915).

Suthern, O. C. "Minstrelsy and Popular Culture." Journal
of Popular Culture, Vol. 3, No. 4 (1971): 669-670.

Obituaries

Billboard (April 10 1954): 53.

Musical America (May 1954): 26.

New York Age-Defender (April 3 1954): 1-2.

New York Times (March 26 1954): 22.

Variety (March 31 1954): 71.

JAMES FURMAN (1937-   )

Southern, Eileen. Biographical Dictionary of Afro-American and African Musicians. Westport, CT: Greenwood Press, 1982, p. 141.

Tischler, Alice. "James Furman." In Fifteen Black American Composers: A Bibliography of Their Works. Detroit, MI: Information Coordinators, 1981, pp. 135-147.

NEWPORT GARDNER (1746-1826)

Battle, Charles. Negroes on the Island of Rhode Island. Newport, RI, 1932. 39pp.

Brooks, Howard. The Negro in Newport. Newport, RI, 1946.

Mason, George Champlain. "Newport Gardner" (excerpt from Reminiscences of Newport. Newport, RI, 1884). In Readings In Black American Music, ed. Eileen Southern. 2nd ed. New York: Norton, 1983, pp. 36-40.

Southern, Eileen. Biographical Dictionary of Afro-American and African Musicians. Westport, CT: Greenwood Press, 1982, pp. 142-143.

Wright, Josephine, and Eileen Southern. "Newport Gardner (1746-1826)." The Black Perspective in Music (July 1976): 202-207.

CARLOS GOMES (1836-1896) - Brazil

Behague, Gerard. "Gomes, (Antonio) Carlos." In The New Grove Dictionary of Music and Musicians, Vol. 7, pp. 517-518.

Bettencourt, Gastao de. A Vida Asiosa e Atormentada de um Genio (Antonio Carlos Gomes). Lisboa: Livraria Clasica, 1945. 118pp.

_____. Temas de Musica Brasileira; conferencias realizadas em Lisboa. Rio de Janeiro: Ed. "A. Noite", 1941. Contains chapter on Gomes.

Brant, Celso. Poetas da Musica. Rio de Janeiro: Ministerio da Educacao e Cultura, Servicio de Documentacao, 1958. 161pp.

Brito, J. Carlos Gomes. Rio de Janeiro, 1956.

Castro, Enio de Freitas e. Carlos Gomes. Porto Alegre: Ed. A Nacao, 1941. 32pp.

Cerquera, Paulo. Carlos Gomes. Sao Paulo: Inteligencia, 1944. 31pp. (Edicoes culturais, No. 3)

Correa de Azevedo, Luiz Heitor. Relacao das Operas de
Autores Brasileiros. Rio de Janeiro: Servico Grafico do
Ministerio da Educacao e Saude, 1938. 116pp.

Escragnolle Taunay, Alfredo de. Dous Artistas Maximos, Jose
Mauricio e Carlos Gomes. Sao Paulo: Comp. Melhoramentos de
S. Paulo, 1930.

Fernandes, Juvenal. Do Sohno a Conquista. Sao Paulo:
Fermata do Brasil, 1978. 251pp.

Gomes, Carlos. Antonio Carlos Gomes: Carteggi Italiani.
Raccolti e Comentati da Gaspare Nello Vetro. Milano: Nuove
Edizioni, 1977. 285pp.

"Gomes, Antonio Carlos." In Encyclopedia of Latin America,
ed. Helen Delpar. New York: McGraw-Hill, 1974, p. 252.

Hare, Maud Cuney. Negro Musicians and Their Music.
Washington, D.C.: Associated Publishers, 1936, pp. 305-307.

Mariz, V. A Cancao Brasileira: Erudita, Folclorica e
Popular. 2nd ed., revista e aumentada. Rio de Janeiro:
Ministerio da Educacao e Cultura, Servico de Documentacao,
1959. 305pp.

Marques, Gabriel. O Homem da Cabeca de Leao Carlos Gomes:
Suas Musicas e Seus Amores. Sao Paulo: Empresa Grafica da
Revista dos Tribunais, 1971. 205pp.

Martins de Andrade, Andre. Carlos Gomes: Escorco
Biographico Homenagens Posthumas a Musica. Rio de Janeiro:
Pongetti, 1939. 177pp.

Rogers, J. A. "Carlos Gomes: First Great Operatic Composer
of the New World." In World's Great Men of Color. New
York: Macmillan, 1972, Vol. 2, pp. 200-202.

Ruberti, Salvatore. O Guarani e Colombo de Carlos Gomes:
Estudo Historico e Critico, Analise Musical. Rio de
Janeiro: Editora Laudes, 1972. 212pp.

Silva, Francisco Pereira de. Carlos Gomes; sua vida e sua
obra. Curitiba: Centro de Letras do Parana, 1951. 20pp.
(Edicoes do Centro de Letras do Parana, Vol. 21)

Vaz de Carvalho, Itala Gomes. Vida de Carlos Gomes. Rio de
Janeiro: A. Noite, 1937. 285pp.

Vieira Souto, Luiz Felippe. Antonio Carlos Gomes. Rio de
Janeiro: Typ. do Jornal do Commercio, Rodrigues & c., 1936.
43pp.

Articles

"Algumas cartas...ao Visconde de Taunay." Instituto
Historico e Geografico Brasileiro. Revista (Rio de
Janeiro), 80, tomo 73, parte 2 (1911): 35-86.

Armond Marchant, Annie d'. "Carlos Gomes, Great Brazilian
Composer, July 11, 1836-July 11, 1936." Pan American Union
Bulletin (Washington, D.C.), Vol. 70 (1936): 767-776.

Bandeira, Antonio Ragel. "Carlos Gomes no Centenario de Il
Guarany." Revista do Arquivo Municipal (Sao Paulo), Vol.
181, No. 33 (abril-junho 1970): 16-35.

Bernardini, Giulia. "Carlos Gomes nei Ricordi della
Figlia." Opera e i Giorni [Genova] (1937): 47-52.

Celso, Affonso, and J. Luso. "Centenario de Carlos Gomes."
Academia Brasileira de Letras, Rio de Janeiro. Revista (Rio
de Janeiro), Vol. 51 (1936): 419-427.

Murizy, Andrade. "Contribuicao do Brasil a Musica
Universal." Panorama, Vol. 2, No. 5 (1953): 42-56.
Discussion of the contributions of Joaquim Manuel, C. Gomes,
and H. Villa-Lobos to Western music.

Rezende, Carlos Penteado de. "O ano de 1859 na Vida de
Carlos Gomes." Revista Brasileira, ano 6, no. 20 (abril
1948): 91-110.

Revista Brasileira de Musica, Vol. III (1936). [Gomes
centenary issue].

Ruberti, Salvatore. "Maneira Pela Qual Nao Se Deve Cantar A
Aria Come Serenamente El Mar De "Lo Schiavo" De Carlos
Gomes." Revista Brasileira de Musica (Rio de Janeiro), Vol.
5 (1940): 54-64.

White, Clarence Cameron. "Antonio Carlos Gomez." Negro
History Bulletin, Vol. IV, No. 5 (February 1941): 104, 110.

SHIRLEY GRAHAM (DuBois) (1907-1977)

Abdul, Raoul. "Operas by Black Composers." In Blacks in
Classical Music. New York: Dodd, Mead & Co., 1977, pp.
123-124.

Davis, Russell H. Blacks in Cleveland. Washington, D.C.:
Associated Publishers, 1972, p. 301. Short sketch of
Graham's "Tom Tom" (1932) the "first Negro opera ever
produced".

Hare, Maud Cuney. Negro Musicians and Their Music.
Washington, D.C.: Associated Publishers, 1936, p. 345.

Southern, Eileen. Biographical Dictionary of Afro-American
and African Musicians. Westport, CT: Greenwood Press, 1982,
p. 152.

Articles

"Graham, Shirley." Current Biography 1946, pp. 221-222.

Perkins, K. A.   "The Unknown Career of Shirley Graham."
Freedomways, Vol. 25, No. 1 (1985): 6-17.

Peterson, B. L.   "Shirley Graham DuBois: Composer and
Playwright." The Crisis (May 1977): 177-179.

"Tom Tom." Cleveland Plain Dealer (July 1 1932); (July 3
1932); (July 10 1932).

Radio Broadcasts

Graham's opera Tom Tom, premiered in concert form by NBC
Radio - June 26, 1932.

Obituaries

Black Perspective in Music, Vol. 5, No. 2 (Fall 1977): 233.

The Black Scholar, Vol. 8 (May 1977): 12.

Central Service Opera Bulletin, Vol. 20, No. 1 (1977-78): 18.

Current Biography 1977, p. 462.

New York Times (April 5 1977): 36.

ADOLPHUS HAILSTORK (1941-   )

McGinty, Doris Evans. "Hailstork, Adolphus." In The New
Grove Dictionary of American Music, Vol. 2, p. 307.

Southern, Eileen. Biographical Dictionary of Afro-American
and African Musicians. Westport, CT: Greenwood Press, 1982,
pp. 158-159.

Tischler, Alice. "Adolphus Cunningham Hailstork." In
Fifteen Black American Composers: A Bibliography of Their
Works. Detroit, MI: Information Coordinators, 1981, pp.
149-164.

TALIB RASUL HAKIM (Stephen A. Chambers) (1940-   )

Abdul, Raoul. "Recordings: Black Piano Music." In Blacks
in Classical Music. New York: Dodd, Mead & Co., 1977, p. 63.

James, Richard S. "Hakim, Talib Rasul." In The New Grove
Dictionary of American Music, Vol. 2, p. 307.

Johnson, Tom. "Music: Talib Rasul Hakim Has Found His
Music." Village Voice (February 20 1978): 80.

Oliver, Christine E. "Selected Orchestral Works of Thomas
J. Anderson, Arthur Cunningham, Talib Rasul Hakim, and Olly
Wilson: A Descriptive Study." Dissertation (Ph.D.) Florida
State University, 1978.

Southern, Eileen. Biographical Dictionary of Afro-American and African Musicians. Westport, CT: Greenwood Press, 1982, pp. 159-160.

"Talib Rasul Hakim." In The Black Composer Speaks, eds. David N. Baker, Lida N. Belt, and Herman C. Hudson. Metuchen, NJ: Scarecrow Press, 1978, pp. 93-107.

FREDERICK DOUGLASS HALL (1898-1982)

Bowers, Violet G. "In Retrospect: Frederick Douglass Hall: 'He Was My Teacher.'" The Black Perspective in Music (Fall 1980): 215-242.

McGinty, Doris Evans. "Hall, Frederick Douglass." In The New Grove Dictionary of American Music, Vol. 2, pp. 308-309.

Obituary. The Black Perspective in Music, Vol. 11, No. 2 (Fall 1983): 226.

Southern, Eileen. Biographical Dictionary of Afro-American and African Musicians. Westport, CT: Greenwood Press, 1982, pp. 160-161.

Who's Who in Colored America, 1927, pp. 84-85.

ROBERT A. HARRIS (1938-   )

Tischler, Alice. "Robert A. Harris." In Fifteen Black American Composers: A Bibliography of Their Works. Detroit, MI: Information Coordinators, 1981, pp. 167-177.

JUSTIN HOLLAND (1819-1887)

Bone, Philip J. The Guitar and Mandolin: Biographies of Celebrated Players and Composers. London: Schott & Co, 1972, pp. 167-68. (Reprint of 1954 ed.)

Davis, Russell H. Black Americans in Cleveland. Washington, D.C.: Associated Publishers, 1972, pp. 120-121.

Hare, Maud Cuney. Negro Musicians and Their Music. Washington, D.C.: Associated Publishers, 1936, pp. 205-207.

Holland, Justin. Holland's Comprehensive Method for the Guitar. New York: J.L. Peters & Co., 1874.

_____. Holland's Modern Method for the Guitar. Boston: Oliver Ditson, 1876.

Simmons, William J. Men of Mark: Eminent, Progressive and Rising. Chicago: Johnson Publishing Co., 1970, pp. 251-254.

Southern, Eileen. Biographical Dictionary of Afro-American and African Musicians. Westport, CT: Greenwood Press, 1982, p. 186.

_____. "Holland, Justin." In The New Grove Dictionary of Music and Musicians, Vol. 8, pp. 646-647.

_____. "Holland, Justin." In The New Grove Dictionary of American Music, Vol. 2, p. 410.

Trotter, James M. Music and Some Highly Musical People. Chicago: Afro-Am Press, 1969, pp. 114-130. (Orig. 1878)

Articles

Bickford, V. O. "The Guitar in America." Guitar Review, No. 23 (June 1959): 17.

Boyer, Horace Clarence. "A Portfolio of Music: The New England Afro-American School." The Black Perspective in Music, Vol. 4, No. 2 (July 1976): 214-237.

Carroll, Agnes. "Justin Holland." The Negro Music Journal, Vol. 1, No. 13 (September 1903): 13-16.

Cleveland Plain Dealer (December 24 1868).

Danner, P. "American Guitar Music: Some Notes on a Forgotten Repertoire." Creative Guitar International, Vol. 4, No. 1 (1976): 3-5.

Der Freimaurer [Vienna] (February 18 1877).

Indianapolis Freeman (May 18 1889).

Musical World (October 1877).

EDMUND THORNTON JENKINS (1894-1926)

Chilton, John. A Jazz Nursery: The Story of the Jenkins Orphanage Bands. London: Image Publicity, 1980.

Green, Jeffrey. Edmund Thornton Jenkins: The Life and Times of an American Black Composer, 1894-1926. Westport, CT: Greenwood Press, 1982.

Hare, Maud Cuney. Negro Musicians and Their Music. Washington, D.C.: Associated Publishers, 1936, pp. 261, 345-346.

Southern, Eileen. Biographical Dictionary of Afro-American and African Musicians. Westport, CT: Greenwood Press, 1982, pp. 202-203.

Articles

Bennett, Gwendolyn B. "Edmund T. Jenkins: Musician." Opportunity: Journal of Negro Life, Vol. 3, No. 35 (November 1925): 338-339.

Brawley, Benjamin G.   "Edmund T. Jenkins: An Appreciation."
Opportunity: Journal of Negro Life, Vol. 4, No. 48 (December
1926): 383.

Hillmon, Betty.   "In Retrospect: Edmund Thornton Jenkins.
American Composer: At Home Abroad."   The Black Perspective
in Music, Vol. 14, No. 2 (Spring 1986): 143-180.

New York Age (January 19 1924).

New York Age (October 2 1926).

FRANCIS HALL JOHNSON (1888-1970)

Abdul, Raoul.   "Hall Johnson Remembered."   In Blacks in
Classical Music.   New York: Dodd, Mead & Co., 1977, pp.
207-208.

Downs, Karl E.   Meet the Negro.   Los Angeles, CA: The
Methodist Youth Fellowship, Southern California-Arizona
Annual Conference, 1943, pp. 90-91.

Hare, Maud Cuney.   Negro Musicians and Their Music.
Washington, D.C.: Associated Publishers, 1936, pp. 253-254,
261.

Macmillan Encyclopedia of Music and Musicians (1938).

Robinson, Wilhelmena S.   Historical Afro-American
Biographies (International Library of Afro-American Life and
History).   Washington, D.C.: Associated Publishers, 1976,
pp. 211-212.

Southern, Eileen.   Biographical Dictionary of Afro-American
and African Musicians.   Westport, CT: Greenwood Press, 1982,
p. 207.

_____.   "Johnson, Hall."   In The New Grove Dictionary of
Music and Musicians, Vol. 9, p. 677.

_____.   "Johnson, (Francis) Hall."   In The New Grove
Dictionary of American Music, Vol. 2, p. 579.

Toppin, Edgar A.   A Biographical History of Blacks in
America since 1528.   New York: David McKay, 1971, pp.
331-333.

Troup, Cornelius V.   "Hall Johnson."   In Distinguished Negro
Georgians.   Dallas, TX: Royal Publishing Co., 1962, pp.
88-91.

Who's Who in Colored America, 1941-44.

Articles

Arvey, Verna.   "Hall Johnson and His Choir."   Opportunity,
Vol. 19 (May 1941): 151, 158-159.

Hobson, Charles.   "Hall Johnson: Preserver of Negro
Spirituals."   The Crisis (November 1966): 480-485.

"Johnson, Hall."   Current Biography 1945.

New York Post Magazine (August 11 1943): 39.

Our World (August 1947): 47.   Brief notice on the appearance
of the Hall Johnson Choir on New York television stations.

Simpson, E. T.   "The Hall Johnson Legacy 1889-1970."   Choral
Journal, Vol. 11, No. 5 (1971): 10-11.

Obituaries

Black Perspective in Music, Vol. 1, No. 2 (Fall 1973): 199.

Central Opera Service Bulletin, Vol. 13 (March-April 1971):
22.

Current Biography 1970, p. 474.

Music and Artists, Vol. 3, No. 3 (1970): 48.

New York Times (May 1 1970): 35.

Variety, No. 258 (May 6 1970): 102.

ULYSSES SIMPSON KAY (1917-   )

Abdul, Raoul.   "Ulysses Kay: New Horizons."   In Blacks in
Classical Music.   New York: Dodd, Mead & Co., 1977, pp.
39-40.

Adams, Russell L.   Great Negroes, Past and Present.
Chicago: Afro-Am Publishing Co., 1969, p. 189.

Broadcast Music, Inc.   Ulysses Kay: Catalogue of Works
Composed to 1968.   New York: Broadcast Music, 1968.

Reis, Claire.   Composers in America: Biographical Sketches
of Contemporary Composers with a Record of Their Works.   New
York: The Macmillan Co., 1947, pp. 204-204.

Southern, Eileen.   Biographical Dictionary of Afro-American
and African Musicians.   Westport, CT: Greenwood Press, 1982,
pp. 226-227.

_____.   "Kay, Ulysses (Simpson)."   In The New Grove
Dictionary of Music and Musicians, Vol. 9, pp. 834-835.

_____.   "Kay, Ulysses (Simpson)."   In The New Grove
Dictionary of American Music, Vol. 2, pp. 615-616.

Ulysses Kay (Pamphlet).   New York, 1962.

"Ulysses Simpson Kay." In The Black Composer Speaks, eds.
David N. Baker, Lida N. Belt, and Herman C. Hudson.
Metuchen, NJ: Scarecrow Press, 1978, pp. 139-171.

Dissertations and Unpublished Papers

Caldwell, Hansonia Laverne. "Black Idioms in Opera as
Manifested in the Works of Six Afro-American Composers."
Dissertation (Ph.D.) University of Southern California,
1974. Includes a discussion of Kay's 3 one-act operas: The
Boor; The Juggler of Our Lady; and The Capitoline Venus.

Hadley, Richard T. "The Published Choral Music of Ulysses
Simpson Kay, 1943-1968." Dissertation (Ph.D.) University of
Iowa, 1972. 337pp.

Hayes, Laurence. "The Music of Ulysses Kay, 1939-1963."
Dissertation (Ph.D., Music) University of Wisconsin, 1971.
342pp.

Wyatt, Lucius R. "The Musical Style of Ulysses Kay." Paper
presented at the Meeting of the Southwest Chapter of the
American Musicological Society, San Antonio, Texas, October
19, 1979.

Articles

"Arizona." Violins and Violinists, Vol. 15 (March-April
1954): 75.

Cervetti, S., et al. "Five Questions, Forty-One Answers."
The Composer (US), Vol. 5, No. 1 (1973): 22-27.

Chapin, Louis. "Ulysses Kay." BMI: The Many Worlds of
Music (February 1970): 9.

"Composers in Focus." BMI (Winter 1976): 24-25.

Courier Journal (February 10 1964): 29+.

Daniel, O. "The New Festival." ACA Bulletin, Vol. 5, No. 1
(1955): 15-16.

Dower, Catherine. "Ulysses Kay: Distinguished American
Composer." Musart (January-February 1972): 9-10+.

Hadley, Richard T. "Life and Music of Ulysses Simpson Kay."
Negro Educational Review (January 1975): 42-51.

"In the News." BMI (October 1968): 22.

"Kay to Conduct Work in Tucson." Down Beat (February 24
1954): 17.

Kay, Ulysses. "An American Composer Reports on Russian
Musical Life." NMC Bulletin, Vol. 19 (Winter 1959): 13-14.

_____. "Thirty Days in Musical Russia." (A diary) <u>Hi Fi Review</u>, Vol. 2 (February 1959): 35-38+.

_____. "Where is Music Going?" <u>Music Journal</u>, Vol. 20 (January 1962): 484.

Kyle, M. K. "AmerAllegro." <u>Pan Pipes</u>, Vol. 47 (January 1954): 47.

_____. "AmerAllegro." <u>Pan Pipes</u>, Vol. 48 (January 1956): 56.

_____. "AmerAllegro." <u>Pan Pipes</u>, Vol. 49 (January 1957): 55.

_____. "AmerAllegro." <u>Pan Pipes</u>, Vol. 50 (January 1958): 59.

_____. "AmerAllegro." <u>Pan Pipes</u>, Vol. 51 (January 1959): 70.

_____. "AmerAllegro." <u>Pan Pipes</u>, Vol. 52, No. 2 (1960): 56.

_____. "AmerAllegro." <u>Pan Pipes</u>, Vol. 53, No. 2 (1961): 61-62.

_____. "AmerAllegro." <u>Pan Pipes</u>, Vol. 54, No. 2 (1962): 57.

_____. "AmerAllegro." <u>Pan Pipes</u>, Vol. 55, No. 2 (1963): 56.

_____. "AmerAllegro." <u>Pan Pipes</u>, Vol. 56, No. 2 (1964): 64.

_____. "AmerAllegro." <u>Pan Pipes</u>, Vol. 57, No. 2 (1965): 66.

_____. "AmerAllegro." <u>Pan Pipes</u>, Vol. 59, No. 2 (1967): 82.

_____. "AmerAllegro." <u>Pan Pipes</u>, Vol. 60, No. 2 (1968): 78-79.

_____. "AmerAllegro." <u>Pan Pipes</u>, Vol. 62, No. 2 (1970): 68.

_____. "AmerAllegro." <u>Pan Pipes</u>, Vol. 63, No. 2 (1971): 65.

_____. "AmerAllegro." <u>Pan Pipes</u>, Vol. 64, No. 2 (1972): 63.

_____. "AmerAllegro." <u>Pan Pipes</u>, Vol. 65, No. 2 (1973): 59.

_____. "AmerAllegro." <u>Pan Pipes</u>, Vol. 66, No. 2 (1974): 59.

_____. "AmerAllegro." Pan Pipes, Vol. 67, No. 2 (1975):
67.

_____. "AmerAllegro." Pan Pipes, Vol. 68, No. 2 (1976):
57.

_____. "AmerAllegro." Pan Pipes, Vol. 69, No. 2 (1977):
54.

_____. "AmerAllegro." Pan Pipes, Vol. 70, No. 2 (1978):
48.

_____. "AmerAllegro." Pan Pipes, Vol. 71, No. 2 (1979):
36.

"New York Composer Ulysses Kay Wins Moravian Contest."
Diapason, Vol. 47 (May 1 1956): 2.

New York Times (May 18 1959).

"Return of Ulysses." Time (March 8 1954): 71.

Schonberg, Harold C. "Exchange Composers: Harris, Sessions,
and Kay Discuss Their Forthcoming Trip to Soviet Union."
New York Times (September 21 1958): Sec. 2, p. 11.

Slonimsky, Nicolas. "Ulysses Kay." ACA Bulletin, Vol. 7
(Fall 1957): 3-6.

"The Odyssey of Ulysses." Down Beat (October 2 1958).

"Ulysses Kay." Composers of the Americas, Vol. 7 (1961):
34-45.

"Ulysses Kay." Music Journal Annual 1972 (July 1972): 50.

"Ulysses Kay." Pan Pipes, Vol. 45 (January 1953): 57.

"Ulysses Kay." Pan Pipes, Vol. 47 (January 1955): 51-52.

"Ulysses Kay Appointed to Endowed Chair of Composition
(Brevard Music Center)." Triangle, Vol. 73, No. 2 (1979): 2.

"Wins Rome Prize Fellowship." Musical America (June 1949):
31.

"Writer Kay Named Professor of Music at Hunter College."
Billboard, Vol. 80 (June 8 1968): 40.

Wyatt, Lucius Reynold. "Ulysses Kay's Fantasy Variations:
An Analysis." The Black Perspective in Music, Vol. 5, No. 1
(Spring 1977): 75-89.

THOMAS KERR (1915-   )

Southern, Eileen. Biographical Dictionary of Afro-American
and African Musicians. Westport, CT: Greenwood Press, 1982,
p. 229.

WENDELL LOGAN (1940-   )

Southern, Eileen. Biographical Dictionary of Afro-American and African Musicians. Westport, CT: Greenwood Press, 1982, p. 248.

_____. "Logan, Wendell." In The New Grove Dictionary of American Music, Vol. 3, p. 103.

Tischler, Alice. "Wendell Morris Logan." In Fifteen Black American Composers: A Bibliography of Their Works. Detroit, MI: Information Coordinators, 1981, pp. 179-187.

Wilson, Olly. "Wendell Logan: Proportions." Perspectives in New Music (1970): 135-142.

LENA MCLIN (1929-   )

Ammer, Christine. Unsung: A History of Women in American Music. Westport, CT: Greenwood Press, 1980, pp. 158-159.

Cox, Donna Marie McNeil. "A Descriptive Analysis of Selected Choral Works of Lena Johnson McLin." Dissertation (Ph.D.) Washington University, 1986. 194pp.

Green, Mildred Denby. "A Study of the Lives and Works of Five Black Women Composers in America." Dissertation (Ph.D.) University of Oklahoma, 1975.

_____. "Lena McLin." In Black Women Composers: A Genesis. Boston: Twayne Publishers, 1983, pp. 113-133.

"McLin, Lena." In Keyboard Music by Women Composers: A Catalog and Bibliography. Compiled by Joan M. Meggett. Westport, CT: Greenwood Press, 1981, p. 117.

Southern, Eileen. Biographical Dictionary of Afro-American and African Musicians. Westport, CT: Greenwood Press, 1982, p. 261.

EDWARD H. MARGETSON (1891-1962)

Hare, Maud Cuney. Negro Musicians and Their Music. Washington, D.C.: Associated Publishers, 1936, pp. 262, 347.

Southern, Eileen. Biographical Dictionary of Afro-American and African Musicians. Westport, CT: Greenwood Press, 1982, pp. 263-264.

Articles

New York Amsterdam News (August 19 1930).

New York Amsterdam News (February 3 1962).

New York Amsterdam News (May 28 1977).

Who's Who in Colored America, 1950.

CARMAN MOORE (1936-)

Quist, Ned. "Moore, Carman (Leroy)." In *The New Grove Dictionary of American Music*, Vol. 3, p. 265.

Southern, Eileen. *Biographical Dictionary of Afro-American and African Musicians*. Westport, CT: Greenwood Press, 1982, pp. 278-279.

Tischler, Alice. "Carman Leroy Moore." In *Fifteen Black American Composers: A Bibliography of Their Works*. Detroit, MI: Information Coordinators, 1981, pp. 189-199.

Articles

"Arts: Back-to-Back Triumphs for Carman Moore." *People* (February 10 1975): 57.

Derhen, A. "N.Y. Phil: Moore Premiere." *High Fidelity* (May 1975): 29.

Michener, C. "Double Header." *Newsweek* (February 3 1975): 71.

Moses, Knolly. "Essence Men: Carman Moore." *Essence* (December 1977): 8.

New York Amsterdam News (June 10 1978).

"This Week's Most Wanted Composer: Carman Moore." *New York Times* (January 19 1975): Sec. II, p. 1.

DOROTHY RUDD MOORE (1940-)

Abdul, Raoul. "Black Women in Music." In *Blacks in Classical Music*. New York: Dodd, Mead & Co., 1977, pp. 56-57.

Davis, Peter. "Retrospective Concert of Music by Dorothy Rudd Moore, performed by group and sung by Mrs. Moore." *New York Times* (February 25 1975): 28. Concert review.

McGinty, Doris Evans. "Moore, Dorothy Rudd." In *The New Grove Dictionary of American Music*, Vol. 3, pp. 265-266.

Southern, Eileen. *Biographical Dictionary of Afro-American and African Musicians*. Westport, CT: Greenwood Press, 1982, p. 279.

Tischler, Alice. "Dorothy Rudd Moore." In *Fifteen Black American Composers: A Bibliography of Their Works*. Detroit, MI: Information Coordinators, 1981, pp. 201-210.

UNDINE S. MOORE (1904-   )

Jones, John R. D.   "The Choral Works of Undine Smith Moore:
A Study of Her Life and Work." Dissertation (Ph.D.) New
York University, 1980.

Moore, James Edward.   "The Choral Music of Undine Smith
Moore." Dissertation (Ph.D.) University of Cincinnati, 1979.

McGinty, Doris Evans. "Moore, Undine Smith." In The New
Grove Dictionary of American Music, Vol. 3, p. 269.

Southern, Eileen. Biographical Dictionary of Afro-American
and African Musicians. Westport, CT: Greenwood Press, 1982,
p. 280.

"Undine Smith Moore." In The Black Composer Speaks, eds.
David N. Baker, Lida N. Belt, and Herman C. Hudson.
Metuchen, NJ: Scarecrow Press, 1978, pp. 173-202.

Articles

Beckner, Steve.   "Composer and Teacher - Mrs. Undine Smith
Moore." The Progress-Index [Petersburg, VA] (January 5
1975).

Harris, Carl G. "Conversation with Undine Smith Moore:
Composer and Master Teacher." The Black Perspective in
Music (Spring 1985): 79-90.

_____. "The Unique World of Undine Smith Moore." Choral
Journal (January 1976): 46-47.

"Rare Treat for Retiree: Adieu by Concert." Clavier, Vol.
11, No. 8 (1972): 43.

JALALU-KALVERT NELSON (1951-   )

Los Angeles Times (October 14 1981).

New York Times (January 22 1981).

JOSE MAURICIO NUNES GARCIA (1767-1830) - Brazil

Abdul, Raoul. "Black Brazilian Composers." In Blacks in
Classical Music. New York: Dodd, Mead & Co., 1977, pp.
49-51.

Andrade, Mario de. Musica, Doce Musica. Sao Paulo: L. G.
Miranda, 1934.

Behague, Gerard. "Garcia, Jose Mauricio Nunes." In The New
Grove Dictionary of Music and Musicians, Vol. 7, pp. 153-155.

_____. "Garcia, Jose Mauricio Nunes." In Encyclopedia
of Latin America, ed. Helen Delpar. New York: McGraw-Hill,
1974, p. 247.

Bettencourt, Gastao de. Temas de Musica Brasileira;
conferencias realizadas em Lisboa. Rio de Janeiro: Ed. "A.
Noite", 1941. Contains chapter on Nunes Garcia.

Correa de Azevedo, Luiz Heitor. 150 Anos de Musica no
Brasil (1800-1950). Rio de Janeiro: J. Olympio, 1956.

_____. La Musique a la Cour Portugaise de Rio de Janeiro
(1808-1821). Paris: Fundacao Calouste Gulbenkian, 1969.
(Arquivos do centro cultural portugues, v.1)

Escragnolle Taunay, Alfredo de. Dous Artistas Maximos, Jose
Mauricio e Carlos Gomes. Sao Paulo: Comp. Melhoramentos de
S. Paulo, 1930.

_____. Uma Grande Gloria Brasileira Jose Mauricio Nunes
Garcia (1767-1830). Edicacao Commemorativa do Primeira
Centenario do Passamento do Grande Compositor. Sao Paulo:
Comp. Melhoramentos de Sao Paulo, 1930. 129pp.

Maciel, Joaquim Jose. Catalogo das Musicas Arquivadas na
Capela Imperial de Composicao do Padre Mestre Jose Mauricio
Nunes Garcia. Rio de Janeiro, 1887. 20pp.

Mattos, Cleofe Person de. Catalogo Tematico das Obras do
Padre Jose Mauricio Nunes Garcia. Rio de Janeiro:
Ministerio da Educacao e Cultura, 1970. 413pp.

Nunes Garcia, Jose Mauricio. Matinas do Natal para coro,
soloistas, orquestra e orgao. Rio de Janeiro: FUNARTE-MEC,
Associacao de Canto Coral, 1978. 69pp. (Musical score)
[For English-language summary see Robert Stevenson's
critique in Handbook of Latin American Studies, No. 44, p.
594].

Rio de Janeiro. Biblioteca Nacional. 2o Centenario do
Nascimento de Jose Mauricio Nunes Garcia, 1767-1830;
Exposicao Comemorativa. Rio de Janeiro: Biblioteca
Nacional, Divisao de Publicacoes e Divulgacao, 1967. 95pp.

Southern, Eileen. Biographical Dictionary of Afro-American
and African Musicians. Westport, CT: Greenwood Press, 1982,
pp. 291-292.

Tavares de Lima, Rossini. Vida e Epoca de Jose Mauricio.
Sao Paulo: Livraria Elo, 1941. 113pp.

Articles

Andrade, Mario de. "A Modinha de Jose Mauricio."
Ilustracao Musical, Vol. 1, No. 3 (1930): 160+.

Correa de Azevedo, Luiz Heitor. "O Espirito Religioso na
Obra de Jose Mauricio." Ilustracao Musical, Vol. 1, No. 3
(1930): 75+.

_____. "Obras do Padre Jose Mauricio Nunes Garcia
Exitentes na Biblioteca do Instituto Nacional de Musica."
Ilustracao Musical, Vol. 1, No. 3 (1930): 81+.

_____. "Um Velho Compositor Brasileiro: Jose Mauricio."
Boletin Latino-Americano de Musica, Vol. 1, No. 1 (1935):
133+.

_____. "Jose Mauricio Nunes Garcia (1767-1830), Ensaio
Historico." Resenha Musical, Vol. 6, No. 63/64
(November-December 1943): 4-13.

_____. "Jose Mauricio Nunes Garcia." Resenha Musical,
Vol. 6, No. 65-66 (January-February 1944): 2-4, 6-8, 9-12;
No. 67-68 (March-April 1944): 8. [Reprinted from Boletin
Latino-Americano de Musica, Vol. 1 (1935)].

_____. "O Padre Jose Mauricio." Brasil Musical (Rio de
Janeiro), Vol. 1, No. 6 (June-July 1945): 5, 48.

De Lerma, Dominique-Rene. "The Life and Works of
Nunes-Garcia: A Status Report." The Black Perspective in
Music, Vol. 14, No. 2 (Spring 1986): 93-102.

Lange, Francisco Curt. "Certidao de Batismo de Victoria
Maria de Cruz, Mae do Padre Jose Mauricio Nunes Garcia; 16
de Novembre de 1738." Barroco (Minas Gerais), Vol. 11
(1981): 91-94.

_____. "Estudios Brasilenos (Mauricinas). I. Manuscritos
en la Biblioteca Nacional de Rio de Janeiro." Revista de
Estudios Musicales (Mendoza, Argentina) Vol. 1, No. 3
(1950): 99-194.

_____. "A Musica Erudita na Regencia e no Imperio."
Historia Geral da Civilizacao Brasiliera (Sao Paulo), Vol. 2
(1967).

_____. "Sobre las Dificiles Huellas de la Musica Antigua
del Brasil." Yearbook (Anuario). Inter-American Institute
for Musical Research (New Orleans), Vol. 1 (1965): 15-40.
Analysis of Nunes-Garcia's "Missa Abreviada."

Mattos, Cleofe Person de. "Jose Mauricio, O Barroco e a
Pesquisa da Musica Brasileira." Universitas, Vol. 2 (1969):
21+.

Porto Alegre, M. de Araujo. "Apontamentos Sobre a Vida e a
Obra do Pe: Jose Mauricio Nunes Garcia." Revista do
Instituto Historico e Geografico Brasileiro, Vol. XIX
(1856): 354+.

_____. "Marcos Portugal e Jose Mauricio: Catalogo de
Suas Composicoes Musicais: Copia Fiel do Original em Mao do
Dr. Jose Mauricio Nunes Garcia, ate o dia 6 de Setembro de
1811." Revista do Instituto Historico e Geografico
Brasileiro, Vol. XXII (1859): 257+.

Vieira, F. "Antiquahas e Memorias do Rio de Janeiro."
Revista do Instituto Historico e Geografico Brasileiro, Vol.
LXXXIX (1898): 9+.

COLERIDGE-TAYLOR PERKINSON (1932-   )

Abdul, Raoul. "Spotlight on Black Composers." In Blacks in
Classical Music. New York: Dodd, Mead & Co., 1977, p. 59.

"Coleridge-Taylor Perkinson." In The Black Composer Speaks,
eds. David N. Baker, Lida N. Belt and Herman C. Hudson.
Metuchen, NJ: Scarecrow Press, 1978, pp. 239-275.

Moore, Carman. "Perkinson, Coleridge-Taylor." In The New
Grove Dictionary of American Music, Vol. 3, p. 536.

Southern, Eileen. Biographical Dictionary of Afro-American
and African Musicians. Westport, CT: Greenwood Press, 1982,
p. 303.

JULIA PERRY (1924-1979)

Abdul, Raoul. "Black Women in Music." In Blacks in
Classical Music. New York: Dodd, Mead & Co., 1977, pp.
55-56.

Ammer, Christine. Unsung: A History of Women in American
Music. Westport, CT: Greenwood Press, 1980, pp. 156-158.

Briscoe, James R., ed. Historical Anthology of Music by
Women. Bloomington: Indiana University Press, 1987, pp.
333-334.

Green, Mildred Denby. "A Study of the Lives and Works of
Five Black Women Composers in America." Dissertation
(Ph.D.) University of Oklahoma, 1975.

_____. "Julia Perry." In Black Women Composers: A
Genesis. Boston: Twayne Publishers, 1983, pp. 71-98.

Perry, Julia. 40 Studies for Classroom Musical Composition.
Unpublished MSS, 1969-1970.

"Perry, Julia." In Keyboard Music by Women Composers: A
Catalog and Bibliography. Compiled by Joan M. Meggett.
Westport, CT: Greenwood Press, 1981, pp. 132-133.

Southern, Eileen. Biographical Dictionary of Afro-American
and African Musicians. Westport, CT: Greenwood Press, 1982,
p. 303.

_____. "Perry, Julia." In The New Grove Dictionary of
Music and Musicians, Vol. 14, pp. 548-549.

_____. "Perry, Julia (Amanda)." In The New Grove
Dictionary of American Music, Vol. 3, p. 539.

Articles

Green, Miriam Stewart. "Consider These Creators." <u>American Music Teacher</u>, Vol. 25, No. 3 (January 1976): 12.

<u>New York Amsterdam News</u> (May 16 1964).

Obituary. <u>The Black Perspective in Music</u>, Vol. 7, No. 2 (Fall 1979): 282.

Pool, Jeanne. "America's Women Composers: Up from the Footnotes." <u>Music Educators Journal</u>, Vol. 65, No. 5 (January 1979): 35.

EVELYN PITTMAN (1910-)

Ammer, Christine. <u>Unsung: A History of Women in American Music</u>. Westport, CT: Greenwood Press, 1980, pp. 158.

Green, Mildred Denby. "A Study of the Lives and Works of Five Black Women Composers in America." Dissertation (Ph.D.) University of Oklahoma, 1975.

_____. "Evelyn Pittman." In <u>Black Women Composers: A Genesis</u>. Boston: Twayne Publishers, 1983, pp. 99-112.

<u>New York Amsterdam News</u> (June 16 1962).

Southern, Eileen. <u>Biographical Dictionary of Afro-American and African Musicians</u>. Westport, CT: Greenwood Press, 1982, p. 308.

FLORENCE B. PRICE (1888-1953)

Abdul, Raoul. "Black Women in Music." In <u>Blacks in Classical Music</u>. New York: Dodd, Mead & Co., 1977, pp. 52-53.

Ammer, Christine. <u>Unsung: A History of Women in American Music</u>. Westport, CT: Greenwood Press, 1980, pp. 152-153.

Fayetteville, Arkansas, University of Arkansas Library. Special Collections Division. <u>A Checklist of Source Materials by and About Florence B. Price</u>. Compiler Sam Sizer, 1977. Lists 81 published and unpublished scores; 31 items of correspondence. [Meggett, p. 137]

Green, Mildred. "Florence Price." In <u>Black Women Composers: A Genesis</u>. Boston: Twayne Publishers, 1983, pp. 31-46.

Hare, Maud Cuney. <u>Negro Musicians and Their Music</u>. Washington, D.C.: Associated Publishers, 1936, pp. 263-264.

Jackson, Barbara Garvey. "Price, Florence Beatrice Smith." <u>Notable American Women: The Modern Period</u>. Cambridge, MA: The Belknap Press, 1980, pp. 561-562.

Nachman, Myrna S. [worklist prepared with Barbara Garvey Jackson]. "Price [nee Smith], Florence Bea(trice)." In The New Grove Dictionary of American Music, Vol. 3, pp. 628-629.

"Price, Florence B." In Keyboard Music by American Composers: A Catalog and Bibliography. Compiled by Joan M. Meggett. Westport, CT: Greenwood Press, 1981, pp. 135-137.

Southern, Eileen. Biographical Dictionary of Afro-American and African Musicians. Westport, CT: Greenwood Press, 1982, p. 308.

Dissertations

Brown, Rae Linda. "The Orchestral Music of Florence B. Price (1888-1953): A Stylistic Analysis." Dissertation (Ph.D.) Yale University (In preparation).

Green, Mildred Denby. "A Study of the Lives and Works of Five Black Women Composers in America." Dissertation (Ph.D.) University of Oklahoma, 1975.

Articles

"Florence B. Price." Pan Pipes, Vol. 47 (January 1955): 62.

Graham, Shirley. "Spirituals to Symphonies." Etude (November 1936).

Green, Miriam Stewart. "Consider These Creators." American Music Teacher, Vol. 25, No. 3 (January 1976): 12.

Jackson, Barbara Garvey. "Florence Price, Composer." The Black Perspective in Music (Spring 1977): 31-43.

Kyle, M. K. "AmerAllegro." Pan Pipes, Vol. 46 (January 1954): 56.

Pool, Jeanne. "America's Women Composers: Up from the Footnotes." Music Educators Journal, Vol. 65, No. 5 (January 1979): 35.

Yancy, H. M. "The Contribution of the American Negro to the Music Culture of the Country." School Musician, Vol. 41 (March 1970): 62.

Obituaries

Etude (August 1953): 56.

Musical America (July 1953): 19.

JOHN PRICE (1935-   )

Southern, Eileen. Biographical Dictionary of Afro-American and African Musicians. Westport, CT: Greenwood Press, 1982, p. 313.

Tischler, Alice. "John Elwood Price." In Fifteen Black
American Composers: A Bibliography of Their Works. Detroit,
MI: Information Coordinators, 1981, pp. 213-257.

Articles

"The Black Musician as Artist and Entrepeneur."
Phelps-Stokes Fund, 1974.

"Classical Black." Miami Herald (December 19 1971).

"Profile... Composer on the Threshold of Fame." The Lamp
(magazine of Florida Memorial College, Miami, FL), 1970.

The Sphinx [magazine of Alpha Phi Alpha fraternity, Florida
Memorial College] (Spring 1976). Profile.

"225 Written, 225 More to Go." Miami Herald (December 19
1971).

AMADEO ROLDAN (1900-1939) - Cuba

MSS in Biblioteca Nacional, Havana.

Ardevol, Jose. Musica y Revolucion. La Habana: Ediciones
Union, 1966. 223pp. Collection of Ardevol's music
criticism with many references to Roldan and Caturla.

Roldan, Amadeo. "The Artistic Position of the American
Composer." In American Composers on American Music, ed.
Henry Cowell. Stanford: Stanford University Press, 1933,
pp. 175+.

"Roldan, Amadeo." In Encyclopedia of Latin America, ed.
Helen Delpar. New York: McGraw-Hill, 1974, p. 539.

Southern, Eileen. Biographical Dictionary of Afro-American
and African Musicians. Westport, CT: Greenwood Press, 1982,
pp. 325-326.

Dissertations

Asche, Charles Byron. "Cuban Folklore Traditions and
Twentieth Century Idioms in the Piano Music of Amadeo Roldan
and Alejandro Garcia Caturla." Dissertation (D.M.A.)
University of Texas, Austin, 1983. 101pp.

Articles

"Catalogo Cronologico de las Obras mas Importantes del
Compositor Cubano Amadeo Roldan." Boletin de Musica y Artes
Visuales. Union Panamericana (Washington, D.C.), No. 38
(abril 1953): 18-21.

Compositores de America/Composers of the Americas, ed. Pan
American Union (Washington, D.C.), Vol. 1 (1955): 77+.

Cowell, Henry. "Roldan and Caturla of Cuba." Modern Music,
Vol. 18, No. 2 (January-February 1941): 98-99.

_____. "Motivos de Son, a Series of 8 Songs for Sopranos
with a Small Orchestra." Musical Quarterly, Vol. 36 (1950):
270+.

Leon, Argeliers. "Las Obras para Piano de Amadeo Roldan."
Revista de Musica, Vol. 1, No. 4 (October 1960): 112-123.

"La Muerta del Maestro Amadeo Roldan." Estudios
Afrocubanos, Vol. 3 (1939): 109-121. Obituary.

Valdes de Guerra, Carmen. "Amadeo Roldan, Musico e
Ejemplar." Revista de Musica, Vol. 1, No. 3 (julio 1960):
72-89.

NOAH FRANCIS RYDER (1914-1964)

Johnson, Marjorie S. "Noah Francis Ryder (1914-1964): A
Study of His Life, Works, and Contributions to Music
Education." Thesis (M.A.) Catholic University, 1968.

_____. "Noah Francis Ryder: Composer and Educator." The
Black Perspective in Music (Spring 1978): 18-31.

McGinty, Doris Evans. "Ryder, Noah Francis." In The New
Grove Dictionary of American Music, Vol. 4, p. 115.

Southern, Eileen. Biographical Dictionary of Afro-American
and African Musicians. Westport, CT: Greenwood Press, 1982,
pp. 328-329.

Tischler, Alice. "Noah Francis Ryder." In Fifteen Black
American Composers: A Bibliography of Their Works. Detroit,
MI: Information Coordinators, 1981, pp. 259-276.

CHEVALIER DE SAINT-GEORGES (1739-1799) - France

Abdul, Raoul. "A Chevalier Rediscovered." In Blacks in
Classical Music. New York: Dodd, Mead & Co., 1977, pp.
26-28.

Beauvoir, Roger de. Le Chevalier de Saint-Georges. Paris:
Dumont, 1840. 2 vols. [Novel - Held by the Schomburg
Collection, NYPL, NYC]

La Boessiere. "Notice Historique sur Saint-Georges."
Traite de l'Art des Armes. Paris, 1818.

Brook, Barry S. La Symphonie Francaise dans la Seconde
Moitie du XVIIIe Siecle. Paris: Institut de Musicologie de
l'Universite de Paris, 1962. 3 vols. [Brook's documented
biography occupies Vol. I, pp. 375-386; a catalogue of
Saint-Georges's works, Vol. II, pp. 641-649; a transcription
of the Symphonie Concertante in G, Catalogue No. 10 (1782)
for strings with two solo violins, Vol. III, pp. 147-169].

_____. "Saint-Georges, Joseph Boulogne, Chevalier de."
In Die Musik in Geschichte und Gegenwart. [Contains
extensive bibliography.]

Denys, Odet. Qui Etait Le Chevalier de Saint-Georges,
1739-1799? Paris: Le Pavillon, 1972. 210pp.

Derr, Ellwood. "Saint-Georges, Joseph Boulogne, Chevalier
de." In The New Grove Dictionary of Music and Musicians,
Vol. 16, pp. 391-392.

Fetis, Francois Joseph. Biographie Universelle des
Musiciens. Paris: Firmin-Didot and Cie, 1875-1878. 2nd
ed. Contains biographical sketch of Saint-Georges.

Fleming, Beatrice J., and Marion J. Pryde. "Le Chevalier de
Saint-Georges." In Distinguished Negroes Abroad.
Washington, D.C.: Associated Publishers, 1946, pp. 63-69.

Hare, Maud Cuney. Negro Musicians and Their Music.
Washington, D.C.: Associated Publishers, 1936, pp. 288-292.

La Laurencie, Lionel de. L'Ecole Francaise de Violon de
Lully a Viotti. Etudes d'Histoire et d'Esthetique. Paris:
Delagrave, 1922-1924. 3 vols. [Volume II, pp. 449-500,
contains an expanded and corrected version of La Laurencie's
Musical Quarterly article of 1919 (see below).

Robinson, Wilhelmena S. Historical Afro-American
Biographies (International Library of Afro-American Life and
History). Washington, D.C.: Associated Publishers, 1976,
pp. 15-16.

Rogers, J. A. "Chevalier de St. Georges: Dazzling Black
Nobleman of Versailles (1745-1799)." In World's Great Men
of Color. Vol. II. New York: Macmillan, 1972, pp. 65-73.
(Orig. 1947)

Southern, Eileen. Biographical Dictionary of Afro-American
and African Musicians. Westport, CT: Greenwood Press, 1982,
pp. 330-331.

Dissertations

Braun, Melanie. "The Chevalier de Saint-Georges: An
Exponent of the Symphonie Concertante." Thesis (M.M.) North
Texas State University, 1982. 131pp.

Articles

Brook, Barry S. "The Symphonie Concertante: An Interim
Report." Musical Quarterly, Vol. 47, No. 4 (October 1961):
493-505.

"Le Chevalier de Saint-Georges." Music and Musicians, Vol.
23 (November 1974): 10+.

"The Chevalier de Saint-Georges." Negro History Bulletin
(December 1937): 7.

Courier-Journal Magazine (February 10 1974): 29+.

De Lerma, Dominique-Rene. "The Chevalier de Saint-Georges."
Black Perspective in Music (Spring 1976): 3-21.

_____. "Two Friends Within the Saint-Georges Songs."
The Black Perspective in Music, Vol. 1, No. 2 (Fall 1973):
115-119.

Duncan, John. "The Chevalier de Saint-Georges: Musician
Patriot." Negro History Bulletin (March 1946): 129-130, 142.

La Laurencie, Lionel de. "The Chevalier de Saint-Georges,
Violinist." Trans. by Frederick H. Martens. Musical
Quarterly, Vol. 5, No. 1 (January 1919): 74-85.

Reed, Gladys Jones. "The Chevalier de Saint-Georges."
Negro History Bulletin, Vol. IV, No. 3 (December 1940): 67.

Tuesday (March 1968): 10+.

IGNATIUS SANCHO (1729-1780) - near Guinea, West Africa

Child, Lydia M. "Ignatius Sancho." In The Freedmen's Book.
New York: Arno Press, 1968, pp. 1-12. (Reprint of 1865 ed.)

Fleming, Beatrice J., and Marion J. Pryde. "Ignatius
Sancho." In Distinguished Negroes Abroad. Washington,
D.C.: Associated Publishers, 1946, pp. 118-124.

Hare, Maud Cuney. Negro Musicians and Their Music.
Washington, D.C.: Associated Publishers, 1936, pp. 292-295.

Robinson, Wilhelmena S. Historical Afro-American
Biographies (International Library of Afro-American Life and
History). Washington, D.C.: Associated Publishers, 1976,
pp. 30-31.

"Sancho, Ignatius." In The Dictionary of National
Biography. Vol. 17, pp. 732-733.

Sancho, Ignatius. Letters of the Late Ignatius Sancho, an
African. To Which are Prefixed, Memoirs of His Life. 5th
ed. London: Printed for W. Sancho by Wilke and Taylor,
1803. 310pp.

Scobie, Edward. Black Brittania: A History of Blacks in
Britain. Chicago: Johnson Publishing Co., 1972, pp. 95-100.

Southern, Eileen. Biographical Dictionary of Afro-American
and African Musicians. Westport, CT: Greenwood Press, 1982,
p. 331.

Wright, Josephine. Ignatius Sancho (1729-1780): An Early
African Composer in England. The Collected Editions of His
Music in Facsimile. New York: Garland Publishing Co.,
1981. 90pp.

Articles

Edwards, P. "Ignatius Sancho." History Today, Vol. 31
(September 1981): 44.

Wright, Josephine. "Ignatius Sancho (1729-1780), African
Composer in England." The Black Perspective in Music (Fall
1979): 133-167.

ALVIN SINGLETON (1940-   )

Montague, Stephen. "Singleton, Alvin (Elliot)." In The New
Grove Dictionary of American Music, Vol. 4, p. 234.

Wyatt, Lucius. "Conversation with...Alvin Singleton,
Composer." The Black Perspective in Music (Fall 1983):
178-189.

HALE SMITH (1925-   )

Abdul, Raoul. "Hale Smith's Rituals." In Blacks in
Classical Music. New York: Dodd, Mead & Co., 1977, pp.
42-43.

Davis, Russell H. Black Americans in Cleveland.
Washington, D.C.: Associated Publishers, 1972, p. 402.

"Hale Smith." In The Black Composer Speaks, eds. David N.
Baker, Lida N. Belt, and Herman C. Hudson. Metuchen, NJ:
Scarecrow Press, 1978, pp. 313-336.

Smith, Hale. "Here I Stand." In Readings in Black American
Music, ed. Eileen Southern. 2nd ed. New York: Norton,
1983, pp. 323-326.

Southern, Eileen. Biographical Dictionary of Afro-American
and African Musicians. Westport, CT: Greenwood Press, 1982,
p. 344.

_____. "Smith, Hale." In The New Grove Dictionary of
Music and Musicians, Vol. 17, p. 414.

_____. "Smith, Hale." In The New Grove Dictionary of
American Music, Vol. 4, p. 246.

Dissertations

Breda, Malcolm Joseph. "Hale Smith: A Biographical and
Analytical Study of the Man and His Music." Dissertation
(Ph.D., Music Education) University of Southern Mississippi,
1975. 240pp.

Spence, Martha Ellen Blanding. "Selected Song Cycles of
Three Contemporary Black American Composers: William Grant
Still, John Duncan and Hale Smith." Dissertation (D.M.A.)
University of Southern Mississippi, 1977. 143pp.

Articles

Caldwell, Hansonia L.   "Conversation with Hale Smith: A Man of Many Parts." The Black Perspective in Music (Spring 1975): 58-76.

"The Changing Scene." Music Educators Journal, Vol. 50, No. 6 (1964): 14.

Cleveland News (March 12 1953).

Cleveland Plain Dealer (March 27 1968).

Cleveland Plain Dealer (December 25 1968).

"Contemporary Composers and Their Works." Music and Artists, Vol. 4, No. 2 (1971): 10.

"Hale Smith." BMI: The Many Worlds of Music (March 1963).

Scanlan, R.   "Spotlight on Contemporary American Composers: Hale Smith." The NATS Bulletin, Vol. 33, No. 4 (1977): 40-41.

Smith, Hale.   "The Commercial Composer Enters the School Music Field - A Phenomenon of Our Times." Instrument, Vol. 22 (November 1967): 88-89.

FELA SOWANDE (1905-   ) - Nigeria

Abdul, Raoul.   "Fela Sowande's Seventieth Birthday."   In Blacks in Classical Music. New York: Dodd, Mead & Co., 1977, pp. 32-33.

Southern, Eileen.   Biographical Dictionary of Afro-American and African Musicians. Westport, CT: Greenwood Press, 1982, pp. 354-355.

"Sowande, Fela." The New Grove Dictionary of Music and Musicians, Vol. 17, p. 780.

Articles

Edet, Edna M.   "An Experiment in Bi-Musicality." Music Educators Journal, Vol. 52, No. 4 (1966): 144.

"Honored Composer." Music: the AGO and RCCO Magazine, Vol. 6 (February 1972): 14.

Levinson, L.   "Fela Sowande of Nigeria at Carnegie; Music More Western Than African." Variety (June 6 1962): 2+.

New York Times (June 2 1962): 9.   Review of NY concert.

Southern, Eileen.   "Conversation with Fela Sowande." The Black Perspective in Music, Vol. 4, No. 1 (Spring 1976): 90-104.

WILLIAM GRANT STILL (1895-1978)

Arvey, Verna. Studies of Contemporary American Composers:
William Grant Still. New York: J. Fischer, 1939. 48pp.

_____. In One Lifetime: The Biography of William Grant
Still. Fayetteville: University of Arkansas Press, 1984.

Detels, Claire, ed. William Grant Still Studies at the
University of Arkansas: A 1984 Congress Report.
Fayetteville: University of Arkansas, 1985. 65pp.

Haas, Robert Bartlett, ed. William Grant Still and the
Fusion of Cultures in American Music. Los Angeles: Black
Sparrow Press, 1972. 202pp.

Books with Sections on W.G. Still

Abdul, Raoul. Blacks in Classical Music. New York: Dodd,
Mead & Co., 1977, pp. 28-32, 124-125.

Arvey, Verna. "The Ballets of William Grant Still."   In
Choreographic Music. New York: Dutton, 1941.

Embree, Edwin R. "Music Maker." In 13 Against the Odds.
New York: The Viking Press, 1944, pp. 197-210.

Goss, Madeleine. "William Grant Still."   In Modern Music
Makers. New York: Dutton, 1952, pp. 207-221.

Hare, Maud Cuney. Negro Musicians and Their Music.
Washington, D.C.: Associated Publishers, 1936, pp. 333-336.

Hughes, Langston. "William Grant Still." In Famous Negro
Music Makers. New York: Mead & Co., 1955, pp. 83-89.

Martin, Fletcher, ed. Our Great Americans: The Negro
Contribution to American Progress. Chicago: Gamma
Corporation, 1954, p. 14-15.

Richardson, Ben, and William A. Fahey. "William Grant
Still." In Great Black Americans. 2nd ed. New York:
Thomas Y. Crowell Co., 1976, pp. 3-11.

Rossi, Nick, and Robert A. Choate. Music of Our Time.
Boston: Crescendo Publishing Company, 1969, pp. 236-244.

Still, William Grant. "The Structure of Music." In Readings
in Black American Music, ed. Eileen Southern. New York:
Norton, 1983. 2nd ed., pp.314-317. (Orig. published in
Etude Music Magazine, March 1950.)

Biographical Dictionaries

ASCAP Biographical Dictionary. New York: 1948, 1952, 1966.

Ewen, David. Composers of Today. New York: H. W. Wilson,
1934, pp. 270-271.

_____. American Composers Today. New York: H. W.
Wilson, 1949, pp. 232-233.

_____. Composers Since 1900. New York: H. W. Wilson,
1969, pp. 545-547.

International Cyclopedia of Music and Musicians (1939).

Negro Yearbook, 1952. New York: William H. Wise & Co. for
Tuskegee Institute, p. 62.

Pierre Key's Musical Who's Who.

Robinson, Wilhelmena S. Historical Afro-American
Biographies (International Library of Afro-American Life and
History). Washington, D.C.: Associated Publishers, 1976,
pp. 250-251.

Southern, Eileen. Biographical Dictionary of Afro-American
and African Musicians. Westport, CT: Greenwood Press, 1982,
pp. 359-361.

_____. "Still, William Grant." In The New Grove
Dictionary of Music and Musicians, Vol. 18, pp. 145-146.

_____. "Still, William Grant." In The New Grove
Dictionary of American Music, Vol. 4, pp. 311-312.

Toppin, Edgar A. "William Grant Still." In A Biographical
History of Blacks in America since 1528. New York: David
McKay, 1971, pp. 415-418.

Who is Who in Music, 1951.

Who's Who in Colored America.

Who's Who in America. All editions 1942 to 1976.

Films

William Grant Still: Trailblazer From the South. 30 min.
University of Arkansas, Fayetteville, 1984. Author Alex
Haley is host and narrator.

Dissertations

Miles, Melvin N. "A Transcription for Concert Band of the
First Movement from William Grant Still's Afro-American
Symphony." Thesis (M.A.) Morgan State University, 1978.

Simpson, Ralph Ricardo. "William Grant Still, The Man and
His Music." Dissertation (Ph.D., Music) Michigan State
University, 1964. 331pp.

Slattery, Paul Harold. "A Comparative Study of the First
and Fourth Symphonies of William Grant Still." Thesis
(M.A.) San Jose College, 1969.

Spence, Martha Ellen Blanding. "Selected Song Cycles of
Three Contemporary Black American Composers: William Grant
Still, John Duncan, and Hale Smith." Dissertation (D.M.A.)
University of Southern Mississippi, 1977. 143pp.

Thompson, Leon Everett. "A Historical and Stylistic
Analysis of the Music of William Grant Still and a Thematic
Catalogue of His Work." Dissertation (D.M.A.) University of
Southern California, 1966. 177pp.

Magazine Articles

Ardoyno, Doris. "William Grant Still." High Fidelity
(October 1984): MA18-20.

Arvey, Verna. "William Grant Still: Creative Aspects of His
Work." Dillard University Arts Quarterly (January-March
1938).

_____. "William Grant Still, Creator of Indigenous
American Music." Chesterian (London) (May-June 1939).

_____. "William Grant Still, American Composer." Co-Art
Turntable [Beverly Hills, CA] (February 1942).

"A Birthday Offering to William Grant Still." The Black
Perspective in Music (May 1975). Special WG Still issue.

"Classified Chronological Catalogue of Works by the United
States Composer, William Grant Still." Composers of the
Americas, Vol. 5 (1959): 85-97. (In Spanish and English).

Cook, J. Douglas. "Visits to the Homes of Famous Composers,
No. 3: William Grant Still." Opera, Concert and Symphony
(November 1946).

Douglass, Fannie Howard. "A Tribute to William Grant
Still." The Black Perspective in Music, Vol. 2, No. 1
(Spring 1974): 51-53.

Hains, F. "William Grant Still...An American Composer Who
Happens to Be Black." High Fidelity (March 1975): 27.

Headlee, J. A. S. "William Grant Still: A Voice Still High
Sounding." Music Educators Journal (February 1984): 24-30.

Gehrkens, K. W. "How About William Grant Still?" Etude
(August 1948): 478.

Hudgins, Mary D. "An Outstanding Arkansas Composer, William
Grant Still." Arkansas Historical Quarterly (Winter 1965).

"In Memoriam: William Grant Still (1895-1978)." The Black
Perspective in Music (Fall 1979): 235-243.

Jones, Isabel Morse. "Meet the Composer: William Grant
Still." Musical America (December 25 1944). [Reprinted as
"From Tin Pan Alley to Opera." Negro Digest (May 1945)].

Lippey, Joyce, and Walden E. Muns. "William Grant Still." Music Journal (November 1963).

Mathews, Miriam. "Pylon Profile: William Grant Still - Composer." Phylon (2nd Qtr, 1951): 106-112.

Moe, Orin. "William Grant Still: Songs of Separation." Black Music Research Journal (1980): 18-36.

Morgan, L. M. "An Interview with William Grant Still." Pan Pipes, Vol. 53, No. 2 (1961): 35+.

"New Native Ballet and Opera Given in Rochester." Musical America, Vol. LI, No. II (June 1931): 13. Review of premiere of Still's "Sahdji."

Pilcher, J. M. "Negro Spiritual, Lively Leaven in the American Way of Life." Etude (April 1946): 194+.

Robinson, Louie. "38 Years of Serious Music." Ebony (February 1964): 102-106.

Southern, Eileen. "William Grant Still: List of Major Works." The Black Perspective in Music (May 1975): 235-238.

"Still, William Grant." Current Biography 1941.

Still, William Grant. "The Art of Musical Creation." The Mystic Light (Rosicrucian Magazine) (July 1936).

_____. "Can Music Make A Career?" Negro Digest (December 1949): 79-84.

_____. "For Finer Negro Music." Opportunity, Vol. 27, No. 5 (May 1939): 137.

_____. "How Do We Stand in Hollywood? " Opportunity, Vol. 23 (1945): 74-77.

_____. "Music, A Vital Factor in America's Racial Problems." The Australian Musical News (November 1 1948).

_____. "On Composing for the Harp, as told to Verna Arvey." American Harp Journal, Vol. 4, No. 4 (Winter 1974): 32-33.

_____. "The Composer Needs Determination and Faith." Etude (January 1949): 7-8.

_____. "The Composer's Creed." Music of the West, Vol. 17 (October 1961): 13-15.

_____, and Verna Arvey. "Our American Musical Resources." Showcase (Music Clubs Magazine), Vol. 41 (1961): 7-9.

_____. "The Lost Audience for New Music." Music Journal (1966 Annual): 38-39.

_____ . "Answer to a Questionnaire." Arts and Society (1968). Special "Arts in the Black Revolution" issue.

"William Grant Still." Flash! (November 15 1938). Photographs.

"William Grant Still." Jet (May 14 1984): 19.

"William Grant Still." Music Journal (January-February 1949): 21.

Newspaper Articles

Butler, Henry. "Still Is Grateful for Tin Pan Alley Days." Indianapolis News (March 6 1970).

Fleming, John. "Composer Proves There's No Color Line in Music World." Arkansas Gazette (August 9 1953).

Greene, Patterson. "Bridging a Musical Gap." Los Angeles Herald-Examiner (September 8 1963).

Hudgins, Mary D. "William Grant Still, The Dean of Negro Composers." Arkansas Gazette (January 30 1966).

Kennan, Clara B. "Native of Little Rock is Widely Celebrated Negro Composer." Arkansas Gazette (August 5 1951).

Monson, Karen. "Still Has Lived Through Musical Changes." Los Angeles Herald-Examiner (January 24 1970).

Nelson, Boris. "William Grant Still: 50 Years of Music." Toledo (Ohio) Blade (May 2 1965).

New York Age (April 9 1938): 7.

New York World-Telegram (June 8 1940): 8.

New York Times (May 26 1940): Sec. IX, p. 5. Discussion of Still's composition "And They Lynched Him on a Tree."

Seidenbaum, Art. "Harmony Aim of Negro Composer." Los Angeles Times (September 7 1963).

Still, William Grant. "Fifty Years of Progress in Music." The Pittsburgh Courier (November 11, 1950): 15.

Obituaries

Billboard (December 16 1978): 83.

Black Perspective in Music, Vol. 7, No. 2 (Fall 1979): 283.

Cadence (January 1979): 44.

Central Opera Service Bulletin, Vol. 21, No. (1978-79): 38.

Chicago Defender Accent (December 16 1978): 3.

Diapason (March 1979): 15.

Down Beat (January 25 1979): 10.

High Fidelity (May 1979): 19.

International Musician (January 1979): 18+.

Melody Maker (January 13 1979): 39.

Music Clubs Magazine, Vol. 58, No. 2 (1978-79): 31.

Music Educators Journal (March 1979): 76.

Music Trades (January 1979): 116.

The Musical Times (March 1979): 244.

Opera News (May 1979): 51.

School Musician (February 1979): 57.

Sepia (February 1979): 8.

Symphony News, Vol. 30, No. 1 (1979): 47.

"Still, William Grant." Current Biography 1979, p. 474.

Variety (December 13 1978): 111.

"William Grant Still Black, 83, Composer." New York Times (December 6 1978): B-6. Obituary.

HOWARD SWANSON (1907-1978)

Abdul, Raoul. "The Black Experience in Sound." In Blacks in Classical Music. New York: Dodd, Mead & Co., 1977, pp. 34-38.

Davis, Russell H. Black Americans in Cleveland. Washington, D.C.: Associated Publishers, 1972, pp. 400-401.

"Howard Swanson." In The Black Composer Speaks, eds. David N. Baker, Lida N. Belt, and Herman C. Hudson. Metuchen, NJ: Scarecrow Press, 1978, pp. 337-355.

Southern, Eileen. Biographical Dictionary of Afro-American and African Musicians. Westport, CT: Greenwood Press, 1982, pp. 364-365.

_____. "Swanson, Howard." In The New Grove Dictionary of Music and Musicians, Vol. 18, pp. 396-397.

_____. "Swanson, Howard." In The New Grove Dictionary of American Music, Vol. 4, p. 337.

Dissertations

Ennett, Dorothy.   "An Analysis and Comparison of Selected
Piano Sonatas by Three Contemporary Black Composers: George
Walker, Howard Swanson, and Roque Cordero." Dissertation
(Ph.D., Education) New York University, 1973.

Jackson, Raymond.   "The Piano Music of Twentieth-Century
Black America as Illustrated Mainly in the Works of Three
Composers [Dett, Swanson, and Walker]." Dissertation
(Ph.D.) Juilliard School of Music, 1973.

Porter, Clara Womack.   "A Study of Selected Art Songs of
Howard Swanson (Black Composer)." Dissertation (D.M.A.)
University of Kentucky, 1982. 99pp.

Reisser, Marsha Jean.   "Compositional Techniques and
Afro-American Musical Traits in Selected Published Works by
Howard Swanson." Dissertation (Ph.D.) University of
Wisconsin-Madison, 1982. 320pp.

Articles

Cleveland Orchestra Program Notes (March 6, 8, 1952): 553.
Biographical portrait.

Cleveland Plain Dealer (September 9 1951).

Cowell, Henry.   "Current Chronicle: Short Symphony."
Musical Quarterly (April 1951): 252.

Harman, Carter.   "Composer of Talent." New York Times
(December 3 1950).

Moe, Orin.   "The Songs of Howard Swanson." Black Music
Research Journal (1981-1982): 57+.

New York Amsterdam News (July 2 1977).

Nolan, Robert L.   "The Music of Howard Swanson." Negro
History Bulletin (December 1971): 177-178.

Quillian, J. W.   "Howard Swanson and Sergius Kagen."
Repertoire (November 1951): 92-96.

Reisser, Marsha J.   "Polytonal Considerations in Selected
Works of Howard Swanson." Black Music Research Journal
(1981-1982): 34-56.

Sims, Maxine D.   "An Analysis and Comparison of Piano
Sonatas by George Walker and Howard Swanson." The Black
Perspective in Music (Spring 1976): 70-81.

Spearman, Rawn Wardell.   "The "Joy" of Langston Hughes and
Howard Swanson." The Black Perspective in Music (Fall
1981): 121-137.

"The Swanson Story." Music News (October 1951): 11.

"Year's Best; Short Symphony." Time (January 21 1952): 42+.

Obituaries

Abdul, Raoul. "In Memoriam: Howard Swanson (1895-1978)."
The Black Perspective in Music, Vol. 7, No. 2 (Fall 1979):
244-250.

Billboard (November 25 1978): 108.

Black Perspective in Music, Vol. 7, No. 2 (Fall 1979): 283.

Blau, Eleanor. "Howard Swanson, 71; Musical Compositions
Covered Wide Range." New York Times (November 13 1978): B9.

Variety (November 15 1978): 94.

Washington Post (November 14 1978): C-6.

FREDERICK C. TILLIS (1930-   )

Moore, Carman. "Tillis, Frederick Charles." In The New
Grove Dictionary of American Music, Vol. 4, pp. 394-395.

Southern, Eileen. Biographical Dictionary of Afro-American
and African Musicians. Westport, CT: Greenwood Press, 1982,
pp. 375-376.

Tischler, Alice. "Frederick Charles Tillis." In Fifteen
Black American Composers: A Bibliography of Their Works.
Detroit, MI: Information Coordinators, 1981, pp. 279-295.

BENJAMIN TYAMZASHE (1890-   ) - South Africa

Hansen, Deirdre Doris. Life and Work of Benjamin Tyamzashe:
A Contemporary Xhosa Composer. Grahamstown, South Africa:
Rhodes University Institute of Social and Economic Research,
1968. 33pp. (Occasional paper, 11)

GEORGE T. WALKER (1922-   )

Abdul, Raoul. "George Walker's New Piece." In Blacks in
Classical Music. New York: Dodd, Mead & Co., 1977, pp.
40-42.

"George Theophilus Walker." In The Black Composer Speaks,
eds. David N. Baker, Lida N. Belt, and Herman C. Hudson.
Metuchen, NJ: Scarecrow Press, 1978, pp. 357-378.

Kehler, George. The Piano in Concert. Metuchen, NJ:
Scarecrow Press, 1982. Vol. 2. Contains a brief
biographical sketch of George Walker and his career as a
pianist.

Southern, Eileen. <u>Biographical Dictionary of Afro-American and African Musicians</u>. Westport, CT: Greenwood Press, 1982, p. 387.

_____. "Walker, George." In <u>The New Grove Dictionary of Music and Musicians</u>, Vol. 20, p. 173.

_____. "Walker, George (Theophilus)." In <u>The New Grove Dictionary of American Music</u>, Vol. 4, p. 469.

Dissertations

Delphin, Wilfred. "A Comparative Analysis of Two Sonatas by George Walker: Sonata No. 1 (1953) and Sonata No. 2 (1958)." Dissertation (D.M.A., Performance) University of Southern Mississippi, 1976.

Ennett, Dorothy. "An Analysis and Comparison of Selected Piano Sonatas by Three Contemporary Black Composers: George Walker, Howard Swanson, and Roque Cordero." Dissertation (Ph.D., Education) New York University, 1973.

Jackson, Raymond. "The Piano Music of Twentieth-Century Black Americans as Illustrated Mainly in the Works of Three Composers [Dett, Swanson, and Walker]." Dissertation (Ph.D.) Juilliard School of Music, 1973.

Newson, Roosevelt. "A Style Analysis of the Three Piano Sonatas of George Theophilus Walker." Dissertation (D.M.A.), Peabody Conservatory, 1977.

Thomas, Andre Jerome. "A Study of the Selected Masses of Twentieth-Century Black Composers: Margaret Bonds, Robert Ray, George Walker, and David Baker." Dissertation (D.M.A.) University of Illinois at Urbana-Champaign, 1983. 214pp.

Articles

De Lerma, Dominique. "The Choral Works of George Walker." <u>American Choral Review</u>, Vol. 23, No. 1 (1981). Special issue.

Finn, Terri Lowen. "A Serious Composer Talks About the Path to Success." <u>New York Times</u> (February 8, 1981): Sec. 11, p. 4-5. Profile and interview with George Walker.

"George Walker." <u>Musical America</u> (November 1 1952): 18.

"George Walker." <u>Musical Courier</u> (November 1 1952): 13.

Martin, T. "George T. Walker: Classical Composer with a Touch of Soul." <u>Ebony</u> (March 1985): 124+.

Plaskin, G. "Composer Who Backed into the Business." <u>New York Times Biographical Service</u> (January 1982): 141-142.

Sims, Maxine D. "An Analysis and Comparison of Piano Sonatas by George Walker and Howard Swanson." <u>The Black Perspective in Music</u> (Spring 1976): 70-81.

Walker, George T. "It Is Clear That We Must End This."
Grecourt Review (November 1962): 31.

_____. "Piano Sound in Reproduction." Music Journal,
Vol. 22 (May 1964): 40+.

_____. "Rise from Your Curled Position." Grecourt
Review, Vol. 6 (November 1962): 30.

CLARENCE CAMERON WHITE (1880-1960)

Writings By

Biographical Information about C. C. White, 1906-1938. Reel
1, No. 1 of Papers. Includes official documents,
autobiographical sketches, brochures, and a fragmentary
scrapbook for the Hampton Institute School of Music. [Held
by the Schomburg Collection, NYPL, NYC - Sc Micro R-2474
reel 1]

White, Clarence Cameron. "The Labor Motif in Negro Music."
Modern Quarterly (1927-28): 79-81.

_____. "The Musical Genius of the American Negro." In
Negro, ed. Nancy Cunard. London: Wishart, 1934.

_____. "Negro Music a Contribution to the National Music
of America." Musical Observer, Vol. 18, No. 11 (1919):
18-19; Vol. 19, No. 1 (1920): 16-17; Vol. 19, No. 2 (1920):
50-52; Vol. 19, No. 3 (1920): 13.

_____. Papers, 1901-1940. 13 Containers. Includes
musical works, principally mss. [Held by the Schomburg
Collection, NYPL, NYC. Microfilm copies of Papers held by
the New York Public Library. Microfilm # ZB-592. 10 Reels.]

Writings About

Caldwell, Hansonia Laverne. "Black Idioms in Opera as
Manifested in the Works of Six Afro-American Composers."
Dissertation (Ph.D.) University of Southern California,
1974. Includes a discussion of White's opera Ouanga.

Hare, Maud Cuney. Negro Musicians and Their Music.
Washington, D.C.: Associated Publishers, 1936, pp. 250, 260,
329-333.

Hipsher, Edward E. "Clarence Cameron White." In American
Opera and Its Composers. New York: Da Capo Press, 1978, pp.
423-424. (Reprint of 1927 ed.)

Lemieux, Raymond. "White, Clarence Cameron." In Dictionary
of American Negro Biography, eds. Rayford W. Logan and
Michael R. Winston. New York: W.W. Norton, 1982, pp.
644-645.

Lovingood, Penman. Famous Modern Negro Musicians. New
York: Da Capo Press, 1978. (Reprint of 1921 ed.)

Robinson, Wilhelmena S. Historical Afro-American
Biographies (International Library of Afro-American Life and
History). Washington, D.C.: Associated Publishers, 1976,
pp. 259-260.

Simms, L. Moody, Jr. "White, Clarence Cameron." In
Dictionary of American Biography, Supplement 6, pp. 689-690.

Southern, Eileen. Biographical Dictionary of Afro-American
and African Musicians. Westport, CT: Greenwood Press, 1982,
pp. 398-400.

_____. "White, Clarence Cameron." In The New Grove
Dictionary of Music and Musicians, Vol. 20, p. 382.

_____. "White, Clarence Cameron." In The New Grove
Dictionary of American Music, Vol. 4, p. 515.

Magazine Articles

Allen, William Duncan. "Correspondence." The Black
Perspective in Music (Spring 1983): 97. Letter on Clarence
Cameron White.

"Bispham Memorial Medal Awarded to Clarence Cameron White."
Musical Courier (October 15 1949): 19.

"Clarence Cameron White." Pan Pipes, Vol. 45 (January
1953): 70.

"Clarence Cameron White." Violins and Violinists, Vol. 15
(May-June 1954): 140.

"Clarence Cameron White Wins Benjamin Award." Musical
Courier, No. 149 (April 1 1954): 27.

"Dr. Clarence C. White." Pan Pipes, Vol. 47 (January 1955):
71.

"Dr. Clarence Cameron White." Violins and Violinists
(November-December 1949): 324.

"Dr. Clarence Cameron White." Violins and Violinists
(May-June 1950): 179.

"Domestic Tranquility." Time (March 29 1954): 37.

Edwards, Vernon H., and Michael L. Mark. "In Retrospect:
Clarence Cameron White." The Black Perspective in Music
(Spring 1981): 51-72.

"Haitian Napoleon." (Ouanga) Opera News, Vol. 22 (November
5 1956): 20.

"How an Opera Came to be Written told by the Composer of Ouanga." Musical Courier (October 15 1949): 19.

Jet (August 11 1966): 11.

Mathews, J. F. "Ouanga: My Venture in Libretto Creation." CLA Journal (June 1972): 428-444.

"Music Study in Paris." Etude (February 1931): 89-90.

Musical Courier (December 15 1949): 3. Biographical sketch.

"Musical Pilgrimage to Haiti." Etude (July 1929): 505-506.

Negro History Bulletin (February 1939): 36. Biographical sketch.

"Negro Musician Honored: Clarence Cameron White." Southern Workman, Vol. 62 (January 1933): 13-14.

"Negro Opera: Ouanga." Variety (May 30 1956): 60.

"Notes About People; Winner of Benjamin Award for Tranquil Music." Recreation (May 1954): 311.

"Opera "Ouanga" Composer's Masterpiece." Negro History Bulletin (June 1952): 194-195.

"Ouanga, Negro Opera, Has New York Premiere." Musical America (June 1956): 18.

"Ouanga, Opera by White Premiered in South Bend." Musical Courier (July 1949): 27.

Pan Pipes (January 1952).

Pan Pipes (January 1956).

Pan Pipes (January 1957).

Pan Pipes (January 1958).

Pan Pipes (January 1960).

Shirley, Wayne D. "In Retrospect: Letters of Clarence Cameron White in the collections of the Music Division of the Library of Congress." The Black Perspective in Music (Fall 1982): 189-212.

Simms, L. M., Jr. "Clarence Cameron White: Violinist, Composer, Teacher." Negro History Bulletin (October-December 1980): 95-96.

Variety (July 31 1940): 51.

Newspaper Articles

Chicago Defender (April 24 1920).

Indianapolis Freeman (May 15 1897).

Indianapolis Freeman (October 16 1915).

New York Age (September 26 1926).

New York Age (January 15 1936).

"Prize Winner" (Benjamin Award for Tranquil Music). New
York Times (March 28 1954): Sec. 2, p. 7.

Obituaries

ASCAP News (October 1960): 4.

Jet (July 21 1960): 62.

Journal of Negro History (October 1960): 286-287.

Musical America (August 1960): 40.

New York Times (July 2 1960): 17.

Variety, No. 219 (July 20 1960): 63.

Violins and Violinists, Vol. 21, No. 4 (July-August 1960):
175.

IKOLI HARCOURT WHYTE (1905-1977) - Nigeria

Achinivu, Achinivu Kanu. Ikoli Harcourt Whyte, the Man and
His Music: A Case of Musical Acculturation in Nigeria.
Hamburg: Karl Dieter Wagner, 1979. 2 vols. (Beitrage zur
Ethnomusikologie, Bd. 7).

HENRY F. WILLIAMS (1813-1889)

Boyer, Horace Clarence. "A Portfolio of Music: The New
England Afro-American School." The Black Perspective in
Music (July 1976): 213-237.

Indianapolis Freeman (May 18 1889).

Simmons, William J. Men of Mark: Eminent, Progressive and
Rising. Chicago: Johnson Publishing Co., 1970, pp. 182-188.
(Reprint of 1887 ed.)

Southern, Eileen. Biographical Dictionary of Afro-American
and African Musicians. Westport, CT: Greenwood Press, 1982,
p. 405.

_____. "Williams, Henry F." In The New Grove Dictionary
of Music and Musicians, Vol. 20, p. 435.

_____. "Williams, Henry F." In The New Grove Dictionary
of American Music, Vol. 4, p. 531.

Trotter, James M. _Music and Some Highly Musical People_.
Chicago: Afro-Am Press, 1969, pp. 106-113.

OLLY WILSON (1937-   )

Abdul, Raoul. "Olly Wilson and Good Company." In _Blacks in
Classical Music_. New York: Dodd, Mead & Co., 1977, pp.
44-45.

"Olly Woodrow Wilson." In _The Black Composer Speaks_, eds.
David N. Baker, Lida N. Belt and Herman C. Hudson.
Metuchen, NJ: Scarecrow Press, 1978, pp. 379-401.

Southern, Eileen. _Biographical Dictionary of Afro-American
and African Musicians_. Westport, CT: Greenwood Press, 1982,
pp. 409, 410.

_____. "Wilson, Olly." In _The New Grove Dictionary of
Music and Musicians_, Vol. 20, p. 444.

_____. "Wilson, Olly." In _The New Grove Dictionary of
American Music_, Vol. 4, p. 539.

Wilson, Olly. "The Black American Composer." In _Readings
in Black American Music_, ed. Eileen Southern. 2nd ed. New
York: Norton, 1983, pp. 327-332. [Orig. published in _The
Black Perspective in Music_, Vol. 1, No. 1 (Spring 1973).]

Dissertations

Oliver, Christine E. "Selected Orchestral Works of Thomas
J. Anderson, Arthur Cunningham, Talib Rasul Hakim, and Olly
Wilson: A Descriptive Study." Dissertation (Ph.D.) Florida
State University, 1978.

Articles

"Emscope." _Electronic Music Review_, Vol. 5 (January 1968):
6.

Logan, Wendell. "Olly Wilson: _Piece for Four_."
Perspectives of New Music (Fall-Winter 1970): 126-134.

Southern, Eileen. "Conversations with Olly Wilson." _The
Black Perspective in Music_, Vol. 5, No. 1 (Spring 1977):
90-103; Vol. 6, No. 1 (Spring 1978): 57-70.

Wilson, Olly. "Contemporary Music Today; A Composer's
View." _American Organist_, Vol. 14, No. 4 (April 1980):
46-48.

_____. "The Significance of the Relationship Between
Afro-American Music and West African Music." _The Black
Perspective in Music_, Vol. 2, No. 1 (Spring 1974): 3-22.

3
Symphony and Concert Artists

CONDUCTORS

Bockman, Chris, and Nick J. Hall. "New Black Symphony Conductors." Sepia (October 1974): 18-29.

Hughes, Allen. "For Black Conductors, A Future? Or Frustration?" New York Times (March 15 1970): Sec. 2, pp. 19, 32.

"Masters of the Baton." Sepia (July 1981): 32-34.

CLAUDIO JOSE DOMINGO BRINDIS DE SALAS (1800-1872) - Cuba

Calcagno, Francisco. Diccionario Biografico Cubano. New York: Imprenta y Libreria de N. Ponce de Leon, 1878-1886.

Enciclopedia Universal Ilustrada Europeo-Americana. Madrid: Espasa-Calpe, S.A. Tomo IX, p. 859.

LaBrew, Arthur. "The Brindis de Salas Family." Afro-American Music Review (Detroit, MI), Vol. 1, No. 1 (1981): 15-57.

Southern, Eileen. Biographical Dictionary of Afro-American and African Musicians. Westport, CT: Greenwood Press, 1982, p. 48.

GEORGE BYRD

"Byrd Leads Harlem Unit of Intercultural Choir." New York Herald Tribune (August 1 1949).

Henahan, Donal. "Music: Symphony of the New World." New York Times (June 26 1972).

Mason, B. S. "And the Beat Goes On." Essence (November 1972): 51. (Profile)

Musical America (September 1959): 10. Note on G. Byrd's becoming the first black American to conduct the Berlin Philharmonic.

Strauss, Noel. "Choir Impresses in First Concert." New York Times (August 1 1949).

DENNIS DE COTEAU (1930-   )

"Orchestrally Speaking." CMEA News, Vol. 26, No. 6 (September-October 1973): 12.

"Speaking of People." Ebony (June 1975): 7. Brief bio.

LEONARD DE PAUR (1914-   )

Abdul, Raoul. "An Award for Leonard de Paur." In Blacks in Classical Music. New York: Dodd, Mead & Co., 1977, pp. 210-211.

De Lerma, Dominique-Rene. "De Paur, Leonard." In The New Grove Dictionary of American Music, Vol. 1, p. 605.

Negro Yearbook 1952, p. 53.

Southern, Eileen. Biographical Dictionary of Afro-American and African Musicians. Westport, CT: Greenwood Press, 1982, p. 100.

Articles

"De Paur to Westchester." Billboard (May 24 1969): 22.

"De Paur Infantry Choir: America's Most-Booked Concert Unit Comes Long Way Since Birth in Back Room." Ebony (December 1951): 42-46, 48-49.

"Leonard De Paur Named Conductor of the Westchester Symphony." Choral Journal, Vol. 10, No. 1 (1969): 6.

New York Age (July 16 1949).

JAMES DE PREIST (1936-   )

Abdul, Raoul. "James De Preist." In Blacks in Classical Music. New York: Dodd, Mead & Co., 1977, pp. 199-205.

Gelles, George. "De Preist, James (Anderson)." In The New Grove Dictionary of Music and Musicians, Vol. 5, p. 380.

_____. "De Preist, James (Anderson)." In The New Grove Dictionary of American Music, Vol. 1, p. 605.

Southern, Eileen. Biographical Dictionary of Afro-American and African Musicians. Westport, CT: Greenwood Press, 1982, p. 100.

Articles

De Preist, James. "Where the Responsibility Lies." Symphony News, Vol. 24, No. 5 (1973): 10-12.

"De Preist Recovering from Polio Attack." Down Beat (December 20 1962): 13.

Hiemenz, J. "Musician of the Month: James De Preist." High Fidelity (March 1977): 8-9.

"James De Preist." New York Philharmonic Program Notes (January 5 1971).

"Polio Fells Conductor on State Department Far East Tour." Variety (September 5 1962): 43.

Spero, B. "De Preist Touts U.S. Symphonies." Biography News (August 1974): 884.

"Spotlight." Music Journal (March 1975): 42.

Stern, W. H. "Music on the Air." Musical Leader (April 1966): 6.

Newspaper Articles

Crutchfield, Will. "Musician's Own Path to Podium." New York Times (July 24 1984): 21.

Denver Post Empire (October 6 1974).

Henahan, Donal. "Music: De Priest Leads." New York Times (January 13 1975): L25.

Washington Post (November 13 1974): B-15.

DEAN DIXON (1915-1976)

Abdul, Raoul. "Dean Dixon: A First." In Blacks in Classical Music. New York: Dodd, Mead & Co., 1977, pp. 191-193.

Adams, Russell L. Great Negroes, Past and Present. Chicago: Afro-Am Publishing Co., 1969, p. 185.

Bontemps, Arna. "Fiddler's Progress: Dean Dixon." In We Have Tomorrow. Boston: Houghton Mifflin Co., 1945, pp. 46-58.

Dunbar, Ernest. "Dean Dixon: Frankfurt." The Black Expatriates: A Study of American Negroes in Exile. New York: Dutton, 1968, pp. 188-200.

Ewen, David. "Dean Dixon." In Dictators of the Baton. New
York: Ziff-Davis, 1948, pp. 275-278.

Fletcher, Martin, ed. Our Great Americans: The Negro
Contribution to American Progress. Chicago: Gamma
Corporation, 1954, p. 17.

Hemming, Roy. Discovering Music. New York: Four Winds
Press, 1974, pp. 19, 293.

Hughes, Langston. "Dean Dixon." Famous Negro Music Makers.
New York: Mead & Co., 1955.

Jacobson, Bernard. "Dixon, (Charles) Dean." In The New
Grove Dictionary of Music and Musicians, Vol. 5, p. 513.

_____. "Dixon, (Charles) Dean." In The New Grove
Dictionary of American Music, Vol. 1, p. 634.

Richardson, Ben, and William A. Fahey. "Dean Dixon." In
Great Black Americans. 2nd ed. New York: Thomas Y. Crowell
Co., 1976, pp. 40-47.

Robinson, Wilhelmena S. Historical Afro-American
Biographies (International Library of Afro-American Life and
History). Washington, D.C.: Associated Publishers, 1976, p.
184.

Southern, Eileen. Biographical Dictionary of Afro-American
and African Musicians. Westport, CT: Greenwood Press, 1982,
pp. 107-108.

Toppin, Edgar A. A Biographical History of Blacks in
America since 1528. New York: David McKay, 1971, p. 281.

Who's Who in Colored America 1950, p. 157.

Magazine Articles

"An American Abroad." Time (May 4 1962): 48.

"Bias vs. Black Tooters Still Practiced by U.S. Symphs.,
Dixon Asserts." Variety, No. 261 (February 3 1971): 53.

Blanks, F. R. "Australia." Musical Times (February 1963):
124.

_____. "Australia." Musical Times (November 1967):
1026-1027.

"Crusader for the Classics: Dean Dixon Won't Be Happy Until
Sonatas Outdraw Sinatras." Ebony (February 1946): 47-50.

"Cultural Ambassador." America (May 4 1963): 628.

"Dean Dixon." Chicago Symphony Program Notes (March 9
1972): 31.

"Dean Dixon." Kansas City Philharmonic Program Notes (January 19 1971): 6.

"Dean Dixon." London Musical Events (June 1955): 13.

"Dean Dixon." London Musical Events (October 1955): 44.

"Dean Dixon." Musical Events [London] (December 1964): 16.

"Dean Dixon." Musical Opinion (May 1963): 456-457.

"Dean Dixon." New York Philharmonic Program Notes (November 25 1970).

"Dean Dixon." The Strad (May 1963): 33.

"Dean Dixon, American Conductor." The Canon (November 1962): 64-66.

"Dean Dixon and Philharmonic Orchestra." London Musical Events (July 1955): 45.

"Dean Dixon Berth to Eliahu Inbal." Variety (June 9 1971): 40.

"Dean Dixon Conducts NBC Summer Symphony." Opportunity, Vol. 19 (July 1941): 217.

"Dean Dixon, Symphony Orchestra in Request for First Lady." Opportunity, Vol. 19 (June 1941): 182.

"Dean Dixon to Make First American Tour." Variety (January 13 1971): 55.

"Dean Dixon to Reprise Europe Tour in New Bid to Promote U.S. Music." Variety (January 24 1951): 37.

"Dean Dixon Tours American Cities." Negro History Bulletin (April 1971): 93.

Derhen, A. "N.Y. Philharmonic." High Fidelity (October 1970): MA15.

"Disk Bias Charge by Negro Batoneer Dean Dixon Brings Quick Denials." Variety (April 20 1966): 1+.

"Dixon." Newsweek (August 3 1970): 62.

"Dixon, Dean." Current Biography 1943.

"Dixon Exits German Orch After 13 Yrs." Variety (June 5 1974): 57.

"First "Big Time" Symphony Conductor." The Crisis (October 1941): 322.

"German Amer Renews U.S. Negro Conductor." Variety (October 26 1966): 50.

Graham, G. P. "Dean Dixon - Musical Ambassador." The Crisis (June-July 1952): 354-357+.

Hemming, Roy. "Mirrors of Our Time: Black Conductors in Europe and the US." [Interview] Senior Scholastic (March 22 1971): 17.

Jacobson, B. "Conductor Miscast." Music and Musicians (January 1964): 33.

_____. "Soft-Centered Mahler." Music and Musicians (April 1964): 33.

Jet (August 6 1970): 55.

Kolodin, Irving. "First Appearance on the Philharmonic Podium." Saturday Review (December 12 1970): 46.

Kristoffersen, K. "Dean Dixon...Hard Work, Perseverance, Sacrifice, Humility." High Fidelity (August 1970): 18-19.

Lemmon, B. "Democracy in Music." Etude (March 1943): 148+.

Monfried, W. "Maestro Dean Dixon." Negro Digest, Vol. 12 (September 1963): 66-69.

"Musicians in the News." International News (May 1952): 29.

"Negro Conductor." Time (April 21 1941): 94-95.

"New York Philharmonic." High Fidelity (March 1971): MA25.

Potts, J. E. "The Sydney Symphony Orchestra." The Strad (March 1969): 459+.

Sadie, S. "London Music." Musical Times (December 1963): 882.

Schaefer, H. J. "Dean Dixon: ein Schallplattenportrait." Musica (Kassel), Vol. 24, No. 2 (1970): 301+.

"Schlitz Sponsors Dean Dixon." Music and Artists, Vol. 4, No. 4 (1971): 6.

Schweizer, Gottfried. "Dean Dixon." Musica [Cassell, W. Germany] (marz 1959): 186. Interview.

"Signed as Chief Conductor for a German Radio-TV Symphony Orchestra." Jet (March 17 1960): 62.

Simon, D. "Melbourne Concert Reviews." Music and Dance [Australia] (November 1962): 84.

"Spreading the Word." Time (July 21 1952): 81.

Stockholm, George. "Dean Dixon: A Return with Laurels." Music and Artists, Vol. 3, No. 3 (1970): 7+.

"Success Story." Cue, Vol. 10, No. 36 (September 6 1941): 3.

Thompson, E. "Dean Dixon: Conductor without a Country."
Ebony (October 1966): 79-80+.

"Transplanted Conductors." Musical America (April 1963): 52.

Trudeau, N. A. "When the Doors Didn't Open: A Cool
Classicist and a Soldier for Social Equality." High
Fidelity (May 1985): 57-58.

Unwin, A. "Dean Dixon." Music and Dance [Australia] (March
1963): 11.

"U.S. Negro Conducting Sydney Symph Regularly." Variety
(March 24 1965): 2.

"U.S. Negro, Dean Dixon, Sydney Symph Maestro." Variety
(March 6 1963): 45.

"U.S. Negro Will Head German Air Symph." Variety (February
24 1960): 1+.

Wagner, W. "Australia/Demonstrations for Dixon." Musical
America (September 1964): 31.

_____. "Australia." Musical America (December 1964): 94.

Ward, H. "Concert Talk." Music Journal (October 1964): 12.

Woolf, S. J. "Music for Millions." Negro Digest (August
1945): 61-64. [Condensed from June 17, 1945, New York Times
article.]

"World's Foremost Negro Conductor." Ebony (December 1957):
48-56.

"Yank Conductor Dean Dixon Exiting Sydney Symph, Hits Work
Conditions." Variety (July 26 1967): 77.

"Young Maestro from Harlem Conducts NBC Symphony at 26."
Newsweek (June 30 1941): 48+.

Newspaper Articles

Chapin, L. "Dean Dixon - Battle for Music." Christian
Science Monitor (August 26 1970): 13.

Chicago Defender (June 7 1975): 3.

Chicago Tribune (March 5 1972): 2.

Detroit Free Press (December 12 1971): B-9.

Detroit News (December 12 1979): C-9.

Evening Bulletin [Philadelphia, PA] (April 4, 1975).

New York Age (December 2 1944).

New York Herald Tribune (August 11 1941): 7.

New York Herald Tribune (March 23 1952).

New York Post (June 13 1941): 13.

New York Post (May 11 1942): 23.

New York Sun (August 12 1941): 15.

New York Times (August 10 1941): Sec. IX, p.5.   Portrait.

New York Times (January 11 1942): Sec. IX, p.6.   On career.

Taubman, H.   "Conductor Abroad."   New York Times (April 6 1952): Sec. II, p. 9.

Woolf, S. J.   "In the Groove with Bach and Beethoven."   New York Times Magazine (June 17 1945): 16+.

Obituaries

Black Enterprise (December 1976): 86-87.

Black Perspective in Music, Vol. 4, No. 3 (Fall 1976): 345.

Central Opera Service Bulletin, Vol. 20, No. 1 (1977-78): 17.

Chicago Defender (November 8 1976).

"Dixon, Dean."   Current Biography 1977, p.462.

"Dixon Dies in Exile."   Billboard (November 27 1976): 67.

Music Educators Journal (February 1977): 109.

The Musical Times (January 1977): 64.

Smothers, Ronald.   "His 'Maestro' Was Hard Won."   New York Times (November 5 1976): A22.

Symphony News, Vol. 27, No. 6 (1976): 28-29.

Variety   (November 10 1976): 71.

The Washington Star (November 5 1976).

W. RUDOLPH DUNBAR (1907-   ) - British Guiana

De Lerma, Dominique-Rene.   "Dunbar, W. Rudolph."   In The New Grove Dictionary of American Music, Vol. 1, pp. 659-660.

Dunbar, Rudolph.   4 Festivals de Musique Symphonique Americaine Diriges par Rudolph Dunbar a Paris...1945. Paris: Imprime sur les Presses de Curial-Archereau, 1946. 89pp. (Contents. - Documentary accounts of the American festivals of music in Paris, by Rudolph Dunbar. - Presentation of the programmes in the four concerts of the

American festivals of music in Paris, by Rudolph Dunbar. -
Opinion of the French press.) [Held by the Schomburg
Collection, NYPL, NYC]

_____. Treatise on the Clarinet (Boehm system). St. Mary
Cray [Eng.] J.E. Dallas, 1941. 141pp.

Rogers, J. A. World's Great Men of Color. New York:
Macmillan, 1972, Vol. 2, pp. 563.

Southern, Eileen. Biographical Dictionary of Afro-American
and African Musicians. Westport, CT: Greenwood Press, 1982,
p. 117.

Articles

Arvey, Verna. "Britain Applauds Rudolph Dunbar."
Opportunity, Vol. 20 (1942): 330.

"Clarinet Virtuoso Rudolph Dunbar Returns, To Teach."
Melody Maker (July 8 1950): 6.

"Debut in the Bowl." Time (September 2 1946): 41-42.

"Dunbar, W. Rudolph." Current Biography 1946, pp. 164-166.

Howard, T. "Dunbar and Yank Music Open Some Paris Ears."
Newsweek (October 29 1945): 111.

Prattis, P. L. "Rudolph Dunbar." Our World, Vol. 1, No. 1
(April 1946): 3.

"Rhythm in Berlin." Time (September 10 1946): 64.

Southern, Eileen. "In Retrospect: W. Rudolph Dunbar,
Pioneering Orchestra Conductor." The Black Perspective in
Music (Fall 1981): 193-225.

"U.S. Negro Conducts Berlin Orchestra; Opera Resumes."
Musical Courier (October 1 1945).

Newspaper Articles

Chicago Defender (January 9 1943).

De Lerma, Dominique-Rene. "Rudolph Dunbar, Conductor."
Baltimore Afro-American (June 17 1978): 17.

"Dunbar Scores in London." New York Times (April 27 1942).

New York Age (May 9 1925).

New York Amsterdam News (September 8 1945).

New York Post (August 19 1946): 31.

"Paris Hears Concert of American Music." New York Times
(October 14 1945).

JAMES FRAZIER, JR. (1940-1985)

Southern, Eileen. Biographical Dictionary of Afro-American and African Musicians. Westport, CT: Greenwood Press, 1982, p. 138.

Articles

Applebaum, S. and S. "Music in America." The Strad (March 1970): 533.

Bims, Hamilton. "A New Breed Maestro." Ebony (May 1972): 140-142, 144, 146, 148-149.

"Black Baton Master to Electrify TV Audiences." Jet (January 15 1976): 58. Preview of James Frazier's WNBC-TV special "Soul and Symphony."

"Black Yank Conductor Woos Spanish Patrons with German 'Messiah'." Variety (November 28 1973): 57.

"The Guest Conductor." Detroit Symphony Program Notes (November 7 1968): 165.

"Here and There." High Fidelity (February 1972): MA2.

"James Frazier, a Black Detroit Conductor Who Made His Debut in 1964 as a Conductor of the Detroit Symphony Orchestra, Won the Cantelli Prize in Milan, Italy Conducting the La Scala Orchestra." Jet (December 11 1969): 62.

Jet (December 17 1970): 61. Notice upon James Frazier's becoming the first black American to conduct the National Symphony.

Jet (August 29 1974): 18.

Kazakova, V., and L. Butir. "Frazier Conducts in Yaroslavl." Music Journal (March 1972): 48.

"The Musical Whirl." High Fidelity (June 1970): 23.

"New Man at the National." Ebony (December 1972): 127-128+.

Thomas, C. "Detroit Acclaims James Frazier." Negro History Bulletin (November 1964): 28.

Webster, D. "National Afro-American Philharmonic." High Fidelity (October 1978): 40-41+.

"Young Conductor." Negro Digest (July 1968): 24-25.

Newspaper Articles

"A Black Conductor Pushes the Cause of Music." New York Times (November 30 1975): 142.

Chicago Defender (October 20 1973): 19.

Chicago Defender Accent (February 24 1979): 2.

Chicago Defender Accent (June 30 1979): 4.

Detroit Free Press (January 5 1969): B-7.

Detroit Free Press (November 23 1969): A-3.

Detroit News (November 14 1971): C-23.

Detroit News (January 16 1972): 13-17+.

Detroit News (June 11 1972): A-28.

Detroit News (October 21 1973): J-4.

Ericson, Raymond. "Music: Black Symphony." New York Times
(May 24 1978): C21. Article on the debut of the National
Afro-American Philharmonic Orchestra led by James Frazier.

Philadelphia Tribune (April 27 1974).

Obituaries

The Black Perspective in Music, Vol. 13, No. 2 (Fall 1985):
242-243.

"James Frazier, Jr." Variety (March 27 1985): 110.

PAUL FREEMAN (1936-   )

De Lerma, Dominique-Rene. "Freeman, Paul (Douglas)." In
The New Grove Dictionary of American Music, Vol. 2, p. 167.

Southern, Eileen. Biographical Dictionary of Afro-American
and African Musicians. Westport, CT: Greenwood Press, 1982,
pp. 138-139.

Articles

Ardoin, J. "A Black Composers Concert." American Musical
Digest, Vol. 1, No. 5 (1970): 5-6. [Reprinted from The
Dallas Morning News (January 31 1970)].

_____. "The DCO: Good News." High Fidelity (February
1969): MA30.

"Dallas Names Negro as a Conductor." Billboard (June 1
1968): 34.

"Dr. Paul Freeman is to Symphony Music What Jackie Robinson
Was to Baseball." Sepia (April 1968): 37.

Freeman, Paul. "Black Symphonic Music Will Now Be Heard."
Symphony News, Vol. 24, No. 6 (1973-74): 7-10.

_____. "Cultural Exchange: An American in Poland."
Music Journal (November 1964): 55-56.

"Guest Conductor." Buffalo Philharmonic Program Notes
(November 8 1970): 7.

"March's Guest Artists." San Francisco Symphony Program
Notes (March 1967): 9.

"Negro to Baton Symph in South for 1st Time." Variety (June
21 1967): 2.

"Orchestras." Music and Artists, Vol. 3, No. 2 (1970): 40.

"Paul Freeman." Chicago Symphony Program Notes (March 9
1972): 452.

"Spotlight." Music Journal (December 1973): 12-15.

Newspaper Articles

Chicago Defender Accent (March 24 1979): 4.

Courier-Journal Magazine (February 10 1974): 29+.

Detroit Free Press (November 18 1973): B-10.

Detroit News (November 28 1971): B-9.

Detroit News Magazine (October 21 1973): 8.

Henahan, Donal. "Conductor Brings to Light Blacks'
Symphonic Works." New York Times (May 8 1974): 39. Article
on Paul Freeman's interest in classical music by black
composers with comments by Freeman himself.

Pittsburgh Courier (March 11 1978): 7.

MARGARET HARRIS (1943-   )

Ammer, Christine. Unsung: A History of Women in American
Music. Westport, CT: Greenwood Press, 1980, p. 218.

Seed, Suzanne. Saturday's Child. New York: O'Hara, 1973,
pp. 16-20.

Southern, Eileen. Biographical Dictionary of Afro-American
and African Musicians. Westport, CT: Greenwood Press, 1982,
pp. 168-169.

Articles

"Black Women 'Star' Behind Scenes in New York Drama." Ebony
(April 1973): 107, 111. Includes brief mention of Harris in
her role as a conductor of Broadway shows.

Brookmire, P. "Music Prodigy Conducts Life with Ease."
Biography News (April 1974): 408.

Contos, C. "Brava, Maestra!" High Fidelity (May 1971):
MA7-10.

"Female Conductor Blasts Today's Pop Music." Soul (August
28 1972): 16.

Jepson, B. "American Women in Conducting." Music Clubs
Magazine, Vol. 56, No. 1 (1976): 12-16. [Reprinted from The
Feminist Art Journal (Winter 1975/76): 13-18.]

Kuflik, A. "Woman in the Pit." Newsweek (August 21 1972):
82-83.

Senior, E. "Now Only One." Music and Musicians (June
1966): 50.

Tuesday-at-Home (December 1973): 4.

"Young Genius on the Rise in US." US News & World Report
(May 19 1975): 60.

Newspaper Articles

Campbell, Mary. "A 'Hair' Raising Conductor." News and
Observer (June 13 1971): 4-V.

Chicago Defender (September 6 1975): 3.

Chicago Today (July 11 1971): 55.

Cook, Joan. "A Piano Prodigy at 3, Now the Conductor of
'Hair'." New York Times (November 5 1970).

Detroit Free Press (August 3 1975): D-9.

Grand Rapids Press (April 5 1970): B-3.

New York Times (September 13 1947). Brief article on delays
in a proposed concert tour for then 3 year old piano prodigy
Margaret Harris.

Sherman, Robert. "Margaret Harris, Conductor of 'Hair'
Makes Piano Debut." New York Times (November 16 1970).

Taylor, N. E. "Raisin's Conductor Began at Age 3."
Christian Science Monitor (January 13 1976): 14.

DARROLD VICTOR HUNT (1941-   )

Baltimore Symphony Programs, January 25-February 8, 1975, p.
25.

DiPerna, Paul. "Bringing Classical Music to the Community."
Encore American and Worldwide News (June 20 1977).

Southern, Eileen. Biographical Dictionary of Afro-American
and African Musicians. Westport, CT: Greenwood Press, 1982,
p. 190.

Who's Who Among Black Americans.

ISAIAH JACKSON (1945-   )

Hoover, Joanne Sheehy. "Jackson, Isaiah (Allen)." In The
New Grove Dictionary of American Music, Vol. 2, pp. 523-524.

Southern, Eileen. Biographical Dictionary of Afro-American
and African Musicians. Westport, CT: Greenwood Press, 1982,
p. 196.

Articles

"Appointments." High Fidelity (October 1973): MA26.

Baltimore Symphony. Programs, April 24-May 4, 1974, p. 25.

Encore (December 1974): 37.

"Isaiah Jackson III, 24-yr.-Old Ph.D. Candidate, Is The New
Black Musical Director and Conductor of the Youth Symphony
of New York." Jet (September 4 1969): 53.

"The Juilliard School." Music Journal (June 1971): 62.

Kash, S. D. "Isaiah Jackson - A Leader in the Classic
Sense." The Crisis (December 1983): 36-38.

Lewando, R. "In and Out of Tune." Music Journal (March
1971): 82.

Mason, B. S. "And the Beat Goes On." Essence (November
1972): 50.

New Courier [Pittsburgh] (July 6 1974).

EVERETT LEE (1919-   )

Abdul, Raoul. "Everett Lee's Philharmonic Debut." In
Blacks in Classical Music. New York: Dodd, Mead ·& Co.,
1977, pp. 194-197.

Davis, Russell. Black Americans in Cleveland. Washington,
D.C.: Associated Press, 1972, p. 350.

Southern, Eileen. Biographical Dictionary of Afro-American
and African Musicians. Westport, CT: Greenwood Press, 1982,
p. 241.

Magazine Articles

"Bits and Pieces." Arts Reporting Service (September 17
1973): 4.

Cincinnati Symphony Orchestra Program Notes, 2 January 1970,
p. 177.

"Curtain Calls." International Musician (May 1952): 11.

"Everett Lee Joins Dixon and Lewis as U.S. Maestros of Distinction." Variety (June 19 1968): 61+.

"Everett Lee Signed by National Artists." Musical America (May 1956): 12.

Hiemenz, J. "N.A.N.M.: 'Aida.'" High Fidelity (December 1972): MA26+.

Hinton, J. "America: New York." Opera [London] (July 1955): 444.

Humphreys, H. S. "Cincinnati: Zoo Opera Going Strong." High Fidelity (October 1970): MA 23.

Jet (April 22 1965): 11.

"Know Your Conductors." International Musician (April 1956): 50.

Lowe, S. "American Symphony." High Fidelity (April 1969): MA15-16.

Mason, B. S. "And the Beat Goes On." Essence (November 1972): 50-51.

Musician (November 1945): 234. Brief mention of the then 25 year old Lee's taking over of Leonard Bernstein's position on "On the Town."

"Spotlight." Music Journal (March 1976): 34.

"Sweden's Black Conductor Lee 'Ready to Come Home.'" Jet (October 29 1970): 57.

"La Traviata" (the first Negro to conduct at a major opera house in this country). Musical America (May 1955): 31.

Newspaper Articles

Chicago Defender (April 30 1955).

Cleveland Plain Dealer (February 16 1969).

"A Negro Conductor Appeals for a New Kind of Pioneering." New York Times (December 26 1948): Sec. X, p. 7.

New York Age (September 29 1945).

New York Age (October 26 1946).

New York Amsterdam News (January 11 1969).

New York Amsterdam News (October 8 1977).

TANIA LEON (1944-   ) - Cuba

Southern, Eileen. Biographical Dictionary of Afro-American and African Musicians. Westport, CT: Greenwood Press, 1982, pp. 242-243.

Articles

Burns, L. "Tania Leon Discovers the Baton's Force." Encore (October 1980): 47.

Ericson, Raymond. "Notes: A Conductor from Cuba." New York Times (June 22 1980): Sec. II, pp. 19, 23. Profile and interview with Cuban-born conductor Tania Leon.

Iadavaia-Cox, Angela. "Tania Leon: The Tug Between Conducting and Composing." Essence (December 1976): 72+.

HENRY LEWIS (1932-   )

Abdul, Raoul. "Henry Lewis: Another First." In Blacks in Classical Music. New York: Dodd, Mead & Co., 1977, pp. 198-199.

Ewen, David, ed. Musicians Since 1900: Performers in Concert and Opera. New York: H.W. Wilson, 1978, pp. 465-467.

Hemming, Roy. Discovering Music. New York: Four Winds Press, 1974, p. 316.

Rubin, Stephen E. "The Marrieds: Marilyn Horne and Henry Lewis." The New Met in Profile. New York: Macmillan, 1974, pp. 107-117.

Southern, Eileen. Biographical Dictionary of Afro-American and African Musicians. Westport, CT: Greenwood Press, 1982, p. 244.

Steinberg, Michael. "Lewis, Henry." In The New Grove Dictionary of Music and Musicians, Vol. 10, p. 707.

_____. "Lewis, Henry." In The New Grove Dictionary of American Music, Vol. 3, p. 39.

Who's Who in America, 1972-1973.

Articles

Ardoin, J. "Henry Lewis Conducts First New York Concert." Musical America (October 1961): 28.

"Baton Breakthrough." Newsweek (February 26 1967): 93.

"Black Baton Bonanza." Variety (July 5 1972): 44.

Bonin, J. "His Life is Classical Music." Sepia (August 1961): 32-36.

Boucher, A. "San Francisco Spring." Opera News (September 29 1962): 24.

Brozen, M. "Midsummer Mozart and Haydn." High Fidelity (November 1968): MA10.

Buffalo Philharmonic Orchestra Programs, January 26, 1969, p. 7.

"Conductor as Listener." High Fidelity (February 26 1970): 20.

"Conspirators in Algiers." Opera News (December 28 1974): 33.

Eaton, Q. "Introducing Henry Lewis." Opera News (January 20 1973): 22-23.

"February's Guest Artists." San Francisco Symphony Program Notes (February 1968): 15.

"First Again." Time (February 23 1968): 94.

"First Black Conductor in Met Opera Trench Hampered by Leads." Variety (November 8 1972): 48.

Fitzgerald, G. "New York." Opera News (December 16 1972): 32-33.

Fleming, S. "Waterloo Village Music Festival." High Fidelity (September 1968): MA32.

Fuchs, H., et al. "A Mozart-Haydn Festival at Philharmonic Hall." Music and Artists, Vol. 1, No. 4 (1968): 30-31.

Goldberg, A. "Husband, Wife Acclaimed." Musical America (April 1961): 30.

Greenfield, E. "London." High Fidelity (October 1969): 26+.

Gualerzi, G. "Turin." Opera [U.K.] (October 1970): 963.

Hemming, Roy. "Living Arts: The Young Conductors Take Over." Senior Scholastic (May 2 1968): 23.

"Henry Lewis." Detroit Symphony Program Notes (November 19 1970): 232.

"Henry Lewis." Musical Events [London] (March 1970): 13.

"Henry Lewis..." (excerpts from an interview, reprinted from ASOM Conductor's Guild newsletter, Winter 1979). Symphony News, Vol. 30, No. 3 (1979): 28-29.

"Henry Lewis, A Negro Double Bass Player with the Los Angeles Philharmonic Orchestra; Conducts Orchestra When Regular Conductor is Ill." Interracial Review (April 1961): 115.

"Henry Lewis is Named to Head the New Jersey Symphony."
High Fidelity (May 1968): MA8.

"Henry Lewis, 35, First Negro Conductor in U.S., Heads New
Jersey Symph." Variety (February 21 1968): 57.

Hiemenz, J. "Musician of the Month: Henry Lewis." High
Fidelity (September 1972): 4-5.

"Incentive to Try." Time (February 17 1961): 48.

Jet (February 15 1968): 1.

Kolodin, Irving. "West Coast Walkure; East Coast
Conductors." Saturday Review (November 11 1972): 87.

Lawrence, R., and G. Movshon. "The Metropolitan Opera."
High Fidelity (January 1973): MA12-13.

"Lewis, Henry." Current Biography 1973, pp. 248-251.

Lewis, Henry. "The Conductor as Listener." High Fidelity
(February 1970): 26.

"Lewis Resigns as New Jersey Symph Chief." Variety
(November 26 1975): 47.

"Los Angeles Chamber Orchestra." Musical Events (December
1963): 20.

"Maestro on the Rise." Ebony (May 1967): 112-119.

"M and A Reviews: The Press." Music and Artists, Vol. 1,
No. 4 (1968): 44.

Mason, E. "Rising from the Bass." Music and Musicians
(December 1963): 30.

Moore, Sally. "Couples: Henry Lewis and Marilyn Horne:
They're Playing Our Aria." People (October 14 1974): 56-59.

"More Depressing Than a Rainy Day in Newark." Arts
Reporting Service (March 22 1971): 1-2.

Morrden, E. C. "All For Love." (Interview) Opera News
(December 7 1974): 18-19.

"Names, Dates and Places." Opera News (September 1973):
10-11.

"Negro Named Conductor of N.J. Symphony." Billboard (March 2
1968): 40.

"Operatic Concert." Opera (March 1968): 259.

Saal, H. "Henry the First." Newsweek (October 30 1972):
98-99.

Sargeant, Winthrop. "A Composer of Distinction." The New
Yorker (January 24 1970).

"A Sense of Timing." Opera News (December 27 1969-January 3
1970): 18-20.

"This Week's Artists; Two American Conductors." Pittsburgh
Symphony Orchestra Program Notes (January 5 1962): 5.

"Top Face." Time (December 31 1965): 49.

Weinstock, H. "New York." Opera (U.K.) (April 1970):
310-311.

Newspaper Articles

Lewis, Henry. "In The Middle of Newark's Ghetto, A
Symphony." New York Times (July 7, 1968): Sec. 2, p. 11.
On the Afro-American's attitude toward classical music,
bringing music to black children and the author's
contribution to achieving this as a black conductor and
musician.

New York Daily News (February 20 1968): 50.

New York Post (March 6 1968): 47.

New York Post (September 9 1972): 33.

New York Times (February 16 1968).

New York Times (March 5 1971): 24.

Newsday (August 5 1968): A32.

Newsday (September 17 1972): Sec. II, p. 1+.

Schumach, M. "Soprano Goes by Her Own Set of Rules." New
York Times (April 19 1964): Sec. 2, p. 9.

Washington Post (August 2 1971): B-10.

KARL HAMPTON PORTER (1939-   )

Southern, Eileen. Biographical Dictionary of Afro-American
and African Musicians. Westport, CT: Greenwood Press, 1982,
p. 310.

Articles

Alice Tully Hall program (May 5 1974).

Ericson, Raymond. "Harlem Youths in Park Concert. 2
Month-Old Orchestra Is Led by Karl Porter." New York Times
(May 31 1968).

Fraser, C. Gerald. "Symphony Hits Audience Where It Lives." New York Times (September 8 1975): 40.

[See also Orchestras section under Harlem Philharmonic Orchestra.]

CALVIN SIMMONS (1950-1982)

Southern, Eileen. Biographical Dictionary of Afro-American and African Musicians. Westport, CT: Greenwood Press, 1982, p. 339.

Walsh, Michael. "Simmons, Calvin." In The New Grove Dictionary of American Music, Vol. 4, p. 228.

Articles

Conant, J. E. "Musician of the Month: Calvin Simmons." High Fidelity, Vol. 29, No. 3 (March 1979): MA6-7.

Conductor Calvin Simmons is Presumed Drowned in Canoeing Accident on Connery Pond near Lake Placid, NY; Body Has Yet to be Found. New York Times (August 23 1982): Sec. II, p. 6.

Ericson, Raymond. "Young Man with a Baton." New York Times (August 15 1980): Sec. III, p. 5. Profile and interview with conductor Calvin Simmons, music director of the Oakland Symphony Orchestra.

"4 Who Blazed New Career Trails." US News and World Report (May 14 1979): 62.

Heymont, George. "Calvin Simmons: View from the Pit." Essence (January 1981): 12+.

King, Wayne. "Oakland Conductor Shuns The Jazz-and-Blues Groove." New York Times (July 21 1980): Sec. III, p. 16.

"9 Young American Conductors Discuss Limited Opportunities Available to Them." New York Times (January 27 1980): Sec. II.

Ulrich, Alan. "Calvin Simmons: Oakland's Paramount Talent." Focus, Vol. 29, No. 3 (1982): 30+.

Von Buchau, S. "Born Lucky: An Interview with Calvin Simmons." Opera News (December 23 1978): 27-28.

Walsh, M. "Five for the Future." Time (April 19 1982): 86-87.

Obituaries

"Calvin Simmons." Newsweek (September 6 1982): 77.

"Calvin Simmons." Opera News (February 12 1983): 42.

"Calvin Simmons." Time (September 6 1982): 60.

"Conductor's Body is Found in Pond." New York Times
(September 1 1982): Sec. II, p. 3; Funeral services set
(September 3 1982): Sec. IV, p. 14; Rites held, San
Francisco (September 9 1982): Sec. IV, p. 26.

"Maestro Buried." Jet (September 27 1982): 18.

New York Times (August 24 1982): B-10.

Opera (December 1982): 1244.

"Simmons, Calvin Eugene." The Black Perspective in Music,
Vol. 10, No. 2 (Fall 1982): 232.

LEON THOMPSON (1928-1983)

Southern, Eileen. Biographical Dictionary of Afro-American
and African Musicians. Westport, CT: Greenwood Press, 1982,
p. 374.

Articles

Alice Tully Hall programs (May 6, 1974).

"Leon Thompson to Direct Philharmonic Education Unit." New
York Times (October 31 1970).

New York Philharmonic Program Notes (April 16, 1973).

Obituaries

The Black Perspective in Music, Vol. 9, No. 2 (Fall 1983):
226.

The New York Times (June 25 1983): 14.

HAROLD WHEELER

Encore (November 8 1976): 27-29.

Williams, J. "Emotions Motivate Arranger." Billboard
(February 28 1976): 46.

INSTRUMENTALISTS

GENERAL

Campbell, Dick. Statement by the Symphony of the New World on the Status of Minority Musicians in Symphony Orchestras of the U.S.A. New York, 1974.

Handy, D. Antoinette. Black Women in American Bands and Orchestras. Metuchen, NJ: Scarecrow Press, 1981. 319pp.

Taylor, John Armstead. "The Emergence of the Black Performing Musician in the American Symphony Orchestra." Dissertation (D.M.E.) Indiana University, 1976.

Articles

"Another Iron Curtain." Down Beat (February 5 1959): 9. On discrimination in New York symphony orchestras.

Campbell, Dick. "Black Musicians in Symphony Orchestras: A Bad Scene." The Crisis (January 1975): 12-17.

Campbell, M. "The Performer." (Excerpt from Rocky Mountain News 1-18-70) American Musical Digest, Vol. 1, No. 5 (1970): 8+. Deals with Afro-American musicians in American symphony orchestras.

Drexler, G. "Letter to the Editor." Woodwind World (December 1957): 7. LA Philharmonic becomes first major U.S. symphony to hire a Negro musician.

Dunham, B. "New York Philharmonic Gives Workshop for Minority Players." Symphony News, Vol. 22, No. 5 (1971): 12-14.

Goines, Leonard. "The Black Musicians and the Symphony Orchestra." The Feet, Vol. 1, No. 7 (February-March 1971): 4.

Hiemenz, J. "NY Philharmonic Reaches Out for Black
Players." High Fidelity/Musical America, Vol. 22 (September
1972): 18.

Holt, John. "A Color-Blind Test for Musicians." New York
Times Magazine (November 17 1969). (Letter to the Editor)

"Inside Stuff-Music." Variety (May 24 1961): 45. On lack
of Negroes in Washington's National Symphony.

"Jog Symphonies Re Race Bias." Variety, No. 215 (July 1,
1959): 52.

Marshall, M. "What's Behind the Shortage of Blacks in
Symphony Orchestras? Past Discrimination and Limited Access
to Musical Training Are Among the Reasons." Ebony
(September 1985): 36-38+.

"Nine New York Symphony Orchestra Hire Negro Artists for
First Time in 1959 Says Urban League Report; Also Negroes in
11 Broadway Musicals, TV Shows and Orchestras." Jet (March
3 1960): 62.

Raines, E. E. "Behind the Cello Player: Integrating
America's Symphony Orchestras." Civil Rights Digest, Vol.
10 (Spring 1978): 38-46.

"The Walls Come Tumbling Down." Woodwind World (November
1957): 2. A black musician is hired by the Boston Symphony.

Thomas, Fred W. "A Seat in a Symphony Orchestra." Symphony
News, Vol. 23, No. 2 (April 1972): 11-12.

Titcomb, Caldwell. "Black String Musicians: Ascending the
Scale." Black Music Research Newsletter, Vol. 5, No. 1
(Fall 1981): 5-6.

"Work Upbeat for Negro Musicians in Symph, Legit, TV."
Variety (February 10 1960): 57.

Wortham, J. "Shoot the Piano Player and the Cellist, the
Oboist and the Drummer; Blacks in the World of Orchestras."
Black Enterprise, Vol. 7 (December 1976): 31-32, 87.

Newspaper Articles

Allen, Sanford. "Why Hasn't the Negro Found a Place in the
Symphony?" New York Times (June 25 1967): Sec. 2, p. 13.

Dixon, Lucille. "Is It 'Artistic Judgement' Or Is It
Discrimination?" New York Times (August 1 1971): Sec. 2,
pp. 11, 18. Refutation of continuing argument that lack of
black representation in symphony orchestras is due simply to
questions of artistic merit.

_____. "Put Down." New York Times (May 30 1971): D12.
[Letter to the Editor]

Garekian, Barbara. "Black Music Competition Spurs
Recognition of Young Artists." New York Times (January 16
1980): Sec. 3, p. 21. On National Black Music Colloquium.

Henahan, Donal. "An About Face on Black Musicians at the
Philharmonic." New York Times (June 11, 1972): D15.

_____. "Philharmonic Plans Workshop, It's First to Train
Minorities." New York Times (August 27 1971): 17.

Hughes, Allen. "New Faces for Tonight's Philharmonic." New
York Times (September 11, 1971): 15.

_____. "Without Regard for Color." New York Times
(February 21, 1965).

Kaye, Evelyn. "Why Are There So Few Blacks in Symphony
Orchestras Today?" Boston Globe [New England Magazine] (May
15, 1977): 22, 25, 27, 30, 32.

Taubman, H. "An Even Break: Negro Instrumentalists Ask for
Chance to Earn Way into Major Ensembles." New York Times
(April 22 1956): Sec. 2, p. 9.

INDIVIDUAL INSTRUMENTALISTS

ARMENTA ADAMS - Piano

Kehler, George, comp. The Piano in Concert. Metuchen, NJ: Scarecrow Press, 1982. Vol. 1. Contains a brief biographical sketch of Armenta Adams.

Southern, Eileen. Biographical Dictionary of Afro-American and African Musicians. Westport, CT: Greenwood Press, 1982, p. 5.

Articles

Adams, Armenta. "Africa Re-Visited." High Fidelity (August 1967): 26-27.

"Armenta Adams." Musical America (March 1960): 36.

Chissell, J. "Leeds." The Musical Times (November 1963): 803.

"A Look at the Future: Nine Young Artists." Musical America (July 1963): 10.

[New York Recital] Musical America (January 1962): 248.

Newspaper Articles

A[llen] H[ughes]. "Armenta Adams in Piano Recital." New York Times (February 13 1960).

Grand Rapids Press (February 27 1972): H-7.

Henahan, Donal. "Armenta Adams Plays Memorial." New York Times (October 13 1970): 54.

Hughes, Allen. "Music: Armenta Adams Piano Recital." New York Times (January 8 1966).

New York Amsterdam News (June 27 1964).

Parmenter, Ross. "The World of Music." New York Times
(August 6 1961): Sec. 2, p. 7.

_____. "Armenta Adams Repeats 1959 Season's Success in
Recital at Town Hall." New York Times (November 20 1961).

Schonberg, Harold C. "Piano Debut is Made by Armenta
Adams." New York Times (? 1959).

ELWYN ADAMS (1933-   ) - Violin

Davis, Russell H. Black Americans in Cleveland.
Washington, D.C.: Associated Publishers, 1972, p. 401.

Southern, Eileen. Biographical Dictionary of Afro-American
and African Musicians. Westport, CT: Greenwood Press, 1982,
p. 4.

Tribune [Tampa, Florida] (April 18 1970).

Video and TV

Positively Black, WNBC-TV, 1974.

SANFORD ALLEN (1939-   ) - Violin

Abdul, Raoul. "Distinguished Music Making." In Blacks in
Classical Music. New York: Dodd, Mead & Co., 1977, pp.
183-187.

Southern, Eileen. Biographical Dictionary of Afro-American
and African Musicians. Westport, CT: Greenwood Press, 1982,
p. 10.

Articles

Henahan, Donal. "Only Black in Philharmonic is Resigning
After 15 Years." New York Times (August 29 1977): C36.

_____. "Philharmonicsville (pop. 106)." New York Times
Magazine (September 28 1969): 134-136.

Liebow, L. A., and A. Slovin. "Music in America." The
Strad (December 1977): 767+.

New York Amsterdam News (April 14 1962).

New York Amsterdam News (October 25 1962).

"Orchestra 'Symbol' Resigns." Richmond Times Dispatch
(August 30 1977): B7.

CAROL ANDERSON (1940-   ) - Violin

"Batoneer of Chi Suburb Symph Quits Over Hiring Ban on Negro
Violinist." Variety (February 13 1963): 2.

"Chicago Suburb Orchestra Moves to Bar Hiring Bias." New
York Times (August 2 1963): 17.

Janson, Donald. "Negro Violinist Wins an Apology." New
York Times (February 13 1963): 6. Article on then 23 yr old
violinist Carol Anderson who was first refused an
opportunity to perform with a suburban Chicago orchestra due
to the protest of local racists and then given an apology
and an invitation to play.

"Negro Girl, Once Rejected by Symphony, Joins Another." New
York Times (June 4 1963): 29. Article on black violinist
Carol Anderson's acceptance into previously all-white
Wheaton, IL summer symphony orchestra.

"Suburban Chi Symphony Solves Audition 'Bias'." Variety
(August 7 1963): 53.

BASILE BARES (1846-1902) - Piano

Christian, Marcus B. "Bares, Basile." In Dictionary of
American Negro Biography, eds. Rayford W. Logan and Michael
R. Winston. New York: W.W. Norton, 1982, pp. 8-9.

Desdunes, Rodolphe. Our People and Our History. Trans. by
Dorothea Olga McCants. Baton Rouge: Louisiana State
University Press, 1973. (Originally published as Nos Hommes
et Notre Histoire. Montreal, 1911).

Hare, Maud Cuney. Negro Musicians and Their Music.
Washington, D.C.: Associated Publishers, 1936, pp. 197-198.

La Tribune de la Nouvelle-Orleans. Various issues.

Southern, Eileen. Biographical Dictionary of Afro-American
and African Musicians. Westport, CT: Greenwood Press, 1982,
p. 27.

Trotter, James M. Music and Some Highly Musical People.
Chicago: Afro-Am Press, 1969, p. 341. (Orig. 1878)

THOMAS GREEN BETHUNE ["Blind Tom"] (1849-1908) - Piano

Brawley, Benjamin. The Negro Genius. New York: Biblo and
Tannen, 1969, pp. 121-133. (Reprint of 1937 ed.)

Derricotte, Elise P. Word Pictures of Great Negroes.
Washington, D.C.: Associated Publishers, 1964, pp. 13-21.

Fisher, Renee B. Musical Prodigies: Masters at an Early
Age. New York: Association Press, 1973, pp. 69-72.

Hare, Maud Cuney. Negro Musicians and Their Music.
Washington, D.C.: Associated Publishers, 1936, p. 215.

Jay, Ricky. Learned Pigs and Fireproof Women. New York:
Villard Books, 1986, pp. 74-81.

Kehler, George, comp. The Piano in Concert. Metuchen, NJ:
Scarecrow Press, 1982. Vol. 1. Contains a brief
biographical sketch of Blind Tom.

The Marvelous Musical Prodigy, Blind Tom, the Negro Boy
Pianist, Whose Performances at the Great St. James and
Egyptian Halls, London, and Salle Hertz, Paris, Have Created
Such a Profound Sensation: Anecdotes, Songs, Sketches of the
Life, Testimonials of Musicians and Savans, and Opinions of
the American and English Press of "Blind Tom". New York:
French and Wheat, 1867. 30pp. [Held by the Schomburg
Collection, NYC -- Sc Rare F 82-45]

Robinson, Wilhelmena S. Historical Afro-American
Biographies (International Library of Afro-American Life and
History). Washington, D.C.: Associated Publishers, 1976, p.
51.

Scrapbook [Boston, 1918]. 29pp. Newspaper clippings and
magazine articles concerning Blind Tom. [Held by the Boston
Public Library, Music Collection. Call # M.409.92]

Simmons, William J. Men of Mark: Eminent, Progressive and
Rising. Chicago: Johnson Publishing Co., 1970, pp. 557-560.
(Reprint of 1887 ed.)

Southall, Geneva. Blind Tom: The Post Civil War Enslavement
of a Black Musical Genius. Book I. Introduction by Samuel
A. Floyd. Minneapolis, MN: Challenge Productions, 1979.
108pp.

_____. The Continuing "Enslavement" of Blind Tom, the
Black Pianist--Composer (1865-1887). Book II. Foreword by
T.J. Anderson. Minneapolis, MN: Challenge Productions, 1983.

_____. "Bethune, Thomas Greene [Blind Tom]." In
Dictionary of American Negro Biography, eds. Rayford W.
Logan and Michael R. Winston. New York: W.W. Norton, 1982,
pp. 43-44.

_____. "Bethune (Green), Thomas [Blind Tom]." In The
New Grove Dictionary of Music and Musicians, Vol. 2, 1980,
pp. 663-664.

_____. "Bethune (Green), Thomas [Blind Tom]. In The New
Grove Dictionary of American Music, Vol. 1, 1986, pp.
203-204.

Southern, Eileen. Biographical Dictionary of Afro-American
and African Musicians. Westport, CT: Greenwood Press, 1982,
pp. 33-34.

Trotter, James M. Music and Some Highly Musical People.
Chicago: Afro-Am Press, 1969, pp. 141-159. (Orig. 1878)

Articles

Abbott, E. B.   "The Miraculous Case of Blind Tom."   The
Etude, Vol. 37 (August 1940): 517+.

Andreu, Enrique.   "Tragedia de un Beethoven Negro."   Revista
Musical Chilena (October-November 1947): 24-29.

Becket, John A'.   "Blind Tom As He Is To-day."   The Black
Perspective in Music, Vol. 4, No. 2 (July 1976): 184-188.
(Reprinted from Ladies Home Journal, Vol. 15 (September 18
1898): 13-14.)

"Blind Tom."   Dwight's Journal of Music, Vol. 22 (1862):
250-252.

"Blind Tom, The Musical Prodigy."   All The Year Round
(London), Vol. 8, (18??): 126.

Cleveland Gazette (August 1 1885).

Davis, Rebecca Blaine Harding.   "Blind Tom."   Atlantic
Monthly, Vol. 10 (1862): 580-585.

F. H. Parmelee's Musical Monthly (New London, CT), No. 13
(June 1885): 4.   [Held by the Performing Arts Research
Center at Lincoln Center, Music Division.]

Indianapolis Freeman (June 1 1889).

Juhn, Kurt.   "Black Beethoven."   Negro Digest (June 1945):
33-38.   [Condensed from April 1945, Pageant article.]

King, Anita.   "Blind Tom: A Child Out of Time."   Essence
(August 1973): 11.

Nixon, L. E.   "Blind Tom...The Incredible Imitator."   Music
Journal (October 1971): 40+.

"The Remarkable Case of the Late 'Blind Tom'.   How An
Imbecile Blind Negro Pianist Amazed Scientists and Musicians
the World Over."   The Etude, Vol. 26, No. 8 (August 1908):
532.

Riis, Thomas.   "The Cultivated White Tradition and Black
Music in Nineteenth-Century America: A Discussion of Some
Articles in J. S. Dwight's Journal of Music."   The Black
Perspective in Music, Vol. 4, No. 2 (July 1976): 161-166,
172-173.

Robinson, Norborne T. N., Jr.   "Blind Tom, Musical Prodigy."
Georgia Historical Quarterly, Vol. 51 (1967): 336-358.

Southall, Geneva.   "Blind Tom: A Misrepresented and
Neglected Pianist-Composer."   Black Perspective in Music,
Vol. 3, No. 2 (May 1975): 141-159.

Stoddard, Tom.   "Blind Tom-Slave Genius."   Storyville, No.
28 (1970): 134-138.

"Thomas Greene Bethune (1849-1908)." The Black Perspective in Music, Vol. 4, No. 2 (July 1976): 177-183.

"Thomas Green (Blind Tom)." Jet, Vol. 64 (May 30 1983): 24.

Thornton, E. M. "Strange Case of Blind Tom." Music Journal (November 1957): 16+.

_____. "The Mystery of Blind Tom." The Georgia Review, Vol. 15 (1961): 395+.

Tutein, A. "The Phenomenon of 'Blind Tom'." The Etude, Vol. 37 (1918): 91.

Obituaries

Musical America, Vol. VIII, No. 6 (1908): 8. (See also "Mephistos Musings", p. 13 of this same issue.)

New York Age (June 18 1908).

New York Age (July 2 1908).

New York Dramatic Mirror, Vol. 59, No. 1539 (1908): 5. [Held by the Performing Arts Research Center at Lincoln Center, Music Division.]

CAROL BLANTON (1911-1974) - Piano

Southern, Eileen. Biographical Dictionary of Afro-American and African Musicians. Westport, CT: Greenwood Press, 1982, p. 38.

Articles

New York Age (January 25 1919).

Obituary. Baltimore Afro-American (February 19-23 1974).

Obituary. The Black Perspective in Music, Vol. 2, No. 2 (Fall 1974): 225.

ALAN BOOTH (1920-   ) - Piano

Baumel, R. B. "An Integrated Trio Goes South." High Fidelity (July 1970): 26-27+.

Southern, Eileen. Biographical Dictionary of Afro-American and African Musicians. Westport, CT: Greenwood Press, 1982, p. 42.

ARTHUR L. BOYD (d.1986) - Violin

Obituary. The Black Perspective in Music, Vol. 14, No. 2 (Fall 1986): 322-323.

GEORGE A. P. BRIDGETOWER (1779-1860) - Violin - Biala, Poland

Abdul, Raoul. "The African Prince." In <u>Blacks in Classical</u>
<u>Music</u>. New York: Dodd, Mead & Co., 1977, pp. 175-178.

Adams, Russell L. <u>Great Negroes, Past and Present</u>. Chicago:
Afro-Am Publishing Co., 1969, p. 172.

Bridgetower, George A. P. <u>Diatonica Armonica for the</u>
<u>Pianoforte</u>. London, 1812.

"Bridgetower, George Augustus Polgreen." In <u>The Dictionary</u>
<u>of National Biography</u>. Vol. 2. London: Oxford University
Press, 1917, pp. 1231-1232.

Fleming, Beatrice, and Marion Pryde. "George Polgreen
Bridgetower." In <u>Distinguished Negroes Abroad</u>. Washington,
D.C.: Associated Publishers, 1946, pp. 160-165.

Groves, George. "Bridgetower, George (Augustus) Polgreen."
In <u>The New Grove Dictionary of Music and Musicians</u>, Vol. 3,
pp. 281-282.

Hare, Maud Cuney. <u>Negro Musicians and Their Music</u>.
Washington, D.C.: Associated Publishers, 1936, pp. 296-303.

Robinson, Wilhelmena S. <u>Historical Afro-American Biographies</u>
(International Library of Afro-American Life and History).
Washington, D.C.: Associated Publishers, 1976, pp. 55-56.

Rogers, J. A. "George A. P. Bridgetower: Musical Genius and
Comrade of Beethoven (1789-1860)." In <u>World's Great Men of</u>
<u>Color</u>. New York: Macmillan, 1972, pp. 92-97. (Orig. 1947)

Scobie, Edward. <u>Black Brittania: A History of Blacks in</u>
<u>Britain</u>. Chicago: Johnson Publishing Co., 1972, pp. 110-114.

Southern, Eileen. <u>Biographical Dictionary of Afro-American</u>
<u>and African Musicians</u>. Westport, CT: Greenwood Press, 1982,
pp. 47-48.

Articles

<u>Bath Journal</u> [U.K.] (December 5 1789).

De Lerma, Dominique-Rene. "Bridgetower: Beethoven's Black
Violinist." <u>Your Musical Cue</u> (1968-70): 7-9.

Edwards, F. G. "George P. Bridgetower and the Kreutzer
Sonata." <u>Musical Times</u>, Vol. 49 (May 1 1908): 302+.

Fikes, R., Jr. "They Made the Violin Sing: Three Black
Virtuosos." <u>The Crisis</u> (May 1982): 29-31.

<u>Gentleman's Magazine</u>, No. 2 (1811): 158.

Hare, Maud Cuney. "George Polgren Bridgetower." <u>The Crisis</u>
(June 19 1927): 137-138.

_____ . "The Kreutzer Sonata and Beethoven's Mulatto Friend." Musical America, Vol. 34, No. 17 (1921): 5.

LaBrew, Arthur. "George Augustus Polgreen Bridgetower." Afro-American Music Review (Detroit, MI), Vol. 1, No. 1 (July-December 1981): 127-164.

London Advertiser (February 20 1790).

London Chronicle (February 20 1790).

London Times (June 30 1811).

Mathews, Betty. "George Polgreen Bridgetower." The Music Review, Vol. 29 (February 1968): 22-26.

Morgan-Browne, H. P. "George Bridgetower." Strad, Vol. 41 (January 1931): 463-464.

St. Laurent, Philip. "The Negro in World History: George A. P. Bridgetower." Tuesday (August 1968).

Wright, J. R. B. "George Polgreen Bridgetower: An African Prodigy in England 1788-1799." Musical Quarterly (January 1980): 65-82.

CLAUDIO J.D. BRINDIS DE SALAS (1852-1917) - Violin - Cuba

Enciclopedia Universal Ilustrada. Madrid: Espasa-Calpe, S.A. Tomo IX, p. 859.

Guillen, Nicolas. Claudio Jose Domingo Brindis de Salas (El Rey de las Octavas) Apuntes Biograficos. Havana: Municipio de la Habana, 1935. 43pp. [Cuaderno de Historia Habanera, No. 3].

Hare, Maud Cuney. Negro Musicians and Their Music. Washington, D.C.: Associated Publishers, 1936, pp. 318-320.

Marchena, Enrique de. Del Areito de Anacaona al Poema Folklorico: Brindis de Salas en Santo Domingo. Ciudad Trujillo [Santo Domingo]: Editora Montalvo, 1942. 99pp. (An english-language synopsis of this book is provided in Robert Stevenson's A Guide to Caribbean Music History. Lima: Ediciones Cultura, 1975, pp. 40-41).

Rogers, J. A. "Claudio J.D. Brindis de Salas: German Baron and Court Violinist (1852-1911)." In World's Great Men of Color. New York: Macmillan, 1972, pp. 142-145. (Orig. 1947)

Southern, Eileen. Biographical Dictionary of Afro-American and African Musicians. Westport, CT: Greenwood Press, 1982, p. 48.

Articles

Anglo African Magazine. New York: Arno Press, 1968, pp. 191-192. (Reprint of 1859 ed.)

Diggs, I. "Brindis de Salas: 'King of the Octaves'." The
Crisis (November 1953): 537-541.

Fikes, R. "They Made the Violin Sing: Three Black
Virtuosos." The Crisis (May 1982): 29-31.

Gacel, Miguel A. "Dos Virtuosos del Violin Brindis de Salas
y White." Revista Musical Chilena [Santiago]
(agosto-noviembre 1949): 44-48.

Hernandez Lopez, Rhazes. "Violinistas en Caracas." Musica
(La Habana), Vol. 63 (Marzo-Abril 1977): 3-7. [Brindis de
Salas and Jose White].

LaBrew, Arthur. "The Brindis de Salas Family." Afro-
American Music Review (Detroit), Vol. 1, No. 1 (1981): 15-57.

La Menestrel (Paris), Vol. 40 (1874): 95, 167.

New York Clipper (June 9 1883).

New York Clipper (August 4 1883).

New York Globe (May 26 1883).

Pou Daubar, G. "El Fin de un Musico Negro y su Violin.
Brindis de Salas." El Mundo Illustrado (March 10 1912).

Reed, Gladys Jones. "Distinguished Negroes of the West
Indies: Brindis de Sala, Negro Violinist." Negro History
Bulletin, Vol. IV, No. 4 (January 1941): 79.

Sanchez de Fuentes y Pelaez, Eduardo. "La Ultima Firma de
Brindis de Salas." Academia Nacional de Artes y Letras.
Anales (Havana), tomo 15 (1930): 331-350; ano 22, tomo 19
(1937): 74-89.

LAWRENCE BROWN (1893-1972) - Piano

Hare, Maud Cuney. Negro Musicians and Their Music.
Washington, D.C.: Associated Publishers, 1936, pp. 342-343.

Southern, Eileen. Biographical Dictionary of Afro-American
and African Musicians. Westport, CT: Greenwood Press, 1982,
p. 51.

Obituaries

Black Perspective in Music, Vol. 1, No. 2 (Fall 1973): 197.

Central Opera Service Bulletin, Vol. 15 (Summer 1973): 21.

New York Times (December 26 1972): 27.

Variety, No. 269 (January 17 1973): 70.

MELVILLE CHARLTON (1880-1973) - Organ

Charlton, Melville. <u>Musical Therapeutics</u>. n.p., 190-?.
7pp. [Held by the Schomburg Collection, NYPL, NYC]

Hare, Maud Cuney. <u>Negro Musicians and Their Music</u>.
Washington, D.C.: Associated Publishers, 1936, pp. 340-341.

Lovingood, Penman. <u>Famous Modern Negro Musicians</u>. 2nd ed.
New York: Da Capo Press, 1978. (Reprint of 1921 ed.)

Southern, Eileen. <u>Biographical Dictionary of Afro-American
and African Musicians</u>. Westport, CT: Greenwood Press, 1982,
p. 69.

<u>Who's Who in Colored America, 1940-1950</u>.

Articles

<u>Chicago Defender</u> (May 29 1920).

<u>Indianapolis Freeman</u> (May 8 1915).

"Musical Happenings." <u>Music: The A.G.O. and R.C.C.O.
Magazine</u>, Vol. 6 (July 1972): 39.

"New Music-Vocal and Instrumental." <u>Musical America</u>, Vol.
XIV, No. 10 (July 15 1911): 10. Critique of Charlton's
"Poeme Erotique."

<u>New York Age</u> (January 19 1905).

<u>New York Age</u> (April 1 1909).

"Synagogue Organist." <u>Ebony</u> (June 1952): 4.

Obituaries

<u>Black Perspective in Music</u>, Vol. 2, No. 2 (Fall 1974): 225.

<u>Diapason</u>, Vol. 65 (January 1974): 16-17.

<u>Music: The A.G.O. and R.C.C.O. Magazine</u> (January 1974): 36.

FRANCES COLE (1937-1983) - Harpsichord

Abdul, Raoul. "Miss Cole Plays the Harpsichord." In <u>Blacks
in Classical Music</u>. New York: Dodd, Mead & Co., 1977, pp.
171-172.

Southern, Eileen. <u>Biographical Dictionary of Afro-American
and African Musicians</u>. Westport, CT: Greenwood Press, 1982,
pp. 75-76.

Articles

Abdul, Raoul. "Miss Cole as 'Magdalena'." <u>New York
Amsterdam News</u> (August 28 1976): D8.

New York Times (October 6 1971).

Obituary. The Black Perspective in Music, Vol. 11, No. 2
(Fall 1983): 225.

Obituary. The New York Times (January 26 1983): A-17.

"Temple University Sponsors Harpsichord Black Artist." The
School Musician (November 1969): 47.

CLARENCE COOPER - French Horn

Southern, Eileen. Biographical Dictionary of Afro-American
and African Musicians. Westport, CT: Greenwood Press, 1982,
p. 83.

Articles

"Denver." Music Journal (October 1970): 73.

Mark, M. "Carnegie Recital Hall." Music Journal (May
1971): 68.

New York Amsterdam News (March 6 1971).

WALTER F. CRAIG (1854-192?) - Violin

Pennsylvania Historical Society. Leon Gardiner Collection,
Box 13G.

Southern, Eileen. Biographical Dictionary of Afro-American
and African Musicians. Westport, CT: Greenwood Press, 1982,
p. 87.

Trotter, James M. Music and Some Highly Musical People.
Chicago: Afro-Am Press, 1969, p. 301. (Orig. 1878)

Articles

Cleveland Gazette (February 27 1886).

New York Age (November 16 1889).

New York Age (May 24 1919).

MARION CUMBO (1899-   ) - Cello

Southern, Eileen. Biographical Dictionary of Afro-American
and African Musicians. Westport, CT: Greenwood Press, 1982,
p. 89.

Articles

Chicago Defender (August 28 1920).

New York Age (October 16 1920).

New York Amsterdam News (August 12 1944).

MARC D'ALBERT (1908-1975) - Piano

Southern, Eileen. Biographical Dictionary of Afro-American and African Musicians. Westport, CT: Greenwood Press, 1982, p. 91.

Obituaries

Black Perspective in Music, Vol. 4, No. 3 (Fall 1976): 344.

New York Amsterdam News (October 15 1975).

New York Times (October 8 1975).

HARRIETTE DAVISON WATKINS (1923-1978) - Violin

New York Amsterdam News (March 27 1937).

Obituary. The Black Perspective in Music, Vol. 6, No. 2 (Fall 1978): 241.

Southern, Eileen. Biographical Dictionary of Afro-American and African Musicians. Westport, CT: Greenwood Press, 1982.

TOURGEE DE BOSE (1893-1971) - Piano

Hare, Maud Cuney. Negro Musicians and Their Music. Washington, D.C.: Associated Publishers, 1936, p. 261.

Negro Year Book, 1915.

Southern, Eileen. Biographical Dictionary of Afro-American and African Musicians. Westport, CT: Greenwood Press, 1982, p. 99.

Who's Who in Colored America, 1927-1940.

Articles

New York Age (September 2 1922).

New York Age (March 1 1924).

New York Age (April 21 1928).

New York Age (October 31 1931).

JESSIE COVINGTON DENT (1904-   ) - Piano

Southern, Eileen. Biographical Dictionary of Afro-American and African Musicians. Westport, CT: Greenwood Press, 1982, pp. 102-103.

Who's Who in Colored America, 1927-1940.

Articles

Chicago Defender (February 27 1930).

Lundy, Anne. "Conversation with...Ernestine Jessie
Covington Dent: Pioneer Concert Pianist." The Black
Perspective in Music (Fall 1984): 245-265.

New York Age (July 17 1937).

CARL DITON (1886-1962) - Piano

Hare, Maud Cuney. Negro Musicians and Their Music.
Washington, D.C.: Associated Publishers, 1936, pp. 262,
339-340.

Lovingood, Penman. Famous Modern Negro Musicians. 2nd ed.
New York: Da Capo Press, 1978. (Reprint of 1921 ed.)

Southern, Eileen. Biographical Dictionary of Afro-American
and African Musicians. Westport, CT: Greenwood Press, 1982,
pp. 106-107.

Who's Who in Colored America, 1929.

Articles

"Carl Diton, Concert Pianist, Applies for Home Relief. Once
Ranked Seventh Among Negro Musicians, at 53 Has Ill Wife and
No Work." New York Post (August 27 1938).

Diton, Carl. "The Present Status of Negro-American Musical
Endeavor." Musician (November 19 1915): 689.

_____. "The Struggle of the Negro Musician." Etude
(February 1930): 89-90.

Indianapolis Freeman (October 23 1915).

Jet (November 4 1965): 11.

New York Age (February 9 1929).

Obituaries

The Juilliard Review, Vol. 9, No. 2 (1962): 19.

New York Amsterdam News (February 3 1962).

New York Times (January 27 1962): 21.

LUCILLE DIXON (1923-   ) - Contrabass

Handy, D. Antoinette. "Conversation with...Lucille Dixon: Manager of a Symphony Orchestra." The Black Perspective in Music (Fall 1975): 299-311.

Southern, Eileen. Biographical Dictionary of Afro-American and African Musicians. Westport, CT: Greenwood Press, 1982, pp. 108-109.

JOHN THOMAS DOUGLASS (1847-1886) - Violin

Hare, Maud Cuney. Negro Musicians and Their Music. Washington, D.C.: Associated Publishers, 1936, p. 214.

Southern, Eileen. Biographical Dictionary of Afro-American and African Musicians. Westport, CT: Greenwood Press, 1982, pp. 113-114.

Trotter, James M. Music and Some Highly Musical People. Chicago: Afro-Am Press, 1969, p. 301. (Orig. 1878)

Articles

New York Freeman (April 24 1886).

New York Globe (February 17 1883).

New York Times (March 20 1912). [Reprinted in The Black Perspective in Music (Spring 1978)]

JOSEPH DOUGLASS (1871-1935) - Violin

Hare, Maud Cuney. Negro Musicians and Their Music. Washington, D.C.: Associated Publishers, 1936, pp. 229-230.

Lovingood, Penman. Famous Modern Negro Musicians. 2nd ed. New York: Da Capo Press, 1978. (Reprint of 1921 ed.)

Southern, Eileen. Biographical Dictionary of Afro-American and African Musicians. Westport, CT: Greenwood Press, 1982, p. 114.

Who's Who of the Colored Race, ed. Frank Lincoln Mather. Chicago: n.p., 1915.

Articles

Chicago Defender (February 3 1912).

Chicago Defender (September 25 1915).

Chicago Defender (April 17 1920).

Cleveland Gazette (December 29 1894).

Hill, Roy.   "Conversation with Fannie Douglass:
Reminiscences of Yesteryear."   The Black Perspective in
Music (Spring 1974): 54-62.

New York Age (February 13 1892).

New York Age (October 17 1907).

ROY EATON (1930 -   ) - Piano

Kehler, George, comp.   The Piano in Concert.   Metuchen, NJ:
Scarecrow Press, 1982.   Vol. 1.   Contains a brief
biographical sketch of Roy Eaton.

Southern, Eileen.   Biographical Dictionary of Afro-American
and African Musicians.   Westport, CT: Greenwood Press, 1982,
p. 121.

Stein, M. L.   Blacks in Communications.   New York: Julian
Messner, 1972, pp. 162-163.

Who's Who in Harlem.

Articles

"Eaton Soloist at Pop Concert."   Musical Courier (April 15
1951): 20.

Feldman, S.   "Concert Pianist Conquers Germany."   Negro
Digest (August 1950): 71-73.

"Master Musician Scores Ad Success."   Ebony (September
1958): 59-62.

New York Age (November 7 1959).

New York Amsterdam News (June 10 1950).

New York Times (May 10 1965): 44.

"Roy Eaton."   Music News (May 1951): 11.

"Roy Eaton."   Musical America (November 15 1952): 28.

"Roy Eaton."   Musical Courier (November 15 1952): 12.

RENARD EDWARDS (1944-   ) - Viola

"First Blacks Rehearsing in Philadelphia Orchestra."   New
York Times (September 16 1970).

"The Philadelphia Gets First Black.   Violist is the Only
Negro in Orchestra's History."   New York Times (November 11
1969).

"Renard Edwards, 25-year-old Black Violist, Hired for the
1970 Season as the Philadelphia Symphony Orchestra's
Black." Jet (December 11 1969): 62.

Webster, D. "One for Philadelphia." American Musical
Digest, Vol. 1, No. 5 (1970): 10-11. [Excerpted from the
Philadelphia Enquirer (November 23 1969)].

EMIDEE (1775-1835) - Violin - Guinea, West Africa

Buckingham, James Silk. "Emidee, A Negro Musician." The
Black Perspective in Music, Vol. 1, No. 2 (Fall 1973):
175-177.

Southern, Eileen. Biographical Dictionary of Afro-American
and African Musicians. Westport, CT: Greenwood Press, 1982,
p. 127.

SAMUEL GILLIOF - Contrabass

"Samuel Gilliof of Brooklyn Signs as Bassist with Denver
Symphony Orchestra for 1960-1961 Season. Second Negro to
Become a Member of a Major Symphony Orchestra in U.S. Ortiz
Walton was First; with Boston Symphony." Jet (July 14
1960): 58.

HELEN HAGAN (1891-1964) - Piano

Hare, Maud Cuney. Negro Musicians and Their Music.
Washington, D.C.: Associated Publishers, 1936, pp. 276,
375-376.

Lovingood, Penman. Famous Modern Negro Musicians. 2nd ed.
New York: Da Capo Press, 1978. (Reprint of 1921 ed.)

Southern, Eileen. Biographical Dictionary of Afro-American
and African Musicians. Westport, CT: Greenwood Press, 1982,
p. 158.

Articles

Chicago Defender (April 17 1915).

Chicago Defender (April 10 1920).

Chicago Defender (July 16 1921).

New York Age (March 6 1937).

New York Age (September 17 1949).

New York Age (March 14 1964).

KEMPER HARRELD (1885-1971) - Violin

De Lerma, Dominique-Rene. "Harreld, Kemper." In The New
Grove Dictionary of American Music, Vol. 2, pp. 327-328.

Hare, Maud Cuney. Negro Musicians and Their Music.
Washington, D.C.: Associated Publishers, 1936, p. 252.

Lovingood, Penman. Famous Modern Negro Musicians. 2nd ed.
New York: Da Capo Press, 1978. (Orig. 1921)

Southern, Eileen. Biographical Dictionary of Afro-American
and African Musicians. Westport, CT: Greenwood Press, 1982,
p. 167.

Who's Who in Colored America, 1929-1950.

Articles

Chicago Defender (July 1 1909).

Chicago Defender (June 13 1910).

Chicago Defender (May 8 1920).

New York Age (September 17 1914).

New York Age (May 9 1936).

Obituary. Jet (March 18 1971): 17.

HAZEL HARRISON (1883-1969) - Piano

Abdul, Raoul. "Hazel Harrison Remembered." In Blacks in
Classical Music. New York: Dodd, Mead & Co., 1977, pp.
159-160.

Cazort, Jean E., and Constance T. Hobson. Born to Play: The
Life and Career of Hazel Harrison. Westport, CT: Greenwood
Press, 1983. 171pp.

De Lerma, Dominique-Rene. "Harrison, Hazel." In The New
Grove Dictionary of American Music, Vol. 2, p. 327.

Hare, Maud Cuney. Negro Musicians and Their Music.
Washington, D.C.: Associated Press, 1936, pp. 373-375.

Love, Josephine Harreld. "Harrison, Hazel Lucile." In
Notable American Women: The Modern Period, eds. Barbara
Sicherman and Carol Hurd Green. Cambridge, MA: The Belknap
Press, 1980, pp. 317-319.

Southern, Eileen. Biographical Dictionary of Afro-American
and African Musicians. Westport, CT: Greenwood Press, 1982,
pp. 169-170.

Note: According to Raoul Abdul's Blacks in Classical Music "voluminous clippings [on Hazel Harrison may be found] in the special collection of the library at Atlanta University."

Articles

Chicago Defender (November 29 1919).

Chicago Defender (November 14 1931).

Chicago Defender (February 20 1932).

Indianapolis Freeman (October 1 1904).

New York Age (February 15 1910).

New York Age (December 4 1920).

New York Age (October 30 1926).

New York Age (October 29 1944).

New York Times (October 15, 1930).

The Washington Post (May 1 1969). Obituary.

EUGENE HAYNES (1928-   ) - Piano

Kehler, George. The Piano in Concert. Metuchen, NJ: Scarecrow Press, 1982. Vol. 1. Contains a short biography of Eugene Haynes.

Southern, Eileen. Biographical Dictionary of Afro-American and African Musicians. Westport, CT: Greenwood Press, 1982, pp. 173-174.

Articles

"Eugene Haynes." Musical America (January 15 1955): 17.

"Eugene Haynes." Musical America (May 1958): 23.

Haynes, Eugene. "To Russia with Love; or Love for Six Oranges." Music Journal (March 1969): 38+.

GAIL HIGHTOWER (1946-   ) - Bassoon

Davis, Peter G. "Gail Hightower Gives Recital on Bassoon." New York Times (December 23 1979): 32.

NATALIE HINDERAS (1927-   ) - Piano

Abdul, Raoul. "Miss Hinderas's Philharmonic Debut." In Blacks in Classical Music. New York: Dodd, Mead & Co., 1977, pp. 162-164.

Davis, Russell H. Black Americans in Cleveland.
Washington, D.C.: Associated Press, 1972, pp. 402-403.

Gelles, George. "Hinderas, Natalie." In The New Grove
Dictionary of Music and Musicians, Vol. 8, p. 587.

_____. "Hinderas, Natalie." In The New Grove Dictionary
of American Music, Vol. 2, p. 392.

Kehler, George. The Piano in Concert. Metuchen, NJ:
Scarecrow Press, 1982. Vol. 1. Contains a brief biography
and career sketch of Natalie Hinderas.

Southern, Eileen. Biographical Dictionary of Afro-American
and African Musicians. Westport, CT: Greenwood Press, 1982,
p. 182.

Magazine Articles

Chicago Symphony Program Notes, May 16-17, 1974, p. 47.

Clare, Nancy. "Essence Women: Natalie Hinderas." Essence
(February 1976): 32.

Ebony (October 1961): 6. Mention of Natalie Hinderas'
appointment as chairman of the International Program for
Music Exchange.

Felton, J. "Phila. Orch., Hinderas." High Fidelity
(February 1972): MA23.

Fleming, S. "Musician of the Month: Natalie Hinderas."
High Fidelity (October 1973): 4-5.

Hertelendy, P. "Natalie Hinderas: Leading Interpreter of
Black Classical Music." Contemporary Keyboard (August
1977): 22+.

Kolodin, Irving. "Music; Ginastera's Piano Concerto
Revisited." Saturday Review (December 16 1972): 73.

Monson, H. "'Tribute to Black Music' - All-Purposes
Mishmash?" High Fidelity (August 1972): MA16.

"Natalie Hinderas." American Music Teacher, Vol. 24, No. 3
(1975): 26-27.

"Natalie Hinderas." Musical America (December 1 1954): 25.

"Natalie Hinderas Artist and Person." American Music
Teacher (February 1975): 40.

"Negro Concert Pianist on NBC." The Baton, Vol. 3, No. 7
(February 1953): 2.

"Spotlight." Music and Artists, Vol. 5, No. 2 (1972): 26.

Werner, J. "Natalie Hinderas." The Musical Times (February
1958): 93.

Newspaper Articles

Chicago Defender (June 26 1937).

Chicago Defender (August 26 1944).

Ericson, Raymond. "A Colored Girl Like You Can't Play in the Hollywood Bowl." New York Times (November 19 1972): Sec. II, p. 15, 26.

Evening Star [Washington, D.C.] (November 9, 1971).

New York Times (October 20 1974): D-21.

Philadelphia Tribune (January 14 1975).

ANN HOBSON (1943-   ) - Harp

Southern, Eileen. Biographical Dictionary of Afro-American and African Musicians. Westport, CT: Greenwood Press, 1982, p. 184.

Articles

Boston Symphony Orchestra programs, 1969-1970, p. 48.

Kalamazoo Gazette (December 26 1971): D-2.

Merritt, Robert. "Harpist Says Her Profession Worth Trouble." Richmond Times Dispatch (January 23 1978): B6.

RAYMOND T. JACKSON (1933-   ) - Piano

Kehler, George. The Piano in Concert. Metuchen, NJ: Scarecrow Press, 1982. Contains a brief biographical sketch of Raymond Jackson.

Southern, Eileen. Biographical Dictionary of Afro-American and African Musicians. Westport, CT: Greenwood Press, 1982, p. 198.

SAMUEL W. JAMIESON (1855-1930) - Piano

Hare, Maud Cuney. Negro Musicians and Their Music. Washington, D.C.: Associated Publishers, 1936, p. 212.

Southern, Eileen. Biographical Dictionary of Afro-American and African Musicians. Westport, CT: Greenwood Press, 1982, p. 201.

Trotter, James M. Music and Some Highly Musical People. Chicago: Afro-Am Press, 1969, pp. 209-218. (Orig. 1878)

Articles

New York Age (August 16 1890).

New York Globe (July 7 1883).

New York Globe (April 12 1884).

LEONARD JETER (1881-1970) - Cello

Hare, Maud Cuney. Negro Musicians and Their Music. Washington, D.C.: Associated Publishers, 1936, p. 230.

Obituary. International Musician (August 1970): 19.

JOSE MANUEL JIMENEZ BERROA (1855-1917) - Piano - Cuba

Southern, Eileen. Biographical Dictionary of Afro-American and African Musicians. Westport, CT: Greenwood Press, 1982, p. 204.

Articles

Lugo Romero, Americo. "Jose Manuel Jimenez Berroa: El 'Liszt de Ebano' Cubano." Musica (Bogota), Vol. 1, No. 4 (1941): 87-90. Personal reminiscences on the Cuban Negro pianist, Jimenez Berroa, pupil of Marmontel in Paris, who played at the homes of Wagner and Liszt, and settled in Hamburg, where he died in 1917.

Peters Jahrbuch. 1917, p. 88.

Tomas, Guillermo M. "Jose Manuel Jimenez." Musicalia, Vol. 1 (February 1929): 157-161; (March-April 1929): 206-209.

Wright, Josephine. "Das Negertrio Jimenez in Europe." The Black Perspective in Music (Fall 1981): 161-176.

ELAYNE JONES (1928-   ) - Tympany

Ammer, Christine. Unsung: A History of Women in American Music. Westport, CT: Greenwood Press, 1980, p. 209.

Southern, Eileen. Biographical Dictionary of Afro-American and African Musicians. Westport, CT: Greenwood Press, 1982, p. 214.

Articles

The Black Perspective in Music (Fall 1975): 310. Brief note on Jones's struggles with the San Francisco Symphony.

Cioffi, Paul. "The Stuff of Courage." San Francisco (February 1975): 16, 18.

Commanday, Robert. "The Symphony Scandal." High Fidelity/Musical America (September 1974): MA28-MA29.

"Editorial" (re: SF Symphony hirings). High Fidelity (December 1975): MA4.

Epstein, Helen. "Notes from the Orchestra Pit." Ms (March 1976): 21.

Hardison, Inge. "Only Woman Tympanist." Color (Charleston, W. Va.) (February 1953): 18-21.

Harvey, Duston. "People in Percussion." Percussion Notes, Vol. 12, No. 1 (1973): 17. (Reprinted from United Press International (UPI), San Francisco.)

"Votes vs. Notes." Newsweek (June 17 1974): 109-110.

Newspaper Articles

Bloomfield, Arthur. "Sour Notes to and from the Symphony." San Francisco Examiner (May 24 1974): 35.

_____. "The Other Side's View of Symphony Freeze-Out." San Francisco Examiner (May 29 1974): 1.

Boston Globe (September 21 1975).

Chicago Defender (July 6 1974): 4.

Commanday, Robert. "Symphony Buys Time in Players Dispute." San Francisco Chronicle (July 31 1974): 46.

"Elayne Asks New Committee Hearing." San Francico Chronicle (January 18 1975): 9.

Finefrock, James A. "Fired Black Symphony Tympanist to File $1.5 Million Damage Suit." San Francisco Examiner (August 13 1976): 6.

Fosburgh, Lacey. "2 Musicians' Jobs Stir Coast Conflict." New York Times (June 12 1974).

_____. "Two Musicians Reinstated for a Year in Coast Dispute." New York Times (August 2 1974): 12.

Fried, Alexander. "Opera House Cheers for Tenure-Less Pair." San Francisco Chronicle/Examiner (May 26 1974): 7.

Harvey, Duston. "What It's Like Being a Black Female Drummer in a Major Orchestra." Richmond Afro-American (March 24 1973): 6.

Henahan, Donal. "About That Tympanist That Got Drummed Out." New York Times (September 7 1975): D25.

New York Times (August 27 1975).

Video and TV

A Day in the Life of a Musician. WNET-TV, 1965.

HAROLD JONES (1934-   ) - Flute

New York Age (June 27 1959).

Rockwell, John. "Music: Harold Jones in Flute Recital."
New York Times (January 23 1980): C16.

Southern, Eileen. Biographical Dictionary of Afro-American
and African Musicians. Westport, CT: Greenwood Press, 1982,
p. 215.

LOUIA VAUGHN JONES (1895-1965) - Violin

Hare, Maud Cuney. Negro Musicians and Their Music.
Washington, D.C.: Associated Publishers, 1936, pp. 383-384.

Southern, Eileen. Biographical Dictionary of Afro-American
and African Musicians. Westport, CT: Greenwood Press, 1982,
p. 217.

Who's Who in Colored America, 1938-1950.

Articles

Obituary. International Musician, Vol. 63 (May 1965):32.

New York Age (October 25 1930).

Record Research (May 1968): 3-4.

NINA KENNEDY (1960-   ) - Piano

Rockwell, John. "A Violinist and 2 Pianists in Recitals."
New York Times (April 12, 1987): 68. Review of Kennedy's
debut recital.

WILLIAM LAWRENCE (1895-1981) - Piano

Hare, Maud Cuney. Negro Musicians and Their Music.
Washington, D.C.: Associated Publishers, 1936, pp. 367-368.

Southern, Eileen. Biographical Dictionary of Afro-American
and African Musicians. Westport, CT: Greenwood Press, 1982,
p. 238.

Obituaries

The Black Perspective in Music, Vol. 9, No. 2 (Fall 1981):
240.

The New York Times (March 21 1981): 28.

RAYMOND AUGUSTUS LAWSON (1875-1959) - Piano

Hare, Maud Cuney. Negro Musicians and Their Music.
Washington, D.C.: Associated Press, 1936, pp. 376-378.

Lovingood, Penman. Famous Modern Negro Musicians. 2nd ed.
New York: Da Capo Press, 1978. (Reprint of 1921 ed.)

McGinty, Doris E. "Lawson, Raymond Augustus." In
Dictionary of American Negro Biography, eds. Rayford W.
Logan and Michael R. Winston. New York: W.W. Norton, 1982,
pp. 386-387.

Southern, Eileen. Biographical Dictionary of Afro-American
and African Musicians. Westport, CT: Greenwood Press, 1982,
pp. 238-239.

Who's Who of the Colored Race. Chicago: n.p., 1915.

Articles

Hartford (Conn.) newspapers (1900-1959).

Obituary. Music Educators Journal (February-March 1959): 95.

SYLVIA OLDEN LEE (1919-   ) - Piano

Southern, Eileen. Biographical Dictionary of Afro-American
and African Musicians. Westport, CT: Greenwood Press, 1982,
p. 242.

Articles

Jet (April 4 1968): 39.

"Met Opera Coach." Ebony (May 1955): 4.

New York Amsterdam News (July 29 1944).

JOSEPHINE HARRELD LOVE (1914-   ) - Piano

New York Amsterdam News (December 17 1932).

Southern, Eileen. Biographical Dictionary of Afro-American
and African Musicians. Westport, CT: Greenwood Press, 1982,
p. 214.

EARL MADISON (1945-   ) - Cello

Southern, Eileen. Biographical Dictionary of Afro-American
and African Musicians. Westport, CT: Greenwood Press, 1982,
p. 263.

Walton, Ortiz. "Arthur Davis, A Suit Against the New York
Philharmonic." In Music: Black, White and Blue. New York:
Morrow/Quill Paperbacks, 1972.

Articles

"Black and White Notes: Discrimination Charge Against New York Philharmonic by Two Black Musicians."   Newsweek (August 18 1969): 82.

Frederick, R. B.   "N.Y. Philharmonic Rolls New Season With Bias and Acoustics Still Unresolved."   Variety, No. 256 (October 1, 1969): 57.

"Philharmonic Ordered to End Racial Bias/City Human Rights Agency Finds Symphony Guilty of One Charge, Not Guilty of Another."   New York Law Journal (November 19 1969).

Walker, C.   "Making the American Symphony Orchestra Truly American."   Symphony News, Vol. 22, No. 4 (1971): 13.

Williams, J.   "Blacks Draw a Blank in Symphonies."   Billboard (February 12 1971): 1+.

Newspaper Articles

"Bernstein Denies Bias by Philharmonic at Auditions."   New York Times (September 30 1969).

"Bias Ruling Disheartens 2 Musicians."   New York Post (November 17 1970): 26.

"Black Musicians Issue Challenge; Losers in Rights Case Seek to Test Philharmonic Best."   New York Times (November 18, 1970): 40.   Concerns bassist Art Davis and cellist Earl Madison's court challenge to the hiring biases of the NY Philharmonic.

Henahan, Donal.   "Philharmonic's Hiring Policy Defended."   New York Times (July 31 1969): L26.

_____.   "Rights Unit Bars Philharmonic from Filling 2 Disputed Chairs."   New York Times (November 27 1969).

Hentoff, Nat.   "Un-Chic Racism at the Philharmonic."   Village Voice (December 17, 1970): 30.

Klein, Howard.   "Overdoing Benign Neglect?"   New York Times (March 7, 1971): Sec. 12, p. 9.

Klemesrud, Judy.   "Is Women's Lib Coming To The Philharmonic?"   New York Times (April 11, 1971): D-19.

"Musicians Suing for Right to Picket Philharmonic."   New York Times (November 21 1969).

"Rights Unit Clears Philharmonic But Finds Bias in Some Hiring."   New York Times (November 17 1969).

"2 Witnesses Are Heard in Philharmonic Hearing."   New York Times (September 25 1969).

Young, Percy. "Blacks Say Philharmonic Refuses To Get In Tune." New York Post (November 7, 1969): 68.

GERTRUDE MARTIN (1910-1945) - Violin

"Gertrude Martin, Violinist: An Opinion." Negro Woman's World (March 1935): 5.

New York Times (September 9 1945): 46. Brief death notice.

KERMIT MOORE (1929-   ) - Cello

Abdul, Raoul. "Kermit Moore at Alice Tully Hall." In Blacks in Classical Music. New York: Dodd, Mead & Co., 1977, pp. 181-183.

Rosenberg, Deena, and Bernard Rosenberg. "Kermit Moore, Freelance Cellist." Music Makers. New York: Columbia University Press, 1979, pp. 277-288.

Southern, Eileen. Biographical Dictionary of Afro-American and African Musicians. Westport, CT: Greenwood Press, 1982, p. 279.

Articles

"Cello." Village Voice (March 13 1969).

Davis, Peter G. "6 Modern Pieces for Cello Played by Kermit Moore." New York Times (February 16 1969).

Encore (September 1972): 64.

SANDY L. PERRY

"Sandy L. Perry is Only Negro Player in Omaha Symphony Orchestra." Jet (March 17 1960): 49.

GODFREY POWELL - Trumpet

"Godfrey Powell is First Negro to Join Kansas City Philharmonic Orchestra." Jet (March 17 1960): 60.

PHILIPPA DUKE SCHUYLER (1931-1967) - Piano

Abdul, Raoul. "Philippa Schuyler at Carnegie Hall." In Blacks in Classical Music. New York: Dodd, Mead & Co., 1977, pp. 160-162.

Cherry, Gwendolyn, et al. "Philippa Duke Schuyler: Prodigy Who Made Good." In Portraits in Color: The Lives of Colorful Negro Women. New York: Pageant Press, 1962, pp. 72-76.

De Lerma, Dominique-Rene.   "Schuyler, Philippa Duke."   In
The New Grove Dictionary of American Music, Vol. 4, pp.
170-171.

Fisher, Renee B.   Musical Prodigies: Masters at an Early
Age. New York: Association Press, 1973, pp. 72-79.

Kehler, George.   The Piano in Concert.   Metuchen, NJ:
Scarecrow Press, 1982.   Vol. 2.   Contains a brief
biographical sketch.

Negro Year Book, 1941-1946.

"Philippa Duke Schuyler." [Bibliography] In American Black
Women in the Arts and Social Sciences, comp. by Ora
Williams. Revised and Expanded Edition. Metuchen, NJ:
Scarecrow Press, 1978, pp. 166-170.

Robinson, Wilhelmena S.   Historical Afro-American
Biographies (International Library of Afro-American Life and
History). Washington, D.C.: Associated Publishers, 1976, p.
249.

Schuyler, Josephine.   Philippa, The Beautiful American: The
Traveled History of a Troubador. New York: Philippa
Schuyler Memorial Fund, 1969.

Schuyler, Philippa Duke.   Adventure in Black and White.   New
York: R. Speller, 1960.   302pp.

Southern, Eileen.   Biographical Dictionary of Afro-American
and African Musicians.   Westport, CT: Greenwood Press, 1982,
p. 332.

Who's Who in Colored America, 1950.

Articles

"Back from Latin American Tour." Musical Courier (April 15
1953): 24.

"Buenos Aires Series Re-Engages Pianist." Musical America
(February 1 1955): 14.

"Child Piano Prodigy Negro Girl, 6, Also Composes." New
York Age (June 3 1937).

Courcy, J. de.   "Bonjour Philippa!" Musical Courier
(December 15 1957): 7.

Delta (March 1964): 45.

Ferguson, C. W.   "Americans Not Everyone Knows." PTA
Magazine (December 1967): 12-14.

"Harlem Prodigy." Time (June 22 1936).

McIntosh, India. "Harlem Prodigy." Negro Digest (September 1944): 67-68. [Condensed from New York Herald-Tribune article of August 2, 1944.]

"Meet the George Schuyler's; America's Strangest Family." Our World, Vol. 6 (April 1951): 22-26.

"Music by Philippa." Newsweek (August 14 1944): 84.

New York Age (July 18 1936).

"Original." Time (March 25 1946): 62.

"Philippa Duke Schuyler." The Crisis (May 1950): 276-334.

"Philippa Duke Schuyler." The Crisis (April 1954): 207.

"Philippa Schuyler." Musical Courier (May 1959): 12. Biographical sketch.

"Philippa Schuyler Back from Europe." Musical Courier (January 1 1954): 20.

"Philippa Schuyler Makes Orchestral Debut in Buenos Aires." The Crisis (December 1954): 600-602.

Rogers, J. A. "World Traveler." The Crisis (January 1961): 57-59. Review of P. D. Schuyler's autobiography Adventures in Black and White.

Schuyler, Josephine L. "My Daughter Philippa." Sepia (May 1959): 8-12.

_____. "17 Years of Mixed Marriage." Negro Digest (July 1946): 61-65. [Condensed from American Mercury, March 1946.]

Schuyler, Philippa. "My Adventures in Black and White." Sepia (March 1960): 44-48.

_____. "My Adventures in Black and White." Sepia (May 1960): 63-67.

_____. "My Black and White World." Sepia (June 1962): 10-15.

"Spotlight on Philippa Schuyler, Pianist." Musical Events [London] (March 1965): 22-23.

Sullivan, Dee. "Teen-aged Genius." Negro Digest (August 1945): 27-30.

"Super-Girl: Philippa Schuyler is a Musical Genius but Bobby-Soxer at Heart." Ebony (March 1946): 21-25.

Talalay, Kathryn. "Philippa Duke Schuyler, Pianist Composer/Writer." The Black Perspective in Music (Spring 1982): 43-68.

"Uncle Sam's Top Genius Prodigy of a Black and White
Marriage Whose Mentality Baffles Science." Color
[Charleston, W. Va.] (December 1952): 18-21.

"Up and Down the Guild Keyboard." Musical Courier (June
1956): 51.

"Why I Don't Marry." Ebony (July 1958): 78-84.

"Young Artist Abroad." Musical Courier (January 1 1956): 2.

Concert Reviews

"London Recital." Musical Events (May 1965): 30.

"Philippa Duke Schuyler." Musical America (May 1954): 30.

"Philippa Duke Schuyler." Musical America (July 1959): 26.

"Philippa Duke Schuyler." Musical Courier (October 1954):
28.

"Philippa Schuyler." Musical America (June 1953): 24.

"Philippa Schuyler." Musical Opinion (February 1957): 263.

"Town Hall Recital." Musical America (November 15 1956): 20.

Obituaries

The Crisis (June 1967): 248+.

Delta Newsletter (May 1967): 1-2.

Gramophone (July 1967): 58.

High Fidelity (August 1967): MA14.

Music Educators Journal (October 1967): 27.

Music Journal (November 1967): 4.

The Musical Times (July 1967): 641.

National Review (May 30 1967): 559.

New York Times (May 10 1967): 1+; (May 19 1967).

Newsweek (May 22 1967): 72.

Sepia (July 1967): 14.

Time (May 19 1967): 112.

Variety (May 24 1967): 63.

Washington Post (May 10 1967): A-18.

HARRY SMYLES (1917-   ) - Oboe

"An Even Break." New York Times (April 22 1956).

"The Negro and the North." Life (March 11 1957).

Southern, Eileen. Biographical Dictionary of Afro-American and African Musicians. Westport, CT: Greenwood Press, 1982, p. 351.

ROY WILFRED TIBBS (1888-1944) - Piano

Diapason (June 1 1944): 4. Obituary.

Diapason (January 1 1945): 6. Obituary.

Musical America (April 1944): 24. Obituary.

JESSE GERALD TYLER (ca. 1879-1938) - Piano

Cotter, John. "The Negro in Music in St. Louis." Thesis (M.A.) Washington University, 1959.

Hare, Maud Cuney. Negro Musicians and Their Music. Washington, D.C.: Associated Publishers, 1936, p. 350.

Southern, Eileen. Biographical Dictionary of Afro-American and African Musicians. Westport, CT: Greenwood Press, 1982, pp. 379-380.

Articles

Chicago Defender (March 20 1920).

New York Age (April 29 1909).

New York Age (March 13 1920).

FRANCES WALKER (1924-   ) - Piano

Kehler, George. The Piano in Concert. Metuchen, NJ: Scarecrow Press, 1982. Vol. 2. Contains a brief biographical sketch.

Concert Reviews

Davis, Peter G. "Pianist: Frances Walker." New York Times (September 15 1981).

Henahan, Donal. "Music: Tasteful Survey of Black Spirit." New York Times (September 15 1975).

New York Herald Tribune (November 29 1965).

Sherman, Robert. "Mellow Piano by Miss Walker." New York Times (January 27 1974).

Strongin, Theodore. "Frances Walker Offers Solid Piano
Program." New York Times (January 25 1971).

Village Voice (February 11 1971).

RACHEL WASHINGTON - Piano/Organ

Hare, Maud Cuney. Negro Musicians and Their Music.
Washington, D.C.: Associated Publishers, 1936, p. 213.

Scruggs, Lawson A. Women of Distinction. Raleigh, NC: the
Author, 1893, pp. 273-274.

Southern, Eileen. Biographical Dictionary of Afro-American
and African Musicians. Westport, CT: Greenwood Press, 1982,
pp. 392-393.

Trotter, James M. Music and Some Highly Musical People.
Chicago: Afro-Am Press, 1969, pp. 288-290. (Orig. 1878)

ANDRE WATTS (1946-   ) - Piano

Abdul, Raoul. "Andre Watts at Lincoln Center." In Blacks
in Classical Music. New York: Dodd, Mead & Co., 1977, pp.
164-171.

Dubal, David. "Andre Watts." In Reflections from the
Keyboard: The World of the Concert Pianist. New York:
Summitt Books, 1984, pp. 324-329.

Ewen, David, ed. Musicians Since 1900: Performers in
Concert and Opera. New York: H.W. Wilson, 1978, pp. 941-943.

Hemming, Roy. Discovering Music. New York: Four Winds
Press, 1974, p. 346.

Kehler, George. The Piano in Concert. Metuchen, NJ:
Scarecrow Press, 1982. Vol. 2. Contains a brief
biographical sketch.

Mach, Elyse. "Andre Watts." In Great Pianists Speak for
Themselves. New York: Dodd & Mead, 1980, pp. 178-189.

Southern, Eileen. Biographical Dictionary of Afro-American
and African Musicians. Westport, CT: Greenwood Press, 1982,
p. 393.

Steinberg, Michael. "Watts, Andre." In The New Grove
Dictionary of Music and Musicians, Vol. 20, p. 235.

_____, and Dennis S. McIntire. "Watts, Andre." In The
New Grove Dictionary of American Music, Vol. 4, pp. 491-492.

Magazine Articles

"Andre Watts: Prodigious Talent." Clavier, Vol. 3, No. 1
(1964): 18-19. (Interview)

"Andre Watts: A Universe of Music." Sepia (March 1974):
48-53.

Andrews, P. "Totally Freaked Out on Music." Horizon
(December 1977): 10-16.

Berg, Gene. "Andre Watts: A Promise Fulfilled." Encore
(May 9 1977): 32-34.

Black, D. "Andre Watts: World's No. 1 Black Concert
Pianist." Sepia (March 1972): 20-26.

Bredemann, D., and G. Ackerman. "'The Point is to Make
Music': An Interview with Andre Watts." Piano Quarterly,
Vol. 21, No. 81 (1973): 12-15.

"Classical Music Prodigy Turns 40." Ebony, Vol. 42 (April
1987): 44+.

Cusumano, R. "The Prep School Days of Andre Watts."
International Musician, Vol. 67 (April 1969): 5+.

Darden, N. "My Man Andre." Saturday Review (July 26 1969):
43-45.

Dietrich, J. "Pianist Watts Fancies Cuban Cigars, Rare
Records." Biography News (January 1975): 220.

Doerschuk, B. "Andre Watts." (Interview) Contemporary
Keyboard, Vol. 3 (December 1977): 12-14+.

Encore (July 1973): 54.

Fahrer, A. "An Interview with Andre Watts." American Music
Teacher, Vol. 21, No. 5 (April 1972): 18-19.

Fleming, S. "And We Quote; Interview." High Fidelity
(February 1968): 19.

Gaines, J. R. Biographical piece on A. Watts. People (June
26 1978): 48-50+.

"Giant and A Prince." Time (February 8 1963): 60.

Grunwald, David. "Andre Watts is Only 28 and 'At the Very
Top'." People (August 19 1974): 52-54.

Hampden, Laurence. "Andre Watts: A Study in Black and
White." After Dark (August 1970): 16-18.

Hiemenz, J. "Musician of the Month: Andre Watts." High
Fidelity (February 1973): 4-5.

Kammerer, R. "High-Voltage Mr. Watts." American Record
Guide (May 1963): 718.

Karp, V. "Master Watts Comes of Age." Music and Artists,
Vol. 1, No. 2 (1968): 30-31+.

Kolodin, Irving. "Destiny Has No Prejudice." Saturday
Review (February 1973): 52.

_____. "Rising Star of Andre Watts." Saturday Review
(February 16 1963): 53-54.

Mason, E. "Young Lion." Music and Musicians, Vol. 17
(January 1969): 40-41.

Massaquoi, H. J. "Andre Watts: A Giant Among Giants at Age
22." Ebony (May 1969): 90-98.

Mayer, M. "Prodigies." Esquire (March 1964): 106-107+.

"Music, Youth, Racial Equality: Voices of Pianist Andre
Watts." US News & World Report (June 6 1977): 69.

Nagy, C. A. "Aristocrat of Virtuosos: Andre Watts."
Clavier, Vol. 18, No. 9 (1979): 12-19.

New Lady (June 1971): 10-14.

"Newsmakers." Newsweek (August 30 1971): 48.

Phillips, H. E. "Musician of the Month: Andre Watts." High
Fidelity (December 1978): 4-5.

"Real Pro." Newsweek (February 11 1963): 58.

Rich, A. "Young Excitement in Music." House Beautiful
(July 1967): 102-103+.

Russell, F. "Andre Watts Interview." Piano Quarterly, No.
57 (Fall 1966): 16-21.

Saal, Hubert. "Beautiful Innocence." Newsweek (January 29
1968): 81.

Sargeant, Winthrop. "Musical Events; Recital in
Philharmonic Hall." New Yorker (November 5 1966): 234.

"A Teenager Rocks Hall of Great Music." Life (February 15
1963): 30.

"Ten Outstanding Single Men." Ebony (August 1972): 96.

Tuesday-at-Home (July 1973): 13-14+.

"Virtuoso on the Rise." Ebony (April 1963): 124-126.

"Watts, Andre." Current Biography 1968, pp. 422-425.

"What Music Means to Me." Seventeen (January 1964): 22.

"Young Genius on the Rise in US." US News & World Report
(May 1975): 57-58.

Newspaper Articles

Chicago Defender (November 4 1978): 5.

Chicago Defender Accent (July 7 1979): 1+.

Conaway, J.   "Andre Watts on Andre Watts: I'm Doing All
Right But I'm Never Good Enough, But I'm Not Standing
Still." New York Times Magazine (September 19 1971): 14-15+.

Detroit Free Press (April 24 1971): B-8.

New York Sunday News Magazine (July 7 1963): 16.

New York Times [Western Edition] (February 2 1963): 3.

New York Times (October 23 1966): Sec. II, p.17. Interview.

FELIX FOWLER WEIR (1884-1978) - Violin

Southern, Eileen. Biographical Dictionary of Afro-American
and African Musicians. Westport, CT: Greenwood Press, 1982,
pp. 395-396.

Articles

Chicago Defender (May 17 1919).

Indianapolis Freeman (November 28 1896).

Indianapolis Freeman (October 28 1916).

New York Age (March 4 1915).

New York Age (September 13 1966).

Obituary. The Black Perspective in Music, Vol. 6, No. 2
(Fall 1978): 241.

JOSE SILVESTRE WHITE (1836-1918) - Violin - Cuba

Abdul, Raoul. "A Master Violinist." In Blacks in Classical
Music. New York: Dodd, Mead & Co., 1977, pp. 179-180.

Du Pont, Paul. Biography of Jose White. Paris: n.p., 1874.

Hare, Maud Cuney. Negro Musicians and Their Music.
Washington, D.C.: Associated Publishers, 1936, pp. 303-305.

Rogers, J. A. World's Great Men of Color. New York:
Macmillan, 1972, Vol. 2, pp. 557-558.

Southern, Eileen. Biographical Dictionary of Afro-American
and African Musicians. Westport, CT: Greenwood Press, 1982,
p. 400.

Trotter, James M. Music and Some Highly Musical People.
Chicago: Afro-Am Press, 1969, pp. 224-240. (Orig. 1878)

Articles

Argote, Joaquin J. "White." Revista de la Biblioteca
Nacional (Havana), 2nd series, Vol. 4, No. 2 (April-June
1953): 80-99. (For an English-language synopsis of this
article see Robert Stevenson's A Guide to Caribbean Music
History. Lima: Ediciones Cultura, 1975, pp. 2-3.)

Burke, Inez. "Jose White." Negro History Bulletin (January
1941): 79-81.

Fikes, R. "They Made the Violin Sing: Three Black
Virtuosos." The Crisis (May 1982): 29-31.

France Musicale (March 3 1867).

Gacel, Miguel A. "Dos Virtuosos del Violin Brindis de Salas
y White." Revista Musical Chilena [Santiago]
(agosto-noviembre 1949): 44-48.

Gazette Musical (August 5 1857).

Hernandez Lopez, Rhazes. "Violinistas en Caracas." Musica
(La Habana), Vol. 63 (Marzo-Abril 1977): 3-7. [White and
Brindis de Salas]

Lopez, Antonio Gonzalez. "Un Gran Violinista Cubano: Jose
White." Academia Nacional de Artes y Letras. Anales
(Havana), ano 22, tomo 19 (1937): 130-165. [See clippings
file, Performing Arts Research Center at Lincoln
Center--Music Division.]

Marti, Jose. "White." Revista de Bellas Artes [Havana]
(junio 1918): 50.

Le Menestrel [Paris] (1861-1876).

New York Times (December 12 1875).

Le Pays (August 5, 1856)

Le Siecle (May 13 1872).

Tuesday (October 1973): 10.

Zertucha, Casimiro. "Jose White." Revista de Bellas Artes
[Havana] (junio 1918): 51.

ORCHESTRAS

Ericson, Raymond. "The Fight for the Integrated Orchestra." New York Times (October 20 1974).

"Los Angeles to Have Negro Symphony Group." Music of the West, No. 8 (October 1952): 13.

BALTIMORE CITY COLORED ORCHESTRA (Baltimore, MD/1929- ?)

Hare, Maud Cuney. Negro Musicians and Their Music. Washington, D.C.: Associated Publishers, 1936, pp. 257-258.

HARLEM PHILHARMONIC ORCHESTRA (New York City/1968- ?)

Davis, Peter G. "Harlem Orchestra Plays at Columbia." New York Times (April 21 1971).

Ericson, Raymond. "Harlem Youths in Park Concert. 2-Month Old Orchestra Is Led by Karl Porter." New York Times (May 31 1968).

Sherman, Robert. "Harlem Orchestra, In Debut, Seeking to Develop Talent." New York Times (December 20 1970).

NATIONAL AFRO-AMERICAN PHILHARMONIC (Philadelphia, PA/1978)

"All Black Orchestra Debuts in Philadelphia." Norfolk Journal and Guide (June 2 1978): 12.

"All Black Symphony to Prem in Philly." Variety (April 19 1978): 2.

Ericson, Raymond. "Music: Black Symphony." New York Times (May 24 1978): 221. Article on debut of National Afro-American Philharmonic.

"National Afro-American Philharmonic." High Fidelity (October 1978): 40-41+.

Orodenker, M. "All-Black Symphony for Philly." Billboard (May 6 1978): 51.

PHILADELPHIA CONCERT ORCHESTRA (Philadelphia, PA/1908-)

Hare, Maud Cuney. Negro Musicians and Their Music. Washington, D.C.: Associated Publishers, 1936, pp. 256-257.

Southern, Eileen. Biographical Dictionary of Afro-American and African Musicians. Westport, CT: Greenwood Press, 1982, p. 306.

Articles

New York Age (December 11 1926).

New York Amsterdam News (January 20 1945).

Philadelphia Tribune (December 20 1913).

SYMPHONY OF THE NEW WORLD (New York City/1965-1976)

Abdul, Raoul. "Symphony of the New World." In Blacks in Classical Music. New York: Dodd, Mead & Co., 1977, pp. 205-207.

Campbell, Dick. Statement by the Symphony of the New World on the Status of Minority Musicians in Symphony Orchestras of the U.S.A. New York, 1974.

Southern, Eileen. Biographical Dictionary of Afro-American and African Musicians. Westport, CT: Greenwood Press, 1982, p. 366.

Symphony of the New World. Miscellaneous Papers, 1965-66. Correspondence, reports, articles, booklets, newspaper clippings, programs, and photos, concerning the groups founding and activities from the papers of Allan Morrison. [Held by the Schomburg Collection, NYPL, NYC--Sc Micro R-3537 reel 3, No. 13].

Articles

Brozen, M. "Symphony of the New World (Steinberg)." High Fidelity (April 1968): 27.

Cumbo, Clarissa, and Marion Cumbo, comp. "In Retrospect: The Symphony of the New World." The Black Perspective in Music (Fall 1975): 312-330.

Handy, D. Antoinette. "Conversation with...Lucille Dixon: Manager of a Symphony Orchestra." The Black Perspective in Music (Fall 1975): 299-311.

Hiemenz, J. "Symphony of the New World." High Fidelity
(January 1974): MA23.

"Lessons of Experience; Members of the Symphony of the New
World." Newsweek (February 1967): 102.

"Music Power." Sepia (April 1968): 38-41.

"New World Symph One-Third Negro." Variety (November 5
1969): 53.

"Symphony of the New World, Friedman." High Fidelity (March
1977): MA24-25.

"Symphony of the New World: Manhattan Orchestra Provides
Training for Talented of All Races." Ebony (November 1966):
39-40, 42-44, 46.

Newspaper Articles

Ericson, Raymond. "Black 'Visions.'" New York Times
(August 8, 1971): Sec. 2, p. 11. Notice of upcoming concert.

_____. "The Fight for the Integrated Orchestra." New
York Times (October 20 1974).

Hughes, Allen. "New World Group Planning Concert. Dispute
Over Director Led to Suspension of Dates." New York Times
(February 26 1972).

"New World Names Lee Music Director." New York Times
(August 14 1973).

"On the Way." New York Times (March 13 1966). Editorial
lauding the efforts of the Symphony of the New World to
create an integrated orchestra.

Peyser, Joan. "The Negro in Search of an Orchestra." New
York Times (November 26 1967): Sec. 2, p. 17.

Concert Reviews

"Beethoven by New World Group." New York Times (November 14
1977).

Davis, Peter G. "Hollander Displays Dazzling Style with
Symphony of the New World." New York Times (November 11
1976).

_____. "New World Delights in a Solid Program of Weber,
Brahms." New York Times (October 21 1974).

_____. "Two Unusual Duets at New World Concert." New
York Times (November 11 1973).

Henahan, Donal. "Music: Much Improved Orchestra." New York
Times (March 14 1977).

_____. "Music: Symphony of the New World." New York Times (June 26 1972).

_____. "Music: Symphony's Malcolm Tribute." New York Times (April 8 1974).

_____. "New World Spirit." New York Times (January 29 1974).

_____. "New World Symphony is Host to Duke." New York Times (June 25 1973).

_____. "Orchestra Opens 7th Season Here." New York Times (October 11 1971).

_____. "Symphony of New World Conducted by De Preist." New York Times (October 23 1967).

_____. "Symphony of the New World at Fisher Hall." New York Times (October 23 1973).

Hughes, Allen. "New World Group Plays at Carnegie." New York Times (February 8 1967).

_____. "Symphony Celebrates Its First Anniversary." New York Times (May 9 1966).

Kastendieck, Miles. "A Symphony's 2nd Anniversary." (New York) World Journal Tribune (May 3 1967): 37.

Klein, Howard. "3-Race Ensemble in Concert Debut. Symphony of the New World Plays at Carnegie Hall." New York Times (May 7 1965).

Molleson, John. "Interracial Symphony Orchestra." New York Herald Tribune (? 1965).

Moore, Carman. "New World." Village Voice (May 8 196?).

Rockwell, John. "Ensemble Directed by Denis de Coteau In Pleasant Concert." New York Times (December 4 1972).

_____. "Ketcham Leads New World in Bruckner." New York Times (January 1 1974).

_____. "Music by Da Costa in Premiere." New York Times (February 7 1977).

_____. "Music: Symphony of the New World." New York Times (December 1 1975).

_____. "Music: Violinist Friedman is Solo Highlight with New World Symphony." New York Times (December 7 1976).

_____. "New World Ensemble: Mixed Luck." New York Times (October 17 1977).

_____. "Opera: A Concert 'Carlo'." New York Times
(April 5 1976).

Sherman, Robert. "Carnegie Concert Salutes Black History
Week." New York Times (February 16 1976).

_____. "Symphony of New World Plays at Carnegie Hall."
New York Times (March 3 1974).

Strongin, Theodore. "Benjamin Steinberg Conducts
Premiere." New York Times (February 5 1968).

"Symphony Hails Black History Week." New York Times
(February 6 1973).

"Symphony of New World Back at Carnegie Hall as
Full-Timer." New York Times (October 20 1975).

4
Concert and Opera Singers

GENERAL

Afro-America Sings. Detroit, MI: Detroit Public Schools, 1971. Contains profiles of vocalists Dorothy Maynor, Roland Hayes, Ollie McFarland, Marian Anderson, McHenry Boatwright, Grace Bumbry, Conwell Carrington, Celeste Cole, Gloria Davy, Carlotta Franzel, Reri Grist, Betty Lane, Paul Robeson, George Shirley, Leontyne Price, Shirley Verrett, William Warfield and Camilla Williams.

Johnson, James Weldon. Black Manhattan. New York: Arno Press, 1968. (Orig. 1930). Contains short sketches of Elizabeth Taylor Greenfield, the Hyers Sisters, Flora Batson, Sissieretta Jones (98-101), Jules Bledsoe (206-208), et al.

Kutsch, K. J., and Leo Riemens. A Concise Biographical Dictionary of Singers; From the Beginning of Recorded Sound to the Present. Trans. by Henry Earl Jones. Philadelphia: Chilton Book Co., 1969. Nearly 1500 singers are covered in this work, 17 of them black. They include the following: M. Anderson, J. Bledsoe, McH. Boatwright, G. Bumbry, E. Davis, G. Davy, M. Dobbs, R. Hayes, V. Little, D. Maynor, L. Price, P. Robeson, S. Verrett, W. Warfield, F. Weathers, C. Williams, and L. Winters.

Majors, Monroe A. Noted Negro Women. Chicago: Donohue & Henneberry Printers, 1971. (Repr. of 1893 ed.) Includes numerous short sketches of 19th century women vocalists.

Petrie, Phil. "The Negro in Opera." In The Negro in Music and Art, ed. Lindsay Patterson. New York: Publishers Company, Inc., 1968, pp. 162-171.

Plant, Richard. "Elective Affinities: American Negro Singers and German Lieder." In The Negro in Music and Art, ed. Lindsay Patterson. New York: Publishers Company, Inc., 1968, pp. 194-198.

Turner, Patricia. Afro-American Singers: An Index and
Preliminary Discography of Opera, Choral Music and Song.
Minneapolis, MN: Challenge Productions, 1977. A bio-
discographical guide to concert and choral singers.

Dissertations and Unpublished Papers

Caldwell, Hansonia Laverne. "Black Idioms in Opera as
Manifested in the Works of Six Afro-American Composers."
Dissertation (Ph.D., Musicology) University of Southern
California, 1974. 285pp.

_____. "The Plight of the Black Composer of Opera
(1890-1970)." Paper presented at ASUC meeting, November 15,
1974, Albuquerque, New Mexico.

Davidson, Celia Elizabeth. "Operas by Afro-American
Composers: A Critical Survey and Analysis of Selected
Works." Dissertation (Ph.D., Theory) Catholic University,
1980. 526pp.

Estill, Ann H. "The Contributions of Selected Afro-American
Women Classical Singers: 1850-1955." Dissertation (D.A.) New
York University, 1982. 145pp.

Jordan, C. "Female Concert Singers of the Nineteenth
Century." Thesis (M.S.) Harvard University, 1982.

Articles

Bernheimer, M. "Yes, But Are We Really Colour Deaf?" Opera
(July 1985): 755-760.

"Black Divas." Essence, Vol. 17 (June 1986): 36.

De Lerma, Dominique-Rene. "Met's Gettin Darker." Baltimore
Afro-American (June 23 1979): 17.

Drury, Theodore. "The Negro in Classic Music; or Leading
Opera, Oratorio, and Concert Singers." The Colored American
(September 5 1902): 324-325.

Duncan, John. "Negro Composers of Opera." Negro History
Bulletin, Vol. 29 (January 1966): 79-80.

Durham, F. "Opera That Didn't Get to the Metropolitan."
South Atlantic Quarterly (October 1954): 497-507.

Ford, C. E. "Negro Singers I Have Heard." Negro History
Bulletin (February 1955): 19-20.

Graham, A. "International Grand Opera in Harlem." Sepia,
Vol. 11 (June 1962): 44-46.

Heymont, George. "Blacks in Opera." Ebony (November 1981):
32-36.

"Hold Down Front Tickets, but 4 Negroes See Met Opera in
Atlanta Balcony." Variety (May 10 1961): 88.

Hopkins, P. E.   "Famous Women of the Negro Race: Phenomenal Vocalists." Colored American Magazine, Vol. 4 (1901-02): 45+.

Hubert, Levi C.   "Harlem WPA Group Singing Opera." The Crisis, Vol. 43 (July 1936): 203, 214.

"Increasing Number of Negro Singers in Opera." The World of Music, No. 4 (August 1960): 77.

Jenkins, Speight.   "When Will the Black Male Make It In Opera?" New York Times (December 3 1972): Sec. II, pp. 15, 30.   Interviews with Francois Clemmons, George Shirley, E. Taylor, Edward Pierson, S. Johnson on the difficulties they face as black male singers.

Landry, R. J.   "Sepia Yanks Hit Operatic Gravy Train--In Europe." Variety (July 18 1956): 1+.

Layng, J.   "Black Images in Opera." Opera Journal, Vol. 2, No. 1 (1969): 28-32.

Lovell, John, Jr.   "The Operatic Stage." The Crisis (February 1948): 42-44, 59-60, 62.

"More Negroes in Grand Opera." Variety (December 27 1967): 48.

Morrison, A.   "Who Will Be First to Crack Met Opera?" Negro Digest (September 1950): 52-56.

Novak, B. J.   "Opening Doors in Music." Negro History Bulletin (January 1971): 10-14.

"Opera's Gain." Newsweek (October 18 1954): 96.   Met breaks the color line.

"Opera Singers." Ebony (November 1959): 27-30+.

Palmer, C.   "Delius's Negro Opera." Opera (May 1972): 403-407.

Redwood, C.   "The First Negro Opera?" Musical Opinion (May 1972): 407+.

Salmaggi, F. W.   "Mail Pouch: Salmaggi Credit." New York Times (January 31 1960): Sec. 2, p. 9.   On Negro artists in grand opera.

Schonberg, Harold C.   "A Bravo for Opera's Black Voices." New York Times Magazine (January 17, 1982): 24-27, 80, 82, 90, 92.   Responses (February 21 1982): Sec. VI, p. 110.

Southern, Eileen.   "In Retrospect: Black Prima Donnas of the Nineteenth Century." The Black Perspective in Music (Spring 1979): 95-106.

"Stations in South Reject NBC Opera with Negro Star." Variety, No. 218 (April 13, 1960): 1.

INDIVIDUAL VOCALISTS

ADELE ADDISON (1925-   )

Abdul, Raoul. "Roland Hayes's Children." In Blacks in Classical Music. New York: Dodd, Mead & Co., 1977, pp. 98-99.

Bernas, Richard. "Addison, Adele." In The New Grove Dictionary of Music and Musicians, Vol. 1, p. 103.

_____. "Addison, Adele." In The New Grove Dictionary of American Music, Vol. 1, p. 7.

Southern, Eileen. Biographical Dictionary of Afro-American and African Musicians. Westport, CT: Greenwood Press, 1982, p. 6.

Articles

"Adele Addison." Musical America (February 1952): 175+.

"Adele Addison." Musical America (December 15 1953): 33.

"Adele Addison." Musical America (July 1959): 4. Bio.

"Adele Addison." Musical Courier (Febuary 1 1952): 25.

"Adele Addison." Musical Courier (March 1 1957): 19.

"Adele Addison." Variety (February 6 1957): 62.

"Adele Addison: American in Moscow." Musical America (May 1963): 19.

Ardoin, J. "Adele Addison Soloist with Collegiate Chorale." Musical America (June 1960): 39.

_____. "Benefit Concert for Project Hope." Musical America (July 1962): 29.

Brozen, M. "Bach Aria Group." Musical America (January 1962): 242.

Durgin, C. "New York City Opera Makes Annual Boston Visit." Musical America (December 1 1955): 10.

Glass, H. "La Boheme." Musical America (November 1961): 27.

Kolodin, Irving. "Music to my Ears." Saturday Review (November 5 1960): 44.

_____. "Sopranos Berger and Addison." Saturday Review (February 2 1952): 33-34.

Kreines, J. "Chicago." Musical America (September 1960): 16.

"Little Orchestra in Berlioz Opera." Musical America (April 1960): 31.

Manzer, C. "Oakland Symphony and Soloists Present Distinguished Concerts." Music of the West (June 1962): 10.

"NCMEA Convention, Houston." Musart, Vol. 20, No. 5 (1968): 48.

New York Amsterdam News (May 10 1947).

New York Amsterdam News (October 28 1950).

[New York Recital] Musical America (January 1964): 53.

Sabin, R. "Foss 'Time Cycle' Has World Premiere." Musical America (December 1960): 34-35.

_____. "Poulenc 'Gloria' in New York Premiere." Musical America (May 1961): 44-45.

Singer, S. L. "Philadelphia." The Music Magazine and Music Courier (December 1961): 67.

"Soprano Soloist at KSC." Negro History Bulletin (May 1953): 184.

Taubman, Howard. "12 Most Promising Negro Singers." Ebony (October 1953): 48-52.

Thimble, L. "Music; New York Chamber Soloists at Carnegie Recital Hall." Nation (February 22 1958): 176.

"This Week." San Francisco Symphony Program Notes (December 23 1965): 7.

"Voice is Born." Our World, Vol. 8 (January 1953): 20-23.

BETTY ALLEN (1930-   )

Abdul, Raoul. "Roland Hayes's Children." In Blacks in Classical Music. New York: Dodd, Mead & Co., 1977, p. 99.

Bernas, Richard. "Allen, Betty." In The New Grove
Dictionary of Music and Musicians, Vol. 1, p. 280.

_____, and Dennis S. McIntire. "Allen, Betty." In The
New Grove Dictionary of American Music, Vol. 1, p. 30.

Southern, Eileen. Biographical Dictionary of Afro-American
and African Musicians. Westport, CT: Greenwood Press, 1982,
p. 8.

Articles

Allen, Betty. "Music--A Religious Experience." Music
Journal (May 1964): 32-33+.

_____. "2 Part Invention." Music Journal (February
1965): 86-87.

"Betty Allen." Detroit Symphony Program Notes (March 2
1972): 422.

"Betty Allen: Sing Out, America!" High Fidelity (May 1976):
28.

Hemming, Roy. "Lively Arts." (Interview) Senior Scholastic
(May 2 1969): 21-22.

Jernstedt, A. T. "The Indomitable Betty Allen." Music
Journal (January 1977): 12-13+.

Jones, R. T. "Betty Allen, Mezzo." High Fidelity (June
1975): 30.

"Mezzo-Soprano Records Rossini's 'Stabat Mater' in Berlin,
Germany; Has Good Spring Season in U.S." Jet (July 14 1960):
59.

"Names, Dates, and Places." Opera News (October 1974): 15.

Petersen, Maurice. "On The Aisle: Spotlight on Betty Allen."
Essence (February 1976): 31.

Sabin, R. "Betty Allen." Musical America (November 1960):
62-3.

"SAI's in Active Roles in American Music." Pan Pipes, Vol.
55, No. 2 (1963): 33.

Smith, P. J. "From France; Classic and Romantic." High
Fidelity (June 1965): 115.

"Soprano is Only American Artist Representing United States
at U.N. Ball at Waldorf-Astoria Hotel, N.Y.C." Jet (November
3 1960): 58.

Wallace, K. D. "Cabrillo Report." High Fidelity (November
1966): MA66.

Zakatiasen, W.   "Gypsy; Interview."   Opera News (January 23 1971): 13.

Newspaper Articles

Chicago Tribune (May 28 1972): 5.

Detroit News (February 27 1972): C-27.

Fraser, C. Gerald.   "Betty Allen Takes Helm at Harlem School of Arts."   New York Times (March 9 1980): 45.

San Francisco Examiner World (December 3 1978): 56.

Concert Reviews

"Betty Allen."   Musical America (January 15 1958): 27.

"Betty Allen."   Musical Courier (December 1 1952): 38.

"Betty Allen."   Musical Courier (September 1954): 30.

"Betty Allen."   Musical Courier (March 1 1957): 25.

"Betty Allen."   Musical Courier (December 1960): 34.

Fleming, S.   "Scott Joplin's 'Treemonisha.'"   High Fidelity (September 1975): 32-3.

"Hillis Conducts Honegger's Judith."   Musical America (February 1957): 185.

Madden, J.   "Mourning Cuts Audience; Archbishop Scenes; Betty Allen Scores."   Variety (April 10 1968): 285.

Manzer, C.   "Three Young Men Pianists Heard in Recitals on Berkeley Campus."   Music of the West (March 1962): 20.

Merkling, F.   "New York."   Opera News (May 1973): 34.

"Mozart-Hindemith List by New York Chamber Soloists." Musical Courier (June 1960): 24.

[New York Recital].   High Fidelity (June 1969): MA16.

[New York Recital].   Musical America (November 1963): 40.

"Revolucion."   Musical America (September 1961): 34.

"Town Hall Recital."   Musical America (January 15 1958): 27.

MARIAN ANDERSON (1902-   )

Anderson, Marian.   My Lord, What A Morning.   New York: Avon Books, 1956.

Newman, Shirlee.   Marian Anderson, The Lady From Philadelphia.   Philadelphia: Westminster Press, 1965.

Sims, Janet. Marian Anderson: An Annotated Bibliography and
Discography. Westport, CT: Greenwood Press, 1981.

Stokes, Anson Phelps. Art and the Color Line: An Appeal Made
May 31, 1939, to the President General and other officers of
the Daughters of the American Revolution to Modify Their
Rules So As To Permit Distinguished Negro Artists Such as
Miss Marian Anderson to be Heard in Constitution Hall.
Printed for the consideration of the D.A.R. at their meeting,
October 23, and for the Marian Anderson committee.
Washington, D.C., 1939.

Vehanen, Kosti. Marian Anderson: A Portrait. New York:
McGraw-Hill, 1941.

Westlake, Neda, and Otto Albrecht, eds. Marian Anderson: A
Catalogue of the Collection at the University of Pennsylvania
Library. Philadelphia: University of Pennsylvania Press,
1981. 89pp.

CORETTI ARLE-TILZ (c.1870s-after 1943)

Hughes, Langston. I Wonder as I Wander: An Autobiographical
Journey. New York: Hill & Wang, 1956, pp. 82-86.

Southern, Eileen. Biographical Dictionary of Afro-American
and African Musicians. Westport, CT: Greenwood Press, 1982,
p. 17.

Articles

Chicago Defender (June 23 1934)

Chicago Defender (December 18 1943).

MARTINA ARROYO (1936-   )

Abdul, Raoul. "Martina Arroyo: A Conversation." In Blacks
in Classical Music. New York: Dodd, Mead & Co., 1977, pp.
107-110.

Blyth, Alan. "Arroyo, Martina." In The New Grove Dictionary
of Music and Musicians, Vol. 1, p. 638.

_____. "Arroyo, Martina." In The New Grove Dictionary of
American Music, Vol. 1, p. 73.

Diamonstein, Barbaralee. "Martina Arroyo." In Open Secrets:
Ninety-four Women in Touch with Our Time. New York: Viking
Press, 1972, pp. 17-22.

Ewen, David, ed. Musicians Since 1900: Performers in Concert
and Opera. New York: H.W. Wilson, 1978, pp. 24-26.

Hemming, Roy. Discovering Music. New York: Four Winds
Press, 1974, p. 277.

Hines, Jerome. "Martina Arroyo." Great Singers on Great
Singing. New York: Doubleday & Co., 1982, pp. 30-34.

Martinez, Al. "Martina Arroyo." Rising Voices: Profiles of
Hispano-American Lives. New York: New American Library,
1974, pp. 13-15.

Southern, Eileen. Biographical Dictionary of Afro-American
and African Musicians. Westport, CT: Greenwood Press, 1982,
p. 19.

Steane, J. B. The Grand Tradition: Seventy Years of Singing
on Record. New York: Scribners, 1974. Includes a brief
assessment of the recorded work of Martina Arroyo.

Articles

"Arroyo, Martina." Current Biography 1971, pp. 11-14.

Arroyo, Martina. "Music Inspires Good Behavior." Music
Journal (March 1967): 33+.

Daniels, R. D. "Full Circle." Opera News (December 11
1965): 26. Biographical portrait.

Gold, Arthur F. "Madame Butterball." Sepia (March 1975):
59-62.

"L'Italiana di Harlem." Time (September 28 1970): 46.

Jacobson, Robert. "If You're Really Famous Why Aren't You on
Ed Sullivan? At Home with Soprano Martina Arroyo." After
Dark (September 1970): 26-28.

Jenkins, Speight. "The Real Martina." Opera News (November
1971): 16-17.

Landry, R. J. "Martina Arroyo Looks Like Met's New Negro
Draw." Variety, No. 254 (February 1 1967): 21.

"A Look at the Future: Nine Young Artists." Musical America
(July 1963): 9.

"Martina Arroyo." The NATS Bulletin, Vol. 35, No. 1 (1978):
21. Biographical portrait.

"Martina Arroyo First Negro Elsa (believed) in "Lohengrin"
History." Variety, No. 249 (January 31 1968): 71.

Movshon, G. "Musician of the Month: Martina Arroyo." High
Fidelity (June 1968): M-5.

"Names, Dates and Places." Opera News (March 23 1968): 4-5.

"Names, Dates and Places." Opera News (March 29 1969): 5.

"Names, Dates and Places." Opera News (December 5 1970): 5.

"Names, Dates and Places." Opera News (Decemember 16 1972): 6-7.

"Names, Dates and Places." Opera News (January 10 1976): 16-17.

"No Nerves." New Yorker (April 8 1967): 33-35.

Phillips, H. E. "Mr. and Mrs. Macbeth." Opera News (February 3 1973): 14-15.

Rogers, E. B. "High Honors." Musical America (January 1961): 182.

Rubin, Stephen E. "Arroyo: A Candid Encounter with the Merry Diva." Opera News (December 18 1976): 22-24, 26.

Saal, Hubert. "Met's Martina." Newsweek (June 14 1971): 73.

"Winning Personalities." Opera News (April 21 1958): 26.

Newspaper Articles

Gruen, John. Article on Martina Arroyo, then preparing to make her first NY appearance since 1978, after being a Metropolitan Opera mainstay from 1958 to 1978. New York Times (April 17 1983): Sec. II, p. 21.

Guardian (February 16 1970): 8.

Levy, A. "Life at the Opera with Madame Butterball." New York Times Magazine (May 17 1972): 20+.

New York Sunday News Magazine (November 8 1970): 4+.

New York Times (April 28 1968): Sec. II, p. 21. Interview.

Concert Reviews

Christian Science Monitor (January 27 1966): 6.

Davis, P. G., and B. Jacobson. "New York." Opera (February 1966): 133-134.

Housewright, W. "Dubrovnik." Musical Courier (August 1961): 29.

Kolodin, Irving. "Music to my Ears." Saturday Review (February 20 1965): 45.

Musical America (April 1961): 67-68.

Musical America (January 1962): 172.

New York Age (March 21 1959).

New York Amsterdam News (July 11 1964).

New York Post (January 27 1968): 21.

New York Post (September 12 1970): 13.

Repass, R.   "'The Ring' Under Leinsdorf."   Opera (March 1962): 170.

Widder, M.   "Cleveland."   Musical Leader (January 1965): 10.

THERMAN BAILEY

Bright, R.   "New Mexico; the Sixth Season."   Musical America (October 1962): 18-19.

CARMEN BALTHROP (1948-   )

Heymont, George.   "Carmen Balthrop: Opera Keeps Her Blowin'."   Essence (May 1980): 12-20+.

Southern, Eileen.   Biographical Dictionary of Afro-American and African Musicians.   Westport, CT: Greenwood Press, 1982, p. 25.

FLORA BATSON (1864-1906)

De Lerma, Dominique-Rene.   "Batson, Flora."   In The New Grove Dictionary of American Music, Vol. 1, p. 160.

Hare, Maud Cuney.   Negro Musicians and Their Music. Washington, D.C.: Associated Publishers, 1936, pp. 219-220.

McGinty, Doris E.   "Flora E. Batson."   In Dictionary of American Negro Biography, eds. Rayford W. Logan and Michael R. Winston.   New York: W.W. Norton, 1982, pp. 32-34.

Millar, Gerard.   Life, Travels, and Works of Miss Flora Batson, Deceased Queen of Song.   n.p.: T.M.R.M. Company, 190?.   92pp.   [Held by the Library of Congress and Boston Public Library, Music Collection.]

Scruggs, Lawson A.   "Madam Flora Batson Bergen."   In Women of Distinction.   Raleigh, NC: The Author, 1893, pp. 26-29.

Southern, Eileen.   Biographical Dictionary of Afro-American and African Musicians.   Westport, CT: Greenwood Press, 1982, p. 30.

Articles

Indianapolis Freeman (December 26 1896).

Indianapolis Freeman (December 24 1898).

Indianapolis Freeman (May 12 1900).

Indianapolis Freeman (February 15 1901).

New York Age (December 3 1887).

New York Age (December 6 1906).

New York Freeman (April 25 1885).

New York Freeman (October 24 1885).

KATHLEEN BATTLE (1948-   )

Dyer, Richard. "Battle, Kathleen." In The New Grove Dictionary of American Music, Vol. 1, p. 160.

Who's Who in America 1984-85.

Articles

"Battle, Kathleen." Current Biography 1984, pp. 23-26.

"A Cincinnati Songbird Named Kathleen Battle is Positively Thrilling from her Perch at the Met." People (March 7 1983): 88-89.

Crutchfield, Will. "Kathleen Battle: The Young Soprano is Remaining Loyal to Her Lyrical Instincts." Ovation (March 1984): 16-19.

"The Most Ravishing Soprano." Vogue, No. 176 (February 1986): 80.

Rich, Alan. "Going for the Gold." Newsweek (December 2 1985): 90-92.

Seebohm, C. "The Performer: Diva." Connoisseur, Vol. 215 (February 1985): 108-109.

Smith, P. J. "Kathleen Battle." High Fidelity (February 1984): 4-5.

Waleson, H. "Fortune's Favorite." Opera News (March 13 1982): 9-11.

Newspaper Articles

Holland, Bernard. "A Very Special Soprano." New York Times Magazine (November 17 1985): 59+.

New York Times (April 11 1982): Sec. III, p. 13. Comment on Kathleen Battle and her prolific singing schedule.

New York Times (February 24 1984): Sec. III, p. 1. Singers Simon Estes, Kathleen Battle, Sherrill Milnes, Leonie Rysanek and Hakan Hagegard discuss their voices and musical approaches.

"Soprano Hopes to Reach New Heights." Los Angeles Times (September 14 1983): Sec. VI, p.3. Interview.

Steinbrink, Mark. "Cautious Road to Vocal Stardom." New York Times (May 2 1982): Sec. II, p. 23+.

ANNABELLE BERNARD

"Annabelle Bernard, Soprano and Graduate of Xavier University (La.); Also Award-Winning Graduate Student of New England Conservatory of Music; Is Acclaimed by East German Newspaper Critics During Recent Concert Tour." Jet (February 23 1961): 60.

Eggler, B.   "New Orleans." Opera News (January 22 1977): 32.

Goodwin, N.   "London." Musical Courier (December 1959): 27.

Jahant, C.   "Washington." Opera (UK) (February 1976): 154-156.

Rothon, G.   "Munich." Opera (UK) (June 1973): 513-514.

Wilson, C.   "Scotland." Musical Times (February 1965): 122.

HAROLYN BLACKWELL

Crutchfield, Will.   "A Soprano and Two Violinists in First Recital Appearances." New York Times (April 5 1987): 61. Review of soprano Harolyn Blackwell's debut recital.

JULES BLEDSOE (1898-1943)

Bishop, Cardell.   Opera at the Hippodrome in New York City. Santa Monica, CA: The Author, 1979, pp. 8, 19-21.

De Lerma, Dominique-Rene.   "Bledsoe, Jules." In The New Grove Dictionary of American Music, Vol. 1, p. 233.

Hare, Maud Cuney.   Negro Musicians and Their Music. Washington, D.C.: Associated Publishers, 1936, pp. 358-362.

Lemieux, Raymond.   "Bledsoe, Jule." In Dictionary of American Negro Biography, eds. Rayford W. Logan and Michael R. Winston.   New York: W. W. Norton, 1982, pp. 47-48.

Southern, Eileen.   Biographical Dictionary of Afro-American and African Musicians.   Westport, CT: Greenwood Press, 1982, pp. 38-39.

Who's Who in Colored America, 1927-1944, p. 16.

[See also Jules Bledsoe clippings file in the Music Division of the Performing Arts Research Center at Lincoln Center.]

Articles

"All-Negro Grand Opera Cast Sings "Emperor Jones" in N.Y." Baltimore Sun (July 14 1934).

"Jules Bledsoe and Abbie Mitchell Open New Deal Presenting
"Emperor Jones", "Cavalleria Rusticana" at the Mecca."   The
Pittsburgh Courier (July 1934?).

"Jules Bledsoe Sings in Town Hall." Musical America
(February 10 1940).

"Negro Opera Singer." News-Week (July 21 1934): 20.

"Negro Opera Singers Appear in Double Bill." New York Herald
Tribune (July 8 1934). Review of productions of "Emperor
Jones" and "Cavalleria Rusticana".

"Recital is Given Here by Bledsoe, Baritone." New York Times
(June 6 1938).

Obituaries

"Bledsoe, Jules." Current Biography 1943.

The Gramophone (November 1945): 73.

"Jules Bledsoe." The Etude (September 1943): 553, 608.

Musical America (July 1943): 19.

Musical Courier (August 1943): 31.

New York Amsterdam News (July 24 1943).

New York Times (July 16 1943): 17.

MCHENRY BOATWRIGHT (1928-   )

Abdul, Raoul. Blacks in Classical Music. New York: Dodd,
Mead & Co., 1977, pp. 118-119.

Eckert, Thor, Jr. "Boatwright, McHenry." In The New Grove
Dictionary of American Music, Vol. 1, p. 251.

Southern, Eileen. Biographical Dictionary of Afro-American
and African Musicians. Westport, CT: Greenwood Press, 1982,
pp. 39-40.

Articles

Ardoin, J. "Boatwright Premieres Kastle Songs." Musical
America (February 1962): 22-23.

_____. "McHenry Boatwright." Musical America (December
1960): 55.

Bloomfield, A. "Baroque Adventure." Musical America
(September 1961): 27.

Chicago Defender (January 25 1958).

Cohn, A., et al. "New York." Music Magazine (February 1962): 24.

"Distinguished Artists to be Heard at San Diego Biennial." Music Clubs Magazine (September 1958): 29+.

Durgin, C. "Boston University Produces Hindemith Opera Premiere." Musical America (March 1956): 5.

_____. "Markevitch, Ormandy Conduct Boston Symphony as Guests." Musical America (April 1957): 13.

Garner, P. "Singer Comes Home." Biography News (December 1974): 1359-1360.

Kolodin, Irving. "Music to my Ears." Saturday Review (January 6 1962): 23.

"McHenry Boatwright." Music Clubs Magazine (April 1959): 42.

"McHenry Boatwright." The Music Magazine and Musical Courier (October 1961): 19. Bio.

"McHenry Boatwright." Musical America (February 1958): 163.

"McHenry Boatwright." Musical Courier (December 1960): 34.

"McHenry Boatwright." Musical Events (London) (April 1969): 8.

"McHenry Boatwright is Concert Click in Japan Despite Lack of 'Name'." Variety (December 3 1958): 13.

Montagu, G. "Splendid Baritone." The Music Magazine and Musical Courier (December 1961): 18.

"The Musical Whirl." High Fidelity (September 1969): MA13.

New York Times (August 24 1975): 43. Black singers Francois Clemons and McHenry Boatwright complain of neglect of black male, but not female singers by US opera companies.

Rapp, B. P. "Schola Cantorum." Musical America (May 1962): 35.

Soria, D. J. "Artist Life." High Fidelity (May 1967): MA6-7.

Taylor, N. E. "'Never Needed Black as a Crutch' Baritone Boatwright Explains His Rise." Christian Science Monitor (September 7 1973): 13.

"Vienna Philharmonic Signed by Vichey." Musical America (November 15 1957): 20.

THOMAS J. BOWERS ["the Colored Mario"] (1826-1885)

Adkins, Aldrich W.   "Bowers, Thomas J."   In Dictionary of
American Negro Biography, eds. Rayford W. Logan and Michael
R. Winston.   New York: W. W. Norton, 1982, p. 54.

De Lerma, Dominique-Rene.   "Bowers, Thomas J."   In The New
Grove Dictionary of American Music, Vol. 1, p. 280.

Hare, Maud Cuney.   Negro Musicians and Their Music.
Washington, D.C.: Associated Publishers, 1936, pp. 199-201.

New York Freeman (October 10 1885).

Pennsylvania Historical Society, Box 13G.

Southern, Eileen.   Biographical Dictionary of Afro-American
and African Musicians.   Westport, CT: Greenwood Press, 1982,
pp. 42-43.

Trotter, James M.   Music and Some Highly Musical People.
Chicago: Afro-Am Press, 1969, pp. 131-137, 310.   (Orig. 1878)

GWENDOLYN BRADLEY

Hughes, Allen.   "Gwendolyn Bradley Sings 'Glitter and Be
Gay.'"   New York Times (June 10 1979).

Who's Who of American Women, 1987-88.

CAROL BRICE (1918-1985)

Abdul, Raoul.   "Roland Hayes's Children."   In Blacks in
Classical Music.   New York: Dodd, Mead & Co., 1977, p. 97.

De Lerma, Dominique-Rene.   "Brice, Carol."   In The New Grove
Dictionary of American Music, Vol. 1, p. 292.

Southern, Eileen.   Biographical Dictionary of Afro-American
and African Musicians.   Westport, CT: Greenwood Press, 1982,
p. 47.

Articles

"Carol Brice."   American Music Teacher, Vol. 25, No. 4
(1976): 43.

"Carol Brice."   Music News (January 1950): 16.

"Carol Brice."   Music News (May 1952): 10.

"Carol Brice."   Musical America (April 1 1952): 18.

"Carol Brice."   Musical America (December 15 1955): 22-23.

"Carol Brice."   Musical America (March 1958): 25-26.

"Carol Brice." Musical Courier (April 15 1952): 13.

"Carol Brice." Musical Courier (January 1 1956): 12.

"Carol Brice: Famed Conductor Commissions New Vocal Symphony for Her." Ebony (December 1946): 46-49.

"New Honorary Members." Pan Pipes, Vol. 66, No. 4 (1974): 16-17.

New York Age (October 27 1945).

New York Age (February 8 1958).

New York Amsterdam News (December 16 1944).

Oklahoma City Symphony Orchestra programs, January 4-5, 1975, p. 149.

Scott, N. "Carol Brice is Just a Typical American Girl." Opportunity: Journal of Negro Life (Spring 1947): 93-94.

"Town Hall Recital." Musical America (December 15 1955): 22.

"Voice Like a Cello." Time (March 11 1946): 74.

Obituaries

The Black Perspective in Music, Vol. 13, No. 2 (Fall 1985): 241.

New York Times (February 19 1985): D-17.

GARNET BROOKS (1936-   ) - Canada

"The Artists." Opera Canada, Vol. 10, No. 3 (1969): 49.

"Canada's Caruso." Ebony (December 1964): 177-185.

"Canadian Opera Touring Company." Opera Canada, Vol. 13, No. 3 (1972): 14-16.

"Canadian Opera Touring Company 1973/74." Opera Canada, Vol. 14, No. 3 (1973): 14-15.

Crichton, R. "Canada." The Musical Times (July 1969): 766.

"Don Giovanni." Opera Canada, Vol. 11, No. 3 (1970): 31.

Donizetti, G. "Lucia di Lammermoor." Opera Canada, Vol. 12, No. 3 (1971): 26.

Forner, J. "Profile: Garnet Brooks." Opera Canada, Vol. 11, No. 2 (1970): 14-15.

Schulman, M. "The Long, Long, Journey to 'Seabird Island.'" Performing Arts Canada, Vol. 14, No. 2 (1977): 30-35.

ANITA PATTI BROWN (1870s-1950s)

Hare, Maud Cuney. Negro Musicians and Their Music.
Washington, D.C.: Associated Publishers, 1936, p. 234.

Southern, Eileen. Biographical Dictionary of Afro-American
and African Musicians. Westport, CT: Greenwood Press, 1982,
pp. 49-50.

Articles

Chicago Defender (June 28 1913).

Chicago Defender (January 7 1922).

Chicago Defender (May 4 1946).

Indianapolis Freeman (June 15 1903).

New York Age (January 28 1915).

New York Age (July 13 1916).

New York Age (May 15 1920).

New York Age (May 25 1929).

ANNE WIGGENS BROWN (1915-   )

Hare, Maud Cuney. Negro Musicians and Their Music.
Washington, D.C.: Associated Publishers, 1936, p. 263.

Southern, Eileen. Biographical Dictionary of Afro-American
and African Musicians. Westport, CT: Greenwood Press, 1982,
p. 50.

Who's Who in Colored America, 1950.

Articles

"Anne Brown Active in Europe." Musical Courier (October 1
1951): 11.

"Anne Brown Becomes a Norwegian." Ebony (September 1948):
26-30.

"Anne Brown Goes to Paris." Ebony (September 1946): 10-13.

Bjarne, R. "Oslo." Musical Courier (July 1955): 30.

Blitzstein, Madelin. "Paris-Bound for a Song." Negro Digest
(September 1945): 57-60.

Brown, Anne. "I Gave Up My Country for My Love." Ebony
(November 1953): 28-38.

Chicago Defender (July 13 1935).

Detroit Symphony Program Notes (February 14, 1946).

Fossum, K. "Oslo." Opera (January 1968): 62.

"Gershwin to Mozart." Newsweek (October 12 1942): 85-87.

New York Age (March 8 1947).

WILLIAM BROWN (1938-   )

Southern, Eileen. Biographical Dictionary of Afro-American and African Musicians. Westport, CT: Greenwood Press, 1982, p. 52.

Articles

Libbey, Theodore W., Jr. "William Brown, Tenor, With Esoteric Program." New York Times (May 16 1982).

"M & A: Festivals." Music and Artists, Vol. 1, No. 3 (1968): 45-46.

"The Musical Whirl." High Fidelity (August 1968): MA8-9.

"The Musical Whirl." High Fidelity (January 1973): 20-21.

"New York." Opera News (November 25 1967): 23.

NELLIE BROWN MITCHELL (1845-1924)

Dannett, Sylvia G. L. Profiles of Negro Womanhood. Yonkers, NY: Educational Heritage, Inc., 1964. Brief biography.

De Lerma, Dominique-Rene. "Brown Mitchell, Nellie." In The New Grove Dictionary of American Music, Vol. 1, p. 310.

Hare, Maud Cuney. Negro Musicians and Their Music. Washington, D.C.: Associated Publishers, 1936, pp. 209, 212, 218-219.

Scruggs, Lawson A. "Miss Nellie E. Brown." In Women of Distinction. Raleigh, NC: The Author, 1893, pp. 82-84.

Southern, Eileen. Biographical Dictionary of Afro-American and African Musicians. Westport, CT: Greenwood Press, 1982, p. 53.

Trotter, James M. Music and Some Highly Musical People. Chicago: Afro-Am Press, 1969, pp. 192-208. (Orig. 1878)

Articles

Cleveland Gazette (October 31 1886).

Cleveland Gazette (April 14 1888).

Indianapolis Freeman (August 23 1890).

New York Freeman (March 14 1885).

New York Freeman (October 24 1885).

New York Freeman (March 20 1886).

New York Globe (1880s-1890s)

JOYCE BRYANT (1928-   )

Southern, Eileen. Biographical Dictionary of Afro-American and African Musicians. Westport, CT: Greenwood Press, 1982.

Articles

Chicago Defender (January 29 1955).

Wilson, John. "Joyce Bryant, After the Age of Silver." New York Times (July 22 1977).

GRACE BUMBRY (1937-   )

Abdul, Raoul. "Miss Bumbry's Met Debut." In Blacks in Classical Music. New York: Dodd, Mead & Co., 1977, pp. 110-111.

Blyth, Alan. "Bumbry, Grace." In The New Grove Dictionary of Music and Musicians, Vol. 3, p. 454.

_____. "Bumbry, Grace." In The New Grove Dictionary of American Music, Vol. 1, p. 325.

Christiansen, Rupert. Prima Donna: A History. New York: Penguin Books, 1986, pp. 233-235.

Ewen, David, ed. Musicians Since 1900: Performers in Concert and Opera. New York: H.W. Wilson, 1978, pp. 109-111.

Hemming, Roy. Discovering Music. New York: Four Winds Press, 1974, p. 283.

Southern, Eileen. Biographical Dictionary of Afro-American and African Musicians. Westport, CT: Greenwood Press, 1982, p. 55.

Steane, J. B. The Grand Tradition: Seventy Years of Singing on Record. New York: Scribners, 1974. Brief assessment of Bumbry's recorded work.

Articles

"America Applauds Grace Bumbry after European Success." Sepia (May 1963): 28-31.

Bailey, Peter A. "Grace Bumbry: Singing is Terrific - But Living is an Art." Ebony (December 1973): 67-68+.

Barker, F. Granville. "Grace Bumbry." Music and Musicians (November 1977): 20-22. Interview.

"Black Venus." Newsweek (August 7 1961): 36.

Blyth, Alan. "Grace Bumbry." Opera (UK), Vol. 21 (June 1970): 506-510.

"Bumbry, Grace." Current Biography 1964, pp. 60-62.

"Dream Come True." Ebony (May 1962): 91-95.

Fischer-Williams, Barbara. "Grace Bumbry: Diva and Enfant Terrible." After Dark (October 1970): 35-37.

Fitzgerald, G. "A New Grace; Interview." Opera News (January 8 1972): 14-16.

"Grace Bumbry: A Singer Comes Home." Look (February 26 1963): 66+.

"Grace Bumbry, the 'Venus' in Bayreuth Festival Production of 'Tannhauser'; 24 year old Negro Mezzo-Soprano from St. Louis, Mo., Signs 5-year 250,000 Contract with Sol Hurok in London for U.S. and Canadian Engagements." Jet (September 14 1961): 59.

Haynes, Howard. "Grace Bumbry: International Opera's Super Star." Sepia (June 1974): 46-48+.

Hoelterhoff, M. "Interview: Grace Bumbry." Music Journal (November 1977): 4-6.

Jenkins, S. "Grace Melzia Bumbry." Stereo Review, Vol. 32 (January 1974): 70-71.

Jet (April 2 1970): 56-57.

Mayer, M. "Musician of the Month: Grace Bumbry." High Fidelity (November 1979): 4-5.

Morsell, F. A. "Grace Bumbry: Interview." The Crisis (November 1977): 446-450.

Movshon, G. "Grace Melzia Bumbry - From Playgirl to Soprano." New York Times Biographical Service (January 1977): 19-21.

Musical America (January 1962): 21. Photo and mention of Grace Bumbry as being the first black to be engaged by the Bayreuth Festival.

"Names, Dates and Places." Opera News (March 2 1968): 4-5.

"Names, Dates and Places." Opera News (April 12 1969): 5.

"Names, Dates and Places." Opera News (April 18 1970): 5.

"Names, Dates and Places." Opera News (April 3 1971): 4-5.

"Names, Dates and Places." Opera News (March 31 1973): 6-7.

"Names, Dates and Places." Opera News (December 8 1973):
10-11.

"Names, Dates and Places." Opera News (April 19 1975): 7.

"Names, Dates and Places." Opera News (October 1977): 8-9.

"Negro Singer Stars as 'Venus' in Wagner Festival's
Production of Opera 'Tannhauser' at Bayreuth, Germany; Is
First Negro to Appear at Bayreuth Festival." Jet (August 10
1961): 60.

"Orfeo Races the Furies." Music Journal (March 1971): 26-27.

"People Are Talking About..." Vogue (February 1 1968): 163.

Rubin, Stephen. "Amazing Grace." Opera News (October 1981):
10-13+.

Silver, E. "People." Essence (January 1971): 48+.

Smith, P. J. "And We Quote; Interview." High Fidelity
(March 1968): 16.

Tuesday-at-Home (December 1973): 10-14+.

"With Our Honorary Artists." Pan Pipes, Vol. 57, No. 4
(1965): 23.

Concert Reviews

Bernheimer, M. "Bayreuth 1961: The Troubles of Tannhauser
(and Others)." Saturday Review (August 26 1961): 42-43.

_____. "Die Schwarze Venus." Opera News (October 28
1961): 21.

"Best in Opera." Music and Musicians [London] (March 1960):
19.

Boucher, A. "San Francisco." Opera News (December 24 1966):
30.

_____. "San Francisco." Opera News (October 14 1967): 23.

Brunner, G. "Bayreuth." Musical Courier (September 1961):
36.

Campbell, A. "San Francisco." Musical Courier (April 1958):
38.

"Command Performance." Time (March 2 1962): 46.

"Dance of Life." Time (December 22 1967): 50.

Emery, J. "Bournemouth Symphony Orchestra." Musical Times
[London] (March 1960): 173.

"Grace Bumbry." Music of the West (March 1958): 19.

Kolodin, Irving. "Bizet or Bizarre, Carmen's the Star."
Saturday Review (December 30 1967): 38-39.

_____. "Music to my Ears; Debut at Carnegie Hall."
Saturday Review (November 24 1962): 43+.

_____. "Music to My Ears." Saturday Review (January 18
1964): 28.

_____. "Music to My Ears." Saturday Review (October 23
1965): 54.

Mackinnon, D. A. "Salzburg Success." Opera News (November
14 1964): 27.

Muller, L. "Progressive Brussels." Opera News (April 8
1961): 32.

Music and Musicians (September 1959): 16. Review of first
London recital.

"New Mezzo." Time (November 16 1962): 70.

"New York." Musical Leader (February 1964): 23.

New York Post (November 8 1962): 28.

[New York Recital] High Fidelity (February 1966): 137.

[New York Recital] Musical America (February 1964): 32.

[New York Recital] Variety (November 24 1965): 64.

Price, G. "Barcelona." Opera (March 1967): 244.

Reid, C. "Notes from Abroad." High Fidelity (November
1961): 28.

Saal, Hubert. "Return of Carmen." Newsweek (December 25
1967): 68.

"Salzburg." The Music Review, Vol. 25, No. 4 (1964): 347.

Salzman, E. "In the Cards." Opera News (December 16 1967):
26-27.

Sargeant, Winthrop. "Musical Events; Second New York Recital
in Carnegie Hall." New Yorker (December 29 1962): 73.

Tassie, P. "San Francisco Music Events." Music of the West
(May 1958): 16.

"Test by Lieder." Newsweek (November 19 1962): 73.

Thomas, E. "Danger Signs." Musical America (September
1961): 57.

_____. "A European Journal." Musical Courier (September 1961): 21.

Tircuit, H. "Tokyo." The Music Magazine and Musical Courier (November 1961): 58-59.

"Wing Personalities." Opera News (April 21 1958): 26.

"Yankee Parsifal." Time (August 4 1961): 47.

MINTO CATO (1900-1979)

Southern, Eileen. Biographical Dictionary of Afro-American and African Musicians. Westport, CT: Greenwood Press, 1982, p. 67.

Articles

Chicago Defender (March 16 1929).

Chicago Defender (December 5 1931).

Chicago Defender (April 3 1937).

Chicago Defender (November 11 1944).

Kahn, H. "Paris Has Produced an All-French 'Negro' Choir." Melody Maker (July 22 1950): 11.

Obituaries

Black Perspective in Music, Vol. 8, No. 2 (Fall 1980): 263.

New York Amsterdam News (November 3 1979).

New York Times (November 2 1979): B-5.

Variety (November 7 1979): 99.

ESTELLE PINCKNEY CLOUGH (c.1860s-1870s-19??)

Southern, Eileen. Biographical Dictionary of Afro-American and African Musicians. Westport, CT: Greenwood Press, 1982, p. 74.

Articles

Chicago Defender (May 10 1919).

"Mme Estelle Clough." The Negro Music Journal, Vol. 1, No. 13 (September 1903): 11-12.

New York Globe (January 6 1883).

CLEOTA COLLINS (1893-1976)

Lovingood, Penman. Famous Modern Negro Musicians. 2nd ed.
New York: Da Capo Press, 1978. (Reprint of 1921 ed.)

Southern, Eileen. Biographical Dictionary of Afro-American
and African Musicians. Westport, CT: Greenwood Press, 1982,
p. 79.

Articles

Chicago Defender (June 12 1920).

Chicago Defender (August 1 1953).

New York Age (March 13 1920).

New York Age (November 5 1927).

Obituary. The Black Perspective in Music, Vol. 4, No. 3
(Fall 1976): 344-345.

CLAMMA DALE (1948-   )

Abdul, Raoul. "A Pair of Sopranos." In Blacks in Classical
Music. New York: Dodd, Mead & Co, 1977, pp. 115-116.

Southern, Eileen. Biographical Dictionary of Afro-American
and African Musicians. Westport, CT: Greenwood Press, 1982,
pp. 92-93.

Articles

"Creative Woman: Success Requires Talent and Dive." Ebony
(August 1977): 137.

"Dale, Clamma." Current Biography 1979, pp. 95-97.

Hiemenz, J. "Musician of the Month: Clamma Dale." High
Fidelity (December 1977): 4-5.

Micklin, Bob. Interview. Newsday (February 20 1977).

Moore, Sally. "Arts: Clamma Rhymes with Drama, and as
Gershwin's Bess She is Broadway's Woman Now." People
(November 22 1976): 43-45.

New York Times (May 2 1976): Sec. II, p. 15. Interview on
the occasion of forthcoming debut.

New York Times (September 29 1976): 28. Interview.

"Pianist and Two Sopranos Win Naumburg Competition." The
School Musician, Vol. 47 (January 1976): 27.

"Welcome to the Great Black Way." Time (November 1 1976):
72+.

BILLIE LYNN DANIEL (1932-   )

Alice Tully Hall. Programs (March 30, 1975).

Davis, Peter G. "Frierson, Miss Daniel Sing a Duo Recital."
New York Times (March 31 1975).

"George Shirley (Tenor), Shirley Verrett-Carter (Soprano),
Billie L. Daniel (Soprano); Among 6 Winners of Opera
Auditions Sponsored by Metropolitan Opera in N.Y.C." Jet
(April 20 1961): 62.

ELLABELLE DAVIS (1907-1960)

Abdul, Raoul. "Roland Hayes's Children." In Blacks in
Classical Music. New York: Dodd, Mead & Co., 1977, pp. 96-97.

De Lerma, Dominique-Rene. "Davis, Ellabelle." In The New
Grove Dictionary of American Music, Vol. 1, p. 584.

Southern, Eileen. Biographical Dictionary of Afro-American
and African Musicians. Westport, CT: Greenwood Press, 1982,
pp. 94-95.

Articles

"Celeste Aida." Time (July 29 1946): 43.

Craig, Mary. "Success Saga." Musical Courier (February 1
1946): 12. Profile.

"Ellabelle Davis." Musical America (January 15 1949): 15.

"Ellabelle Davis." Musical America (January 15 1951): 16.

"Ellabelle Davis." Musical America (March 1954): 30.

"Ellabelle Davis." Musical Courier (January 15 1951): 24.

"Ellabelle Davis." Musical Courier (April 1 1954): 20.

"Ellabelle Davis Making Second Tour of Europe." Musical
Courier (February 15 1949): 21.

"Ellabelle Davis: New Rochelle Soprano is Toast of World
Music Centers." Our World, Vol. 3, No. 8 (August 1948):
38-39.

"Ellabelle Davis Returns after European Successes." Musical
Courier (July 1949): 13. Brief notice.

"Ellabelle Davis Sings Foss Cantata." Musical America
(January 15 1956): 21.

Jet (March 19 1964): 11.

"National Symphony Opens Bargain Series." Musical America
(December 15 1959): 22.

"National Symphony Orchestra." Musical Courier (January 1960): 14.

New York Amsterdam News (1920s-1950s).

"N.Y. Philharmonic-Symphony." Musical Courier (February 1956): 72-73.

Our World (August 1947): 48. Brief feature article.

"Portrait." The Crisis (February 1950): 87.

"Song of Solomon and Foss." Newsweek (March 17 1947): 90.

Obituaries

Jet (December 1 1960): 44.

Musical America (December 1960): 96.

New York Amsterdam News (November 19 1960).

New York Times (November 16 1960): 41.

Opera (March 1961): 191.

Opera News (January 7 1961): 31.

Variety (November 23 1960): 71.

GLORIA DAVY (1931-   )

Bernas, Richard. "Davy, Gloria." In The New Grove Dictionary of Music and Musicians, Vol. 5, p. 284.

_____. "Davy, Gloria." In The New Grove Dictionary of American Music, Vol. 1, p. 589.

Dunbar, Ernest. "Gloria Davy: Berlin." In The Black Expatriates: A Study of American Negroes in Exile. New York: Dutton, 1968, pp. 176-187.

Southern, Eileen. Biographical Dictionary of Afro-American and African Musicians. Westport, CT: Greenwood Press, 1982, pp. 97-98.

Who's Who in America, 1976-77.

Articles

"Aida." Musical America (March 1958): 19.

"'Aida' in Concert Form." Musical America (August 1957): 33.

"American Opera Gives 'Anna Bolena.'" Musical America (November 1 1957): 30.

"Davy Returning to Metropolitan." _Musical America_ (September 1958): 20.

"Double Launching." _Time_ (February 24 1958): 46.

Dragadze, P. "Troilus and Cressida Given Cold Welcome in Milan." _Musical America_ (March 1956): 8.

"Gloria Davy." _Musical America_ (March 1960): 33.

"Gloria Davy and Robert McFerrin with the Philadelphia Grand Opera Company at Academy of Music." _Jet_ (November 17 1960): 60.

"Gloria Davy Ignores Snub of 1957 and Will Sing for La Scala in 'Mahagonny'." _Variety_ (October 9 1963): 1+.

Jack, A. "Stockhausen." _Music and Musicians_ (January 1975): 54-55.

Jet (December 25 1969): 61.

Jolly, C. "Recital by Davy." _Musical America_ (November 1 1958): 8.

Kolodin, Irving. "Debuts of Tchaikovsky and Simionato-City Center." _Saturday Review_ (October 26 1957): 29.

_____. "Kubelik, Munch, and Szell--Brenda Lewis in 'Vanessa'." _Saturday Review_ (March 1 1958): 27.

Landry, R. J. "Gloria Davy's Diva from 'Bess' to 'Aida' at Met; Got Work(s) at Scala." _Variety_ (February 19 1958): 2.

Marcus, M. "Aida." _Music and Musicians_ [London] (July 1960): 26.

"Metropolitan Opera Engages Six New Singers." _Musical America_ (October 1957): 15.

"The Musical Whirl." _High Fidelity_ (August 1973): 10-11.

"Names, Dates and Places." _Opera News_ (May 17 1969): 5.

"New Voices on the Air." _Opera News_ (December 1 1958): 8.

New York Age (January 21 1959).

New York Age (June 8 1974).

Sabin, R. "Little Orchestra Opens with Strauss 'Daphne'." _Musical America_ (November 1960): 49.

"Scherman Revives Gluck Opera." _Musical America_ (February 1959): 266.

"Spotlight." _Music and Artists_, Vol. 2, No. 3 (1969): 32.

"Spotlight." _Music and Artists_, Vol. 3, No. 1 (1970): 53.

"Spotlight." Music Journal (February 1973): 48.

Stuckenschmidt, H. H. "Berlin (West)." Opera (January 1962): 34.

"Two Fine Glorias." Time (March 13 1964): 59.

Weaver, W. "Naples." Opera [London] (April 1959): 248.

MATTIWILDA DOBBS (1925-   )

Bernas, Richard. "Dobbs, Mattiwilda." In The New Grove Dictionary of American Music, Vol. 1, p. 636.

Cherry, Gwendolyn, et al. "Mattiwilda Dobbs: A Gift from the South." In Portraits in Color: The Lives of Colorful Negro Women. New York: Pageant Press, 1962, pp. 94-96.

Dunbar, Ernest. "Mattiwilda Dobbs: Stockholm." In The Black Expatriates: A Study of American Negroes in Exile. New York: Dutton, 1968, pp. 207-223.

Ewen, David, ed. Musicians Since 1900: Performers in Concert and Opera. New York: H.W. Wilson, 1978, pp. 201-202.

Southern, Eileen. Biographical Dictionary of Afro-American and African Musicians. Westport, CT: Greenwood Press, 1982, p. 109.

Troup, Cornelius V. Distinguished Negro Georgians. Dallas, TX: Royal Publishing Co., 1962, pp. 55-56.

Articles

"Atlanta to La Scala." Time (March 16 1953): 54-55.

"Atlanta's Queen." Newsweek (July 12 1954): 54.

Chicago Defender (March 10 1956).

"Contest Winner." International Musician (December 1951): 29.

"Dobbs, Mattiwilda." Current Biography 1955, 172-173.

"Hurok Pacts New Negro Singer for Concert Tour." Variety (February 18 1953): 47.

Jet (March 5 1964): 11.

Jet (September 24 1970): 40.

Jet (September 12 1974): 24.

"Mattiwilda's Life Abroad." Ebony (January 1959): 54-56.

"Met's New Coloratura." Time (November 19 1956): 51.

"Mlle Merit Awards." Mademoiselle (January 1955): 63.

Murdock, C.   "'My Daughter Married a White Man' - J. Wesley Dobbs."   Ebony (January 1954): 86-93.

"Negro Opera Star's Integrated B'ham Biz."   Variety (December 11 1963): 2.

New Courier [Pittsburgh] (August 25 1973).

"New York Debut; Lavish Praise by Critics and 7 Encores Reward Soprano Mattiwilda Dobbs First New York Concert."   Our World (July 1954): 40-43.

Philadelphia Tribune (November 17 1973).

Preece, H.   "Atlanta's Queen of Opera."   Sepia (May 1958): 42-46+.

"Sopranos East and West."   Opera News (March 5 1960): 10-11+.

Taubman, H.   "12 Most Promising Negro Singers."   Ebony (October 1953): 48-52.

"Third Negro Singer Signed by Met Opera."   Variety (February 29 1956): 68.

"Wins Geneva Contest."   Musical Courier (October 15 1951): 17.

"Woman of the World."   Opera News (March 31 1958): 9.

Concert Reviews

"Adelaide."   The Canon (October 1955): 99.

Ardoin, J.   "Rigoletto."   Musical America (April 1961): 56.

Briggs, E.   "Brisbane."   The Canon (October 1955): 94-95.

Chicago Defender (March 10 1956).

"Covent Garden."   Opera [London] (May 1959): 329.

"Dobbs Impresses in Debut as Gilda."   Musical America (December 1 1956): 3.

Dowdy, D., and R. Devries.   "Chicago."   Musical Courier (March 1955): B1.

Eyer, R.   "Dobbs Impresses in Debut as Gilda."   Musical America (December 1 1956): 3.

_____.   "New York."   Opera [London] (February 1958): 99.

Felton, J.   "Philadelphia--Philharmonia Orch.: 'Abduction.'"   High Fidelity (April 1974): 32-33.

Fisher, M. M.   "San Francisco Opera Revives Rimsky-Korsakoff Work; Season Best in Many Years."   Musical America (November 15 1955): 9.

Gilbert, E. "Detroit." Musical Courier (December 1 1957): 27.

Goddard, S. "London Letter." Chesterian (April 1954): 122.

Haggin, B. H. "Music." Nation (February 25 1956): 165.

Hiemenz, J. "N.J. Schola Cantorum, Dobbs." High Fidelity (July 1972): MA26.

Kerman, J. "San Francisco: Glitter and Gold." Opera News (November 14 1955): 5.

Kolodin, Irving. "Bellini and Berlioz, also Mattiwilda Dobbs." Saturday Review (March 27 1954): 26.

_____. "Callas in "Lucia", Gobbi in "Rigoletto." Saturday Review (December 22 1956): 36.

_____. "Mattiwilda Dobbs, "Figaro", Chavez." Saturday Review (February 11 1956): 31.

_____. "Music to My Ears." Saturday Review (February 5 1955): 27.

_____. "Music to My Ears." Saturday Review (March 14 1959): 69.

_____. "Vienna Philharmonic; Byron Janis; M. Dobbs, et. al." Saturday Review (November 24 1956): 71.

"Little Orchestra Society." Musical Courier (April 1 1954): 15-16.

"London Recital." Music and Musicians (June 1961): 20, 26.

"Lucia di Lammermoor." Musical America (January 15 1958): 22-23.

"Lucia di Lammermoor." Musical Times (May 1959): 273.

Matalon, S. "Sinai Campaign Fails to Halt Musical Life in Israel." Musical America (June 1957): 6.

"Mattiwilda Dobbs." Gramophone (May 1954): 472.

"Mattiwilda Dobbs." London Musical Events (November 1953): 35.

"Mattiwilda Dobbs." London Musical Events (December 1954): 52.

"Mattiwilda Dobbs." London Musical Events (April 1959): 15+.

"Mattiwilda Dobbs." Musical America (February 1 1956): 26-27.

"Mattiwilda Dobbs." Musical America (January 15 1960): 17.

"Mattiwilda Dobbs." Musical Courier (February 15 1955): 20-21.

"Mattiwilda Dobbs." Musical Courier (March 1 1956): 19-20.

"Mattiwilda Dobbs." Musical Courier (April 1959): 39.

"Mattiwilda Dobbs." Musical Opinion (November 1954): 71-72.

"Mattiwilda Dobbs." Variety (November 14 1956): 76.

"Mattiwilda Dobbs, Coloratura Soprano, is Praised by Critics for Her Role of Zerlina in "Don Giovanni" at Metropolitan Company, New York City." Jet (February 18 1960): 59.

"Mattiwilda Dobbs Heard in Bach, Handel Program." Musical America (March 1959): 26.

"Mattiwilda Dobbs in Recital." Musical Courier (February 15 1953): 10.

"Melbourne." The Canon (September 1955): 64.

"Negro Coloratura Soprano Acclaimed in Donnizetti's Opera "L'Elisir d'Amore" at England Opera Festival." Jet (June 22 1961): 58.

"New Honorary Members." Pan Pipes, Vol. 67, No. 1 (1974): 29.

Parker, R. "Moscow." Opera (March 1960): 217-218.

Porter, A. "Covent Garden Cockerel." Opera News (March 29 1954): 28+.

"Recitals." London Musical Events (March 1953): 44-45.

Redewill, H. M. "Berkeley-Oakland Music Events." Music of the West (April 1955): 16.

"Rigoletto." Musical Courier (December 1 1956): 11.

Sandberg, I. "Dobbs, Bjoerling, Nilsson in Stockholm Opera Casts." Musical America (April 1957): 5.

Sargeant, Winthrop. "Musical Events." New Yorker (November 17 1956): 210.

Taylor, P. W. "The 25th Edinburgh International Festival." Musical Opinion (October 1971): 17.

"Town Hall Recital." Musical America (February 1 1955): 28.

"Very Busy Met." Newsweek (November 19 1956): 112.

Wagner, W. "Goosens, Barbirolli, Krips Conduct in Australia." Musical America (December 1 1955): 34.

_____. "Sydney." The Canon (August 1955): 29; (September 1955): 65.

R. TODD DUNCAN (1903-   )

De Lerma, Dominique-Rene. "Duncan, (Robert) Todd." In The
New Grove Dictionary of American Music, Vol. 1, pp. 660-661.

Hare, Maud Cuney. Negro Musicians and Their Music.
Washington, D.C.: Associated Publishers, 1936, p. 380.

Robinson, Wilhelmena S. Historical Afro-American Biographies
(International Library of Afro-American Life and History).
Washington, D.C.: Associated Publishers, 1976, pp. 187-188.

Southern, Eileen. Biographical Dictionary of Afro-American
and African Musicians. Westport, CT: Greenwood Press, 1982,
p. 118.

Toppin, Edgar A. A Biographical History of Blacks in America
since 1528. New York: David McKay, 1971, pp. 287-288.

Who is Who in Music 1941.

Articles

"Baritone Made His Name in Gershwin Opera." The Australian
Musical News and Musical Digest (August 1949): 16-17.

Black, Doris. "Yesterday's Hit Makers: Todd Duncan." Sepia
(January 1976): 80.

"Change of Diet." Time (August 15 1949): 39.

"Chicago Concerts." Music News (January 1952): 14-15+.

Craig, Mary. "New Doctor of Letters, Todd Duncan,
Versatile." Musical Courier (July 1950): 16.

_____. "Todd Duncan Speaks for the Recitalist." Musical
Courier (July 1949): 14.

"Duncan, Todd." Current Biography 1942, pp. 223-224.

Duncan, Todd. "South African Songs and Negro Spirituals."
Music Journal (May-June 1950): 19.

_____. "To Sing...But Where?" Opera and Concert (August
10 1950): 8-10.

Flatow, S. "Premiere Porgy." Opera News (March 16 1985):
34-35+.

Greene, M. "It is That Perfection Which I Seek."
Opportunity: Journal of Negro Life (Winter 1947): 24-25.

Lyons, J. "Baritone Saga." Musical America (February 1
1955): 10+.

"Mr. Duncan Returns to B'way." Our World (March 1950): 32-34.

New York Times (April 26 1942): Sec. VIII, p. 1+.

New York Times (February 9 1978): Sec. III, p. 18. Profile and interview with singer Todd Duncan on the occasion of his 75th birthday. Discusses problems faced by black opera singers in the 1930s and 1940s.

"Porgy to Pagliacci." Newsweek (October 8 1945): 92-93.

"Todd Duncan." Chicago Symphony Orchestra Program Notes (December 6 1951): 45.

"Todd Duncan." Musical America (December 15 1951): 12.

"Todd Duncan of 'Lost in the Stars'." Music News (June 1950): 8+.

"Todd Duncan Plans European Tour." Musical America (April 25 1947): 17.

Washington Post Potomac (August 24 1969): 36-40.

"Whatever Happened to Todd Duncan?" Ebony (December 1975): 182.

RUBY ELZY (ca.1910-1943)

Elzy, Ruby. "Spirit of the Spirituals." Etude (August 1943): 495-496.

N. S. "Other Music: Recital by Ruby Elzy." New York Times (October 11 1937).

"Ruby Elzy, Soprano, Gives Her First Recital Here: Sings Operatic Airs, Brahms Lieder at Town Hall." New York Herald Tribune (October 10 1937).

Obituaries

Musical America (July 1943): 31.

Musical Courier (July 1943): 24.

New York Times (June 28 1943): 21.

SIMON ESTES (1938-   )

Abdul, Raoul. Blacks in Classical Music. New York: Dodd, Mead & Co., 1977, pp 118-119.

Bernheimer, Martin. "Estes, Simon." In The New Grove Dictionary of Music and Musicians, Vol. 6, p. 261.

_____. "Estes, Simon." In The New Grove Dictionary of American Music, Vol. 1, pp. 57-58.

Matheopoulos, Helena. Divo: Great Tenors, Baritones and Basses Discuss Their Roles. New York: Harper & Row, 1986, pp. 235-243.

Southern, Eileen. Biographical Dictionary of Afro-American and African Musicians. Westport, CT: Greenwood Press, 1982, p. 127.

Articles

Bims, H. "Here Comes Simon." Ebony, Vol. 27 (February 1972): 84-89.

Blyth, A. "The Creation." The Musical Times (June 1970): 618-619.

Buchau, Stephanie von. "Keeping the Faith." Opera News, Vol. 47 (March 26 1983): 17-19.

"Estes, Simon." Current Biography 1986, pp. 122-125.

Heymont, G. "Musician of the Month: Simon Estes." High Fidelity (January 1982): 4-5.

Lingg, A. M. "After the Price." Opera News (March 30 1968): 14.

"March's Guest Artists." San Francisco Symphony Program Notes (March 1967): 11.

Mills, B. K. "Simon Estes: A Shoeshine Boy Who Left Centerville, Iowa 26 Years Ago Returns as One of Opera's Great Stars." People, Vol. 18 (November 1 1982): 39-40.

"Names." Music Journal, Vol. 36 (September 1978): 19.

"Names, Dates and Places." Opera News (September 20 1969): 5.

"Names, Dates and Places." Opera News, Vol. 43 (August 1978): 8.

"Opera Review." Variety (November 2 1977): 84.

"Profiles." San Francisco Opera Magazine, No. 9 (Fall 1980): 67.

Satz, A. "Simon Estes-On the Threshold of a Big Career." High Fidelity, Vol. 22 (October 1972): 12-13.

Smith, P. J. "Simon Estes, Bass-Baritone." High Fidelity (March 1981): 24-25.

Steinbrink, M. "Simon Estes Come Home." Saturday Review (January 1982): 22-23+.

Stevenson, F. "A Promising Bass-Baritone: Simon Estes." Stereo Review (August 1973): 70-71.

Toms, John. "Wagner Opera Sung by Blacks." Sepia (June 1980): 64-71. Profile/interview with Estes and vocalist Barbara Conrad.

Newspaper Articles

Chicago Defender (September 23 1976).

Libbey, T. W., Jr. "I've Been Ready Since 1974." New York Times (January 3 1982): Sec. 2, p. 15+.

New York Amsterdam News (September 9 1978).

New York Times (February 24 1984): Sec. III, p. 1. Singers Simon Estes, Kathleen Battle, Sherill Milnes, Leonie Rysanek and Hakan Hagegard discuss their voices and musical approaches.

Vecsey, G. "The Athlete at Carnegie Hall." New York Times Biography Service (May 1985): 633.

Concert Reviews

Boaz, R. "Obert." Music and Musicians (March 1977): 50.

Frankenstein, A. "San Francisco Report." High Fidelity (January 1968): 18-19.

Gualerzi, G. "Turin." Opera (UK) (July 1976): 663-664.

Jacobs, A. "San Francisco." Opera (January 1968): 33-35.

Jahant, C. "Vienna, Virginia." Opera (UK) (September 1976): 850.

New York Times (August 13 1978): D-17+.

Videos

Simon Estes. 15 min. Profile and interview with Simon Estes on the occasion of a visit to his alma mater, the University of Iowa. Estes explains some of his struggles as a black singer and his love of the art form. (For more information contact: BRAVO, P.O. Box 999, Woodbury, NY 11797.)

LILLIAN EVANTI (1890-1967)

Hare, Maud Cuney. Negro Musicians and Their Music. Washington, D.C.: Associated Publishers, 1936, pp. 357-358.

Lemieux, Raymond. "Evanti, Lillian." In Dictionary of American Negro Biography, eds. Rayford W. Logan and Michael R. Winston. New York: W.W. Norton, 1982, pp. 215-217.

Southern, Eileen. Biographical Dictionary of Afro-American and African Musicians. Westport, CT: Greenwood Press, 1982, pp. 129-130.

Who's Who in Colored America, 1950.

[See also Lillian Evanti clippings file in the Music Division of the Performing Arts Research Center at Lincoln Center.]

Articles

Jet (December 21 1967): 55.

Jet (August 15 1968): 11.

Kyle, M. K. "AmerAllegro." Pan Pipes (January 1958): 52.

_____. "AmerAllegro." Pan Pipes, Vol. 55, No. 2 (1963):
48.

"Lillian Evanti." Pan Pipes (January 1953): 50.

"Lillian Evanti Heard." Musical Courier (November 1944).

"Lillian Evanti Heard in Opera on Several Continents."
Musical Courier (April 5 1944).

Newspaper Articles

Chicago Defender (November 27 1915).

Chicago Defender (September 11 1943).

"Negro Coloratura to Sing at White House Friday." New York
Herald Tribune (February 6 1934).

New York Age (May 3 1917).

New York Age (March 5 1927).

Thomson, Virgil. "Crooning, Alas." New York Herald Tribune
(October 13 1944). Review of Town Hall recital.

Washington Tribune (March 29 1934).

Obituaries

Music Educators Journal (February 1968): 14.

New York Times (December 9 1967).

Variety (December 13 1967): 63.

Washington Post (December 8 1967): 14.

Washington Post (December 10 1967).

WILHELMINA WIGGENS FERNANDEZ (1949-   )

Black Stars (October 1977): 52-57.

Finn, Terri Lowen. "Diva's Diva in State Debut." New York
Times (November 20 1983): Sec. 11, pp. 28-29. Profile and
interview with soprano Wilhelmina Wiggens Fernandez.

Heaton, M. "On the Move." People (May 9 1983): 105+.

"Keep Your Eye On: Sixteen Young American Artists on the Rise." Opera News (July 1982): 26.

WILLIAM FRANKLIN (1906-   )

Southern, Eileen. Biographical Dictionary of Afro-American and African Musicians. Westport, CT: Greenwood Press, 1982, pp. 137-138.

Articles

Chicago Defender (October 30 1937).

Chicago Defender (February 25 1939).

Chicago Defender (October 25 1941).

New York Amsterdam News (July 3 1948).

ANDREW FRIERSON (1927-   )

Southern, Eileen. Biographical Dictionary of Afro-American and African Musicians. Westport, CT: Greenwood Press, 1982, p. 139.

Articles

Alice Tully Hall Program Notes (March 30 1975).

C. H. "Frierson Offers Recital." New York Times (April 3 1950).

Davis, Peter G. "Frierson, Miss Daniel Sing a Duo Recital." New York Times (March 31 1975).

Horowitz, Joseph. "Recital: Frierson Sings." New York Times (March 15 1980).

"Town Hall Recital." Musical America (March 1955): 29.

ZOILA GALVEZ (1902-   ) - Cuba

Feijoo, Samuel. "Entrevista a la Famosa Cantante Zoila Galvez." Signos (Santa Clara, Cuba), Vol. 26 (September-December 1980): 203-204. Interview with Afro-Cuban singer Zoila Galvez. [For English-language summary see Handbook of Latin American Studies, No. 46, p. 587].

GEORGE ROBERT GARNER (1890-1971)

Hare, Maud Cuney. Negro Musicians and Their Music. Washington, D.C.: Associated Publishers, 1936, p. 379.

Southern, Eileen. Biographical Dictionary of Afro-American
and African Musicians. Westport, CT: Greenwood Press, 1982,
pp. 143-144.

Articles

Chicago Defender (February 16 1924).

Chicago Defender (November 13 1926).

Chicago Defender (May 19 1928).

Chicago Defender (July 4 1936).

Chicago Defender (November 20 1943).

ZELMA WATSON GEORGE (1903-   )

Abdul, Raoul. "Zelma George Integrates Broadway." In Blacks
in Classical Music. New York: Dodd, Mead & Co., 1977, pp.
103-105.

Southern, Eileen. Biographical Dictionary of Afro-American
and African Musicians. Westport, CT: Greenwood Press, 1982,
p. 145.

Who's Who of American Women 1958-59.

Articles

Atkinson, Brooks. "'Medium' Revisited." New York Times
(September 3 1950): Sec. 2, p. 1.

"George, Zelma Watson." Current Biography 1961, pp. 171-173.

"Medium in the Round." Newsweek (July 31 1950): 76-77.

Roy, J. H. "Pin Point Portrait of Zelma Watson George."
Negro History Bulletin (May 1962): 190.

Smith, Cecil. "Menotti Double Bill Returns in Arena-Style
Production." Musical America, Vol. LXX, No. 9 (August 1950):
17. Review of Zelma George's role in Menotti's "The Medium."

"Woman of Courage." Ebony (April 1961): 70-72+.

KATHERINE GRAVES

"Diva in the Making: Marian Anderson Award Winner Katherine
Graves is an Up and Coming Concert Singer." Our World, Vol.
3, No. 12 (December 1948): 48-49.

JOHN GREENE (1901-1960s)

Chicago Defender (March 14 1931).

Chicago Defender (August 22 1931).

Southern, Eileen. Biographical Dictionary of Afro-American and African Musicians. Westport, CT: Greenwood Press, 1982.

ELIZABETH T. GREENFIELD [the 'Black Swan'] (1824-1876)

Austin, William W. "Greenfield, Elizabeth Taylor." In The New Grove Dictionary of American Music, Vol. 2, p. 285.

A Brief Memoir of the 'Black Swan', Miss E.T. Greenfield, the American Vocalist. London, 1853. 16pp.

The Black Swan at Home and Abroad; or, A Biographical Sketch of Miss Elizabeth Taylor Greenfield, the American Vocalist. Philadelphia: W.S. Young, Printer, 1855. 64pp. [Held by the Library of Congress and Boston Public Library, Music Collection]

Dannett, Sylvia G. L. Profiles of Negro Womanhood. Yonkers, NY: Educational Heritage, Inc., 1964. Brief biography.

Hare, Maud Cuney. Negro Musicians and Their Music. Washington, D.C.: Associated Publishers, 1936, pp. 202-204.

LaBrew, Arthur. The Black Swan: Elizabeth T. Greenfield, Songstress: Biographical Study. Detroit, MI: The Author, 1969.

_____. "Elizabeth Taylor Greenfield." In Studies in 19th Century Afro-American Music. Detroit, MI: the Author, 1973, pp. 262+.

Lemieux, Raymond. "Greenfield, Elizabeth Taylor." In Dictionary of American Negro Biography, eds. Rayford W. Logan and Michael R. Winston. New York: Norton, 1982, pp. 268-270.

Pennsylvania Historical Society, Leon Gardiner Collection. Boxes IG, 13G.

Robinson, Wilhelmena S. Historical Afro-American Biographies (International Library of Afro-American Life and History). Washington, D.C.: Associated Publishers, 1976, pp. 84-85.

Scruggs, Lawson A. "Elizabeth Taylor Greenfield." In Women of Distinction. Raleigh, NC: the Author, 1893, pp. 78-82.

Southern, Eileen. Biographical Dictionary of Afro-American and African Musicians. Westport, CT: Greenwood Press, 1982, pp. 153-154.

Spencer, Samuel R., Jr. "Greenfield, Elizabeth Taylor." In Notable American Women, 1607-1950: A Biographical Dictionary, eds. Edward T. James, et al. Vol. II. Cambridge, MA: The Belknap Press, 1971, pp. 87-89.

Stowe, Harriet Beecher. Sunny Memories of Foreign Lands. Boston: Phillips, Sampson, 1854.

Trotter, James M. Music and Some Highly Musical People.
Chicago: Afro-Am Press, 1969, pp. 66-87. (Orig. 1878)

Articles

A. C. "Elizabeth Taylor Greenfield, a Sketch." The Negro
Music Journal, Vol. 1, No. 2 (October 1902): 18-19.

"Black Swan." Record Research (August 1955): 3-4; (October
1955): 5.

Illustrated London News (July 30 1853).

LaBrew, Arthur. "Elizabeth Taylor Greenfield." Afro-American
Music Review, Vol. 1, No. 2 (1984): 1+.

Provincial Freeman [Chatham, Ontario] (April 21 1855).

Richards, Agnes. "The Black Swan." Negro Digest (November
1950): 73-75.

Obituaries

New York Times (April 2 1876): 2.

Philadelphia Public Ledger (April 3 1876).

RERI GRIST (1932-   )

Blyth, Alan. "Grist, Reri." In The New Grove Dictionary of
Music and Musicians, Vol. 7, p. 738.

_____. "Grist, Reri." In The New Grove Dictionary of
American Music, Vol. 2, p. 250.

Dunbar, Ernest. "Reri Grist: Zurich." In The Black
Expatriates: A Study of American Negroes In Exile. New
York: Dutton, 1968, pp. 113-126.

Ewen, David, ed. Musicians Since 1900: Performers in Concert
and Opera. New York: H.W. Wilson, 1978, pp. 320-322.

Southern, Eileen. Biographical Dictionary of Afro-American
and African Musicians. Westport, CT: Greenwood Press, 1982,
p. 155.

Articles

"Absolutely Priceless." Time (November 15 1963): 64.

Brozen, M. "Quote...unquote." Musical America (October
1963): 24.

"Coloratura Soprano, Signs Contract as Permanent Member of
Zurich (Switzerland) Opera. First American Coloratura to
Gain a Yearly Contract with a European House, Also Has Brief
Career in United States." Jet (August 4 1960): 60.

"First American Negro on Yearly Contract in O'seas Opera: Reri Grist." Variety (May 25 1960): 1.

Jacobson, B. "Lyric Opera in the Home Stretch." High Fidelity (February 1969): MA30.

Lingg, A. M. "Close Encounters." Opera News, Vol. 42 (January 7 1978): 27.

Movshon, G. "Musician of the Month: Reri Grist." High Fidelity (January 1970): Sec. II, p. 5.

"The Musical Whirl." High Fidelity (June 1970): 22-23.

"Names, Dates, and Places." Opera News (February 10 1973): 8-9.

New York Age (January 24 1959).

Phillips, H. E. "Reri." Opera News (March 19 1966): 16.

"Reri Grist, Coloratura Soprano, Signs Contracts as Permanent Member of Zurich (Switzerland) Opera." Jet (June 16 1960): 60.

"Reri Grist: Nightingale from Harlem." Look (March 9 1971): M+.

"Reri Grist, 10th Negro to Join Met Opera, Opens in Ritchard's 'Barber'." Variety (March 2 1966): 1+.

"Reri Grist, Toast of Two Continents." Ebony (March 1965): 85-86.

Stockholm, G. "Reri Grist Captures Essence of Pure Song." Music and Artists, Vol. 3, No. 5 (1971): 14-15+.

Concert Reviews

"American Song Program." Musical America (March 1960): 35.

Ardoin, J. "New York." Opera (May 1966): 361-362.

Barnes, C. "Stage Fireworks." Music and Musicians (September 1962): 35.

Bernheimer, M. "Los Angeles." Opera (March 1966): 224.

_____. "Montreal." Opera (November 1967): 910+.

Bloomfield, A. "California." Musical America (January 1964):22.

Blyth, A. "'Ariadne auf Naxos'; Bavarian State Opera at Covent Opera." Opera (UK) (April 1972): 373.

Campbell, F. "Vancouver: Reri Grist's Happy Return." Opera (June 1964): 391.

Crowder, C. "Opera Finale." Musical America (May 1962): 10.

_____. "Stravinsky, Schoenberg." Musical America
(February 1961): 17.

Galatoupoulos, S. "East Coast/West Coast." Music and
Musicians, Vol. 20 (February 1972): 24.

Hutchison, P. "Vienna." Opera (UK) (August 1972): 716-717.

Jacobson, R. "Music to my Ears." Saturday Review (March 28
1970): 54.

Kolodin, Irving. "Music to my Ears." Saturday Review
(February 8 1969): 44.

Legge, W. "Salzburg Report: Festival 1965." High Fidelity
(November 1965): 206-207.

Marcus, M. "Sensual Mozart." Music and Musicians (August
1962): 36.

Mayer, M. "Price's Ballo; Grist and Lorengar Debuts." High
Fidelity (May 1966): 134+.

"Mephisto's Musings." High Fidelity (February 1966): 120-121.

Moor, P. "Alessandro Scarlatti's Pretty Pastoral." High
Fidelity (June 1970): 25.

Movshon, G. "Montreal Report: The Vienna Opera at Expo."
High Fidelity (November 1967): MA20+.

_____. "New "Rosenkavalier" at the Met." High Fidelity
(April 1969): MA32.

_____. "Vienna: "Rosenkavalier": Four Stars for
Bernstein." High Fidelity (July 1968): 26+.

"New York, N.Y." Music and Artists, Vol. 2, No. 2 (1969): 28.

"New York, N.Y." Opera (April 1969): 309.

New York Times (August 8 1971): D-13.

Noble, J. "Vienna." Musical Times (August 1973): 823-825.

Osborne, C. "Vienna: Triumphant Donizetti and Schoenberg."
Opera (UK) (Autumn 1973): 44-49.

"Promenade Concerts." Musical Opinion (September 1962): 712.

"Reri Grist." Musical America (January 1 1959): 44.

"Reri Grist." Musical America (October 1963): 24.

"Reri Grist, Soprano at Town Hall, N.Y.C. in Rossini's "La
Cambiale di Matrimonio"; Critics Praise Her." Jet (March 16
1961): 60.

Rothon, G.   "Munich."   Opera (UK) (July 1970): 660.

Sadie, S.   "Music in London."   Musical Times (January 1972):
22-23.

Smith, P. J.   "NY Philharmonic, Grist (Gielen)."   High
Fidelity (January 1972): 22-23.

Stedman, J.   "Chicago."   Opera News (January 25 1969): 33.

Sutcliffe, J. H.   "Munich's Rare Strauss and Mozart."   Opera
(UK), Vol. 22 (Autumn 1971): 54.

Welsh, C. N.   "Vienna."   Opera (July 1969): 621-622.

E. AZALIA HACKLEY (1867-1922)

Brown, Hallie Q.   "Madam Emma Azalia Hackley."   In Homespun
Heroines. Xenia, OH: Aldine Publishing Company, 1926, pp.
231-236.

Dannett, Sylvia G. L.   Profiles of Negro Womanhood. Yonkers,
NY: Educational Heritage, Inc., 1964. Biographical sketch.

Davenport, M. Marguerite.   Azalia, The Life of Madame E.
Azalia Hackley. Boston: Chapman & Grimes, 1947.

De Lerma, Dominique-Rene.   "Hackley [nee Smith], E(mma)
Azalia."   In The New Grove Dictionary of American Music, Vol.
2, pp. 302-303.

Hackley, E. Azalia.   A Guide in Voice Culture. Philadelphia:
n.p., c.1909. 15pp. [Held by the Detroit Public Library, E.
Azalia Hackley Collection.]

Hare, Maud Cuney.   Negro Musicians and Their Music.
Washington, D.C.: Associated Publishers, 1936, pp. 241-242.

LaBrew, Arthur.   Documentary: Negro Music and Musicians.
Detroit, MI: the Author, 1969. 28pp. Contains excerpts from
"Report on Scholarsip for 1908, by E. Azalia Hackley" and
Annual Azalia Hackley Concerts programs, 1943-1969. [Held by
the Detroit Public Library, E. Azalia Hackley Collection.]

Logan, Rayford W.   "Hackley, [Emma] Azalia [Smith]."   In
Dictionary of American Negro Biography, eds. Rayford W. Logan
and Michael R. Winston. New York: W.W. Norton, 1982, pp.
275-276.

Love, Josephine Harreld.   "Hackley, Emma Azalia Smith."   In
Notable American Women, 1607-1950: A Biographical Dictionary,
eds. Edward T. James, et al. Vol. II. Cambridge, MA: The
Belknap Press, 1971, pp. 106-108.

Lovingood, Penman.   Famous Modern Negro Musicians. New York:
Da Capo Press, 1978. (Reprint of 1921 ed.)

Southern, Eileen. Biographical Dictionary of Afro-American
and African Musicians. Westport, CT: Greenwood Press, 1982,
p. 157.

Articles

Chicago Defender (October 21 1911).

Chicago Defender (October 7 1916).

Indianapolis Freeman (March 23 1901).

Indianapolis Freeman (June 4 1914).

Indianapolis Freeman (January 8 1916).

New York Age (December 31 1914).

New York Age (December 23 1922).

HILDA HARRIS (c.1930-   )

Southern, Eileen. Biographical Dictionary of Africo-American
and American Musicians. Westport, CT: Greenwood Press, 1982,
p. 168.

Articles

Hughes, Allen. "Music: Hilda Harris in Recital." New York
Times (March 13 1983).

Osment, Noel. "Diva is Musical Comedy Graduate. Rejection
for Role Pointed Way." San Diego Union (February 6 1978).

Pittsburgh Symphony Orchestra Program Notes (December 12-13,
1972): 9.

Sherman, Robert. "Miss Harris, Mezzo, Triumphs in Debut."
New York Times (January 23 1967).

ROLAND HAYES (1887-1976)

Abdul, Raoul. "The Art of Roland Hayes." In Blacks in
Classical Music. New York: Dodd, Mead & Co., 1977, pp. 73-82.

Adams, Russell L. Great Negroes, Past and Present. Chicago:
Afro-Am Publishing Co., 1969, p. 184.

Bartlett, R. M. They Dared To Live. New York: Association
Press, 1937, pp. 80-84.

Bullock, Ralph W. In Spite of Handicaps. New York:
Association Press, 1927, pp. 1-4.

Ewen, David, ed. Musicians Since 1900: Performers in Concert
and Opera. New York: H.W. Wilson, 1978, pp. 331-333.

Hare, Maud Cuney. _Negro Musicians and Their Music_.
Washington, D.C.: Associated Publishers, 1936, pp. 262,
352-356.

Harris, Charles Jacob. _Reminiscences of My Days with Roland
Hayes_. Orangeburg, SC: American Negro Authors, 1944. 27pp.

Hayes, Roland. _My Songs: Afro American Religious Folk Songs
Arranged and Interpreted by Roland Hayes_. Boston: Little,
Brown, 1948.

Helm, MacKinley. _Angel Mo' and Her Son, Roland Hayes_.
Boston: Little, Brown and Co., 1942. 289pp.

Henderson, Dorothy. "Roland Hayes." In _Biographical
Sketches of Six Humanitarians Whose Lives Have Been for the
Greater Glory_. New York: Exposition, 1958, pp. 48-82.

Hughes, Langston. "Roland Hayes." In _Famous Negro Music
Makers_. New York: Mead & Co., 1955.

Lahee, Henry Charles. _Famous Singers of Today and
Yesterday_. Rev. ed. Boston: L.C. Page & Co., 1936, pp.
327-343.

Lankard, Frank Glenn. "Roland Hayes." In _Rising Above
Color_, ed. by Philip H. Lotz. Freeport, NY: Books for
Libraries, 1972, pp. 82-89. (Reprint of 1943 ed.)

Lovingood, Penman. _Famous Modern Negro Musicians_. New York:
Da Capo Press, 1978. (Reprint of 1921 ed.)

Martin, Fletcher, ed. _Our Great Americans: The Negro
Contribution to American Progress_. Chicago: Gamma
Corporation, 1954, pp. 27-28.

Ovington, Mary White. "Roland Hayes." In _Portraits in
Color_. New York: Viking Press, 1923, pp. 227-241.

Robinson, Wilhelmena S. _Historical Afro-American Biographies_
(International Library of Afro-American Life and History).
Washington, D.C.: Associated Publishers, 1976, pp. 201-202.

Rogers, J. A. "Roland Hayes." In _World's Great Men of
Color_. New York: Macmillan, 1972, pp. 499-507. (Orig. 1947)

Schauensee, Max de. "Hayes, Roland." In _The New Grove
Dictionary of Music and Musicians_, Vol. 8, p. 414.

_____, and Dennis S. McIntire. "Hayes, Roland." In _The
New Grove Dictionary of American Music_, Vol. 2, pp. 355-356.

Southern, Eileen. _Biographical Dictionary of Afro-American
and African Musicians_. Westport, CT: Greenwood Press, 1982,
p. 173.

Stidger, William LeRoy. _The Human Side of Greatness_. New
York: Harper & Bros., 1940, pp. 28-42.

Toppin, Edgar A. A Biographical History of Blacks in America since 1528. New York: David McKay, 1971, pp. 315-317.

Troup, Cornelius V. Distinguished Negro Georgians. Dallas, Texas: Royal Publishing Co., 1962, pp. 76-78.

Articles

Afro-American Magazine (June 7 1975): 1.

Brown, Sterling. "Roland Hayes--An Essay." Opportunity: Journal of Negro Life, Vol. 3 (June 1925): 173-174.

Carter, Marva Griffin. "In Retrospect: Roland Hayes - Expression of the Soul in Song (1887-1977)." The Black Perspective in Music (Fall 1977): 188-220.

Dunkin, L. E, ed. "What Do They Hear in My Singing?" Etude (February 1939): 125.

Green, Jeffrey P. "Roland Hayes in London, 1921." The Black Perspective in Music (Spring 1982): 29-42.

"Hayes, Roland." Current Biography 1942.

Hayes, Roland. "Lieder is of the People." Musical Courier (December 15 1954): 11.

_____. "Music of Aframerica; My Songs." Music Journal (February 1963): 20-21+.

_____. "My Song is Nothing." Christian Science Monitor (November 22 1947): 6.

Helm, MacKinley. "Angel Mo' and Her Son: Roland Hayes." The Atlantic (August 1942): 1-10; (September 1942): 56-62; (October 1942): 79-85; (November 1942): 102-108.

Henderson, W. "Rise of Roland Hayes." Mentor (May 1926): 46-47.

Knight, A. E. "Roland Hayes." (w/discography) The Record Collector [U.K.] (July 1955): 29-45.

Locke, Alain Leroy. "Roland Hayes: An Appreciation." Opportunity: Journal of Negro Life, Vol. 1 (December 1923): 356-358.

Marr, W., II. "Roland Hayes." The Crisis (June-July 1974): 205-206+.

Mullet, Mary B. "A World-Famous Singer Whose Parents Were Slaves." The American Magazine (June 25 1942): 26-27.

"Negro Artist in Song." Literary Digest (January 5 1924): 30.

Negro History Bulletin (February 1939): 37. Biographical sketch.

"Nobody Was Killed; Hayes Incident." Commonweal, Vol. 36 (July 31 1942): 339-342.

"Performer of Vocal Miracles." Current Opinion (April 1924): 458-459.

Rich, Alan. "A Bouncy Seventy-Five." New York Times (June 3 1962): Sec. 2, p. 7.

"Roland Hayes: A Lifetime on the Concert Stage." Ebony (September 1946): 42-46.

"Roland Hayes at 75." Music Magazine (August 1962): 49.

"Roland Hayes Speaks." National Association of Teachers of Singing Bulletin, Vol. 18, No. 3 (1962): 6.

"Rome Incident." Time, Vol. 40 (July 27 1942): 17.

"Singin' high, Singin' low, Strugglin' for Success." Newsweek (May 4 1935): 34-35.

Stidger, W. L. "Magic of Music." Coronet (December 1950): 150-151. (Reprinted in Negro Digest (August 1951): 32-33.)

Villard, O. G. "Story of Roland Hayes." Saturday Review of Literature, Vol. 25 (November 28 1942): 5-6.

Woolsey, F. W. "Conversation with...Roland Hayes." The Black Perspective in Music, Vol. 2, No. 2 (Fall 1974): 179-185. [Reprinted from the Courier Journal-Louisville Times (May 21 1967)].

Concert Reviews

Atlanta Constitution (August 26 1939): 6.

Chattanooga Free Press (August 27 1939).

Durgin, C. "Boston Symphony Observes Vaughan Williams Birthday." Musical America (December 1 1957): 20.

Jackson News (October 10 1938).

"New York." Music Magazine (July 1962): 52-53.

[New York Recital]. Musical America (July 1962): 29-30.

"Roland Hayes." Musical America (December 15 1950): 32.

"Roland Hayes." Musical America (December 15 1957): 25.

"Roland Hayes." Musical Courier (April 1 1950): 18.

"Roland Hayes." Musical Courier (December 15 1953): 8-9.

"Roland Hayes." Musical Courier (December 1 1954): 21.

"Roland Hayes." Musical Courier (May 1956): 17.

"Roland Hayes." Musical Courier (April 1957): 31.

Straus, H. "Roland Hayes." Nation (December 19 1923): 718.

Wolffers, J. "Boston." Musical Courier (November 15 1955):
23.

Obituaries

Black Perspective in Music, Vol. 5, No. 2 (Fall 1977): 234.

Central Opera Service Bulletin, Vol. 20, No. 1 (1977-78): 19.

"Hayes, Roland." Current Biography 1977, p. 465.

New York Times (January 2 1977): 47.

Saturday Review (March 5 1977): 48.

Time (January 17 1977): 68.

Variety (January 19 1977): 94.

BARBARA HENDRICKS (1948-   )

Forbes, Elizabeth. "Hendricks, Barbara." In The New Grove
Dictionary of American Music, Vol. 2, p. 370.

Articles

Karp, J. "Barbara Hendricks." Fugue, Vol. 3 (January 1979):
37-38.

"Lookout: A Guide to the Up and Coming." People (September
16 1974): 43.

"Names, Dates and Places." Opera News, Vol. 41 (May 1977):
8-9.

People (December 26 1977): 147. Brief biographical portrait.

Waleson, Heidi. "A Singer Whose Personal Life Comes First."
New York Times (October 26 1986): Sec. II, p. 21, 24.
Profile and interview with expatriate singer Barbara
Hendricks on the occasion of her Metropolitan Opera debut.

ESTHER HINDS (1943-   ) - Barbados

Abdul, Raoul. Blacks in Classical Music. New York: Dodd,
Mead & Co., 1977, pp. 118-119.

Articles

"Awards." Opera (UK), Vol. 28 (September 1977): 826.

"Concerted Family Effort." New York Times (November 26 1982).

Strongin, Theodore.   "Esther Hinds Sings in Solo Debut Here." New York Times (January 16 1968).

"Vignettes." Music Clubs Magazine, Vol. 57, No. 1 (1977): 31+.

ALTONELL HINES (Mathews) (1905-1977)

Southern, Eileen. Biographical Dictionary of Afro-American and African Musicians. Westport, CT: Greenwood Press, 1982, p. 183.

Obituaries

Black Perspective in Music, Vol. 5, No. 2 (Fall 1977): 234.

Central Opera Service Bulletin, Vol. 20, No. 1 (1977-78): 21.

New York Times (August 9 1977): 36.

Variety (August 24 1977): 71.

CHARLES HOLLAND (c.1910-   )

Jahant, Charles. "Holland, Charles." In The New Grove Dictionary of American Music, Vol. 2, p. 210.

Southern, Eileen. Biographical Dictionary of Afro-American and African Musicians. Westport, CT: Greenwood Press, 1982, p. 186.

Articles

"Charles Holland, Negro Tenor, Makes First Appearance." Musical America (November 10 1940).

Dunlop, L. "B.B.C. Television: Otello." Opera [London] (December 1959): 828.

Moskowitz, G. "American Negroes Impact on Parisian Show Biz." Variety (January 9 1957): 204.

Swan, A. "Struggle to Be Heard." Newsweek (December 27 1982): 64.

Newspaper Articles

Chicago Defender (February 19 1955).

Crutchfield, Will. "Music: 2 Tenors Perform at Tully Hall." New York Times (May 21 1984).

F. D. P. "Charles Holland Makes His Debut in Town Hall." New York Herald Tribune (October 29 1940).

Henahan, Donal. "Concert a Triumph for Charles Holland." New York Times (October 20 1969).

New York Amsterdam News (February 7 1948).

New York Amsterdam News (March 7 1981).

O. T.   "Charles Holland in Song Recital. Negro Tenor of
Radio and Pictures Heard." New York Sun (October 29 1940).

R. P.   "Charles Holland Heard." New York Times (October 29
1940).

Rothstein, Edward.   "Recital: Charles Holland, Tenor, at
Carnegie Hall." New York Times (December 11 1982).

"U.S. Tenor Bows in Paris." New York Times (January 30 1955).

Village Voice (October 18 1983).

CHARLOTTE HOLLOMAN

"Artists Contribute Services to Association." Negro History
Bulletin (January 1954): 84.

Cartwright, Marguerite.   "A New Star is Born: Charlotte
Wesley Holloman." Negro History Bulletin (April 1954):
153-154.

"Charlotte Holloman." Musical America (March 1954): 264.

"Charlotte Holloman." Musical America (March 1956): 21.

"Charlotte Holloman." Musical America (November 15 1957): 34.

"Charlotte Holloman." Musical Courier (March 15 1954): 15.

"Charlotte Holloman." Musical Courier (March 15 1956): 15-16.

"Charlotte Holloman." Musical Courier (November 15 1957): 19.

"Charlotte Holloman." New York Herald Tribune (February 26
1954). Review of debut.

"Charlotte Holloman, Coloratura Soprano, Gives Third Recital
in Bermuda in Seven Years." Negro History Bulletin (March
1962): 135.

Levinger, H. W.   "On The Threshold of a Great Career."
Musical Courier (March 15 1954): 9.

"Miss Holloman Heard in Recital." New York Herald Tribune
(February 20 1956).

"Miss Holloman Sings. Soprano Presents Her Third Town Hall
Recital." New York Times (November 4 1957).

"Singer of Promise." Music and Musicians [London] (March
1961): 21.

EUGENE HOLMES (1934-   )

Kastendieck, Miles. "Junior Met Wins Spurs." [New York]
World Journal Tribune (January 9 1967).

Kolodin, Irving. "Music to my Ears." Saturday Review (March
27 1971): 16+.

Loveland, K. "Welsh National." Opera (UK) (December 1974):
1119-1121.

Schauensee, Max de. "Philadelphia." Opera (UK) (August
1976): 724-725.

"What They've Been Doing." High Fidelity (July 1971): MA14.

"Young Artists of 1968." High Fidelity (July 1968): MA14.

HYERS SISTERS, THE (1850s- ?)

Beasley, Delilah L. The Negro Trailblazers of California.
Los Angeles: The Author, 1919. (See chapter 17)

Dannett, Sylvia G. L. Profiles of Negro Womanhood. Yonkers,
NY: Educational Heritage, Inc., 1964. Brief biography.

Hare, Maud Cuney. Negro Musicians and Their Music.
Washington, D.C.: Associated Publishers, 1936, pp. 215-218.

Sampson, Henry T. "Hyers Sisters, The." In The New Grove
Dictionary of American Music, Vol. 2, pp. 445-446.

Scruggs, Lawson A. "The Hyers Sisters." In Women of
Distinction. Raleigh, NC: the Author, 1893, pp. 105-108.

Southern, Eileen. Biographical Dictionary of Afro-American
and African Musicians. Westport, CT: Greenwood Press, 1982,
pp. 191-192.

Trotter, James M. Music and Some Highly Musical People.
Chicago: Afro-Am Press, 1969, pp. 160-179. (Orig. 1878)

Articles

Cleveland Gazette (September 15 1883).

Cleveland Gazette (August 25 1894).

Indianapolis Freeman (April 15 1893).

Indianapolis Freeman (December 27 1902).

New York Clipper (1860s-1880s)

New York Freeman (August 14 1886).

New York Globe (May 26 1883).

RHEA JACKSON (1926?-   )

"Rhea Jackson." Musical America (May 1951): 34.

"Rhea Jackson." Musical America (November 15 1958): 24.

"Rhea Jackson." Musical Courier (June 1951): 27.

"Rhea Jackson, Soprano, Gives Town Hall Recital." New York Herald Tribune (February 13 1947). Review of debut recital.

"Social Worker Makes Operatic Debut Monday." New York Herald Tribune (February 14 1953).

Thomson, Virgil. "The Pearl-Fishers." New York Herald Tribune (February 17 1953).

"Two Singers Signed by National Artists." Musical America (November 1 1958): 12.

CATERINA JARBORO (1903-1986)

Bishop, Cardell. Opera at the Hippodrome in New York City. Santa Monica, CA: The Author, 1979, pp. 8-9.

Hare, Maud Cuney. Negro Musicians and Their Music. Washington, D.C.: Associated Publishers, 1936, pp. 362-364.

Negro Year Book, 1941-1946.

Robinson, Wilhelmena S. Historical Afro-American Biographies (International Library of Afro-American Life and History). Washington, D.C.: Associated Publishers, 1976, pp. 210-211.

Southern, Eileen. Biographical Dictionary of Afro-American and African Musicians. Westport, CT: Greenwood Press, 1982, p. 201.

Articles

"Aida without Make-Up." Time (July 31 1933): 28.

"Caterina Jarboro Heard in 2nd Recital of Season." New York Herald Tribune (April 20 1942). Review of Town Hall recital.

"Caterina Jarboro, Soprano." Musical America (March 10 1944).

"Chicago Audience Applauds Debut of Caterina Jarboro." Musical Courier (June 2 1934).

Chicago Defender (March 12 1932).

Chicago Defender (July 18 1936).

Chicago Defender (February 17 1938).

"Miss Jarboro Gives Recital.   Soprano Returns to Carnegie Hall After Season's Absence."   New York Times (February 7 1944).

New York Age (July 22 1933).

New York Times (July 23 1933).   Brief notice of an upcoming concert.

Obituary.   The Black Perspective in Music, Vol. 14, No. 2 (Fall 1986): 324-325.

Sanborn, Pitts.   "Negro Diva is Singing in France."   (New York) World Journal (September 30 1936).

Thomson, Virgil.   "The Last of the Divas."   New York Herald Tribune (January 17 1942).

EUGENE JONES (d.1969)

Obituary.   Variety (June 25 1969): 71.

JUNETTA JONES

Afro-American Magazine (January 21 1967): 1.

"Goldman Band."   Musical America (July 1964): 42-43.

Kolodin, Irving.   "Music to my Ears."   Saturday Review (April 13 1963): 31.

Moed, P.   "Fresh Voices."   Opera News (March 7 1964): 28-9.

SISSIERETTA JONES ("The Black Patti") (1869-1933)

Accooe, William J.   Black Patti Waltzes.   [Held by the Performing Arts Research Center at Lincoln Center, Music Research Division.   Call # *MYD +box.]

Dannett, Sylvia G. L.   Profiles of Negro Womanhood.   Yonkers, NY: Educational Heritage, 1964.   Brief biography.

Daughtry, Willa Estelle.   "Sissieretta Jones: A Study of the Negro's Contribution to Nineteenth Century American Concert and Theatrical Life."   Dissertation (Ph.D., Fine Arts) Syracuse University, 1968.   257pp.

Farewell Appearance of Sissieretta Jones: known as the Black Patti.   Chicago: Star Lecture Course, 1893.   21pp.   (Concert program).   [Held by the New York Public Library]

Hare, Maud Cuney.   Negro Musicians and Their Music. Washington, D.C.: Associated Publishers, 1936, pp. 230-231.

Lichtenwanger, William. "Jones, Matilda Sissieretta Joyner."
In Notable American Women, 1607-1950: A Biographical
Dictionary, eds. Edward T. James, et al. Cambridge, MA: The
Belknap Press, 1971, pp. 288-290.

Logan, Rayford W. "Jones, [Matilda] Sissieretta [Joyner]."
In Dictionary of American Negro Biography, eds. Rayford W.
Logan and Michael R. Winston. New York: Norton, 1982, pp.
367-368.

Scruggs, Lawson A. "Mrs. Sissieretta Jones." In Women of
Distinction. Raleigh, NC: the Author, 1893, pp. 325-331.

Sissieretta Jones, the Black Patti. [MSS in the E. Azalia
Hackley Collection of the Detroit Public Library].

Southern, Eileen. Biographical Dictionary of Afro-American
and African Musicians. Westport, CT: Greenwood Press, 1982,
pp. 217-218.

Wright, Josephine. "Jones [nee Joyner], (Matilda)
Sissieretta ["Black Patti"]. In The New Grove Dictionary of
American Music, Vol. 2, p. 595.

_____, and Eileen Southern, comps. "Sissieretta Jones
(1868-1933)." In Women in Music: An Anthology of Source
Readings from the Middle Ages to the Present, ed. Carol-Neuls
Bates. New York: Harper & Row, 1982, pp. 135-142.
[Reprinted from The Black Perspective in Music (July 1976):
191-201.]

Note: Original material on this singer can also be found in
the Boston Conservatory Library, Massachusetts.

Articles

"An Archival Supplemental Adjunct (RR archives) to Henry
Henricksen's Black Patti Research." Record Research, No.
173-174 (June 1980): 9.

Boston Chronicle (April 2 1932).

Daughtry, Willa Estelle. "Sissieretta Jones: Profile of a
Black Artist." Musical Analysis (Dutton, TX), Vol. 1, No. 1
(Winter 1972): 12-18.

Henriksen, Henry. 'Black Patti.' Record Research, Nos.
165-166 (August 1979): 4-8; Nos. 167-168 (October 1979): 4-8;
Nos. 171-172 (March 1980): 4-5+; Nos. 177-178 (November
1980): 8; Nos. 187-188 (December 1981): 8.

Indianapolis Freeman (December 30 1889).

Indianapolis Freeman (July 28 1894).

Indianapolis Freeman (October 27 1894).

Indianapolis Freeman (May 4 1895).

Kirk, E. K. "Nightingales at the White House (celebrated divas who charmed our nations presidents)." Opera News, Vol. 45 (November 1 1980): 22+.

New York Age (October 14 1915).

Obituaries

Chicago Defender (July 1 1933).

Musical America, Vol. V, No. 4 (1933): 8.

MELVIN JORDAN

Coombs, O. "Melvin Jordan: Lyric Tenor." Essence (February 1972): 40-41.

GWENDOLYN KILLEBREW (c.1942-   )

Forbes, Elizabeth. "Killebrew, Gwendolyn." In The New Grove Dictionary of American Music, Vol. 2, p. 630.

Southern, Eileen. Biographical Dictionary of Afro-American and African Musicians. Westport, CT: Greenwood Press, 1982, p. 230.

Articles

Connolly, R. "Gwendolyn Killebrew." Stereo Review (December 1971): 70-71.

Fleming, S. "Hanover, N.H.: Webern, Krenek, and New Violin." High Fidelity (October 1968): MA23.

"Gwendolyn Killebrew." New York Philharmonic Program Notes (April 22 1971): M.

Hiemenz, J. "City Opera." High Fidelity (December 1971): MA17.

Lingg, A. M. "After the Prize." Opera News (March 30 1968): 13-14.

Sullivan, Dan. "This is Gwen's Day." New York Times (May 15 1966).

JUANITA KING (1924-1974)

Obituary. The Black Perspective in Music, Vol. 2, No. 2 (Fall 1974): 226.

Obituary. New York Amsterdam News (April 27 1974): B-11.

Strongin, Theodore. "Juanita King Offers First Recital Here." New York Times (November 10 1970).

LENORA LAFAYETTE (1926-   )

"Aida for a Night." Time (February 9 1953): 49.

"Lenora Lafayette." London Musical Events (February 1954): 32-33.

Moor, P. "Our Operatic Expatriates." High Fidelity (November 1960): 52.

"New Vaughan Williams Symphony; Barbirolli Conducts Premiere of Antarctica." Musical America (April 1 1953): 7.

"Recitals." London Musical Events (June 1956): 46.

Taubman, H. "12 Most Promising Negro Singers." Ebony (October 1953): 48-52.

BETTY LANE

"Impressive Singing by Betty Lane Has Bright, Free Sound." New York Times (January 29 1974).

GEORGIA ANN LASTER (1928-1961)

"Georgia Ann Laster, 33, Negro Concert Singer; Killed in Labor Day Night Auto Collision Near Lodi, California; Her Mother Killed Also; Her Career Given in Brief." Jet (September 21 1961): 61.

Goldberg, Albert. "The Sounding Board: Bowl's Family Night Stars Young Artists." Los Angeles Times (August 5 1953).

P. G. H. "Georgia Laster, Soprano." New York Times (March 7 1955): 22.

ELLA LEE

"Another Operatic Negro." Variety (March 29 1961): 2.

Bloomfield, A. "San Francisco." Opera (December 1964): 810.

Davidson, H. "Canada/Puccini at the Place." Musical America (March 1964): 21.

"Ella Lee." San Francisco Symphony Program Notes (March 26 1960): 7.

Humphreys, H. S., and E. Bell. "M & A Reviews: The Press." Music and Artists, Vol. 2, No. 1 (1969): 43.

Lee, Ella. "Singing with Felsenstein." Opera (UK) (January 1976): 26-29.

Opera News (March 11 1967). (Concert Review)

_____ (October 10 1967). (Concert Review)

_____ (April 17 1971). (Concert Review)

Posthuma, K. A. "Amsterdam." Opera (February 1964): 122.

Stuckenschmidt, H. H. "Felsenstein Mounts Britten's
'Dream.'" Opera (September 1961): 586-587.

MABEL SANFORD LEWIS (c.1902-1980)

Southern, Eileen. Biographical Dictionary of Afro-American
and African Musicians. Westport, CT: Greenwood Press, 1982,
pp. 245-246.

Articles

Chicago Defender (July 28 1928).

Chicago Defender (September 17 1938).

Chicago Defender (March 18 1939).

VERA LITTLE (1928-   )

Southern, Eileen. Biographical Dictionary of Afro-American
and African Musicians. Westport, CT: Greenwood Press, 1982,
p. 247.

Articles

"Double Launching." Time (February 24 1958): 46.

H. C. S. "Joint Recital Given. Vera Little, Soprano, Heard
with Dorothy Taylor, Violinist." New York Times (March 30
1953).

Hoffman, P. "Memphis Soprano Sings in Vatican." New York
Times (April 5 1959): 81.

HERMIONE HORTENSE LOVE (1910-   )

Chicago Defender (December 13 1979).

Southern, Eileen. Biographical Dictionary of Afro-American
and African Musicians. Westport, CT: Greenwood Press, 1982,
p. 249.

LUCA FAMILY, THE

Hare, Maud Cuney. Negro Musicians and Their Music.
Washington, D.C.: Associated Publishers, 1936, pp. 204-205.

Southern, Eileen. Biographical Dictionary of Afro-American and African Musicians. Westport, CT: Greenwood Press, 1982, p. 251.

Trotter, James M. Music and Some Highly Musical People. Chicago: Afro-Am Press, 1969, pp. 88-105. (Orig. 1878)

SETH MCCOY (1928-   )

"From Mailman to the Met: Talent and Hard Work Lead Seth McCoy to Triumphant Debut." Ebony (May 1979): 48-50.

Southern, Eileen. Biographical Dictionary of Afro-American and African Musicians. Westport, CT: Greenwood Press, 1982, p. 257.

ROBERT McFERRIN (1921-   )

De Lerma, Dominique-Rene. "McFerrin, Robert." In The New Grove Dictionary of American Music, Vol. 3, p. 147.

Southern, Eileen. Biographical Dictionary of Afro-American and African Musicians. Westport, CT: Greenwood Press, 1982, p. 258.

Articles

"Aida." Musical Courier (February 15 1955): 12-13.

Chicago Defender (May 7 1955).

Dierks, D. "San Diego, California." Music and Artists, Vol. 1, No. 2 (1968): 66.

Glassner, Barry. "Yesterday's Hitmakers: Robert McFerrin." Sepia (May 1976): 80.

Kolodin, Irving. "Music to my Ears." Saturday Review (February 12 1955): 29.

Musical America (August 1957): 4. Biographical sketch.

"New Singers on "Met" Roster." Musical Courier (December 15 1954): 24.

New York Age (January 1 1949).

New York Amsterdam News (October 15 1975).

"Robert McFerrin." Musical America (February 1950): 282.

"Robert McFerrin." Musical Courier (January 1 1956): 15.

"Robert McFerrin." Musical Courier (August 1956): 18.

Taubman, H. "12 Most Promising Negro Singers." Ebony (October 1953): 48-52.

"Town Hall Debut." Musical America (January 1 1956): 35.

"Town Hall Recital." Musical America (March 1957): 42.

"Walter to Conduct at Metropolitan." Musical America
(December 15 1954): 6.

"We Present Robert McFerrin." Opera News (February 20 1956):
15.

MONICA MAIS

"Monica Mais is Her Name." Opportunity: Journal of Negro
Life (October-December 1948): 134.

MARIA MARTINEZ (c.1830s-18??) - Cuba

Southern, Eileen. Biographical Dictionary of Afro-American
and African Musicians. Westport, CT: Greenwood Press, 1982.

Articles

LaBrew, Arthur R. "Dona Maria Martinez." Afro-American
Music Review (Detroit), Vol. 1, No. 1 (July-December 1981):
89-98. Afro-Cuban singer.

Le Menestrel (17 avril 1859): 158.

_____ (12 juin 1859): 220-221.

The Musical World, Vol. 25 (June 22 1850): 392+.

Peress y Gonzales, Felipe. "La 'Malibran' Negra - La 'Patti'
Negra." La Ilustracion Espanola y Americana (Madrid), Vol.
49, No. 12 (March 30 1905): 182-183; and No. 13 (April 8
1905): 206-207.

Revue et Gazette Musicale de Paris (9 juin 1850): 194.

_____ (16 juin 1850).

_____ (4 janvier 1852): 6.

_____ (18 avril 1852): 122.

_____ (1 mai 1853): 161.

_____ (29 mai 1853): 194.

_____ (25 decembre 1859): 429.

_____ (5 fevrier 1860): 46.

EDWARD MATTHEWS (1907-1954)

Hare, Maud Cuney. Negro Musicians and Their Music.
Washington, D.C.: Associated Publishers, 1936, p. 381.

Southern, Eileen. Biographical Dictionary of Afro-American
and African Musicians. Westport, CT: Greenwood Press, 1982,
p. 268.

Articles

Bowles, Paul. "Edward Matthews Barytone is Heard in Recital
at Town Hall." New York Herald Tribune (December 25 1945).

Chicago Defender (January 17 1931).

Jet (February 23 1961): 9.

"Mathews in Leading Role in Thomson-Stein Opera." New York
Herald Tribune (January 21 1934).

New York Age (January 16 1932).

New York Age (December 18 1937).

New York Herald Tribune (January 19 1936).   Biographical
sketch.

Obituaries

Musical America (March 1954): 34.

New York Amsterdam News (February 27 1954).

New York Times (February 22 1954): 26.

Variety (February 24 1954): 63.

INEZ MATTHEWS (1917-   )

Southern, Eileen. Biographical Dictionary of Afro-American
and African Musicians. Westport, CT: Greenwood Press, 1982,
p. 268.

Articles

Chicago Defender (March 22 1958).

Craig, M. "Found in the Stars." Musical Courier (August
1954): 6.

"Inez Mathews Appears in Command Performance." Musical
Courier (March 1 1954): 40.

J. S. H. "Inez Matthews, Soprano, Has Debut at Town Hall."
New York Herald Tribune (November 21 1947).

New York Amsterdam News (November 15 1947).

DOROTHY MAYNOR (1910-   )

Abdul, Raoul. "Roland Hayes's Children." In Blacks in
Classical Music. New York: Dodd, Mead & Co., 1977, pp. 95-96.

Cherry, Gwendolyn, et al. "Dorothy Maynor: Singer." In
Portraits in Color: The Lives of Colorful Negro Women. New
York: Pageant Press, 1962, pp. 86-88.

Fletcher, Martin, ed. Our Great Americans: The Negro
Contribution to American Progress. Chicago: Gamma
Corporation, 1954, p. 18.

Rosenberg, Deena, and Bernard R. Rosenberg. "Dorothy Maynor,
Singer." In Music Makers. New York: Columbia University
Press, 1979, pp. 313-324.

Biographical Dictionaries

Ewen, David, ed. Musicians Since 1900: Performers in Concert
and Opera. New York: H.W. Wilson, 1978, pp. 510-512.

Musicians' International Directory and Biographical Record
(1949-50).

Schauensee, Max de. "Maynor, Dorothy." In The New Grove
Dictionary of Music and Musicians, Vol. 11, p. 857.

_____. "Maynor [Mainor], Dorothy (Leigh)." In The New
Grove Dictionary of American Music, Vol. 3, pp. 196-197.

Southern, Eileen. Biographical Dictionary of Afro-American
and African Musicians. Westport, CT: Greenwood Press, 1982,
p. 269.

Who is Who in Music, 1941.

Who's Who in America, 1950-51.

Who's Who in America (Addenda).

Who's Who in Colored America, 1950.

Who's Who Today.

World Biography (1948).

Audiotapes

Destination Freedom: Norfolk Miracle. (Radio Program)
[Audiotape]. Chicago, WMAQ, 1949. Duration: 30 min. A
radio dramatization based on the life of singer Dorothy
Maynor; script by Richard Durham. [Held by the Schomburg
Collection, NYPL, NYC Sc Audio C-326 (Side 1, no. 1)]

Articles

Arthur, J. K. "Women of 1939." Independent Woman, Vol. 19
(January 1940): 4.

"Black Diva." _Time_ (November 27 1939): 58.

Black, Doris. "Classical Arts Come to Harlem." _Sepia_
(October 1971): 21-27.

Chapin, L. "Two Ways to be Advantaged." _Christian Century_
(April 21 1976): 434-436.

Diedrichs, G. "A Respect for Talent: Harlem School of the
Arts." _Opera News_ (October 1974): 39-42.

"Dorothy Maynor." _Musical America_ (December 15 1959): 24.

"Dorothy Maynor." _Variety_ (November 25 1959): 71.

Dreyfus, Sylvia J. "American Songbird - The Success Story of
Dorothy Maynor." _Liberty_, Vol. 17 (November 30 1940): 55-57.

Evans, O. "Making Friends with Music." _Opera News_ (November
5 1966): 15-17.

Ferguson, C. W. "Americans Not Everyone Knows: Dorothy
Maynor." _PTA Magazine_ (November 1969): 10-12.

"Fine Arts School." _Ebony_ (May 1966): 80-86.

Fisher, M. M. "Community Concerts to Community Service."
Music Journal (November 1966): 38-39+.

"Maynor." _The New Yorker_ (November 18 1939): 18.

"Maynor, Dorothy." _Current Biography 1940_.

"Maynor, Dorothy." _Current Biography 1951_, pp. 419-421.

Maynor, Dorothy. "Arts in the Ghetto." _Music Educators
Journal_ (March 1968): 39-40+.

_____. "Looking Back Without Anger, Looking Forward to
Change." _American Symphony Orchestra League Newsletter_ (now
Symphony News), Vol. 22, No. 4 (1971): 17+.

_____. "Why Should Whitey Care About the Ghetto?" _Music
Educators Journal_ (April 1969): 60-62.

"Maynor's Year." _Time_ (November 4 1940): 58.

Milburn, F. "Dorothy Maynor - A Singer Who Has Happily
Combined Her Home Life with A Career." _Musical America_ (May
1956): 16-17.

Miller, P. L. "Ever-Fresh Art of Dorothy Maynor." _American
Record Guide_ (August 1969): 1111.

Musical America (April 1 1953): 15. Biographical Note.

"Native Flagstad?" _Newsweek_ (August 21 1939): 26-27.

"Not By the Pound." _Time_ (June 27 1949): 39-40.

Petersen, Maurice. "Dorothy Maynor: The Musical Whiz of Harlem." Essence (December 1977): 56-61.

Rogers, E. B. "High Honors." Musical America (January 1961): 184.

"Salt at Stockbridge." Time (August 21 1939): 45.

"Scherman Launches Season with 'Comus.'" Musical America (November 1 1958): 16.

Seward, W. "Whatever Became of Dorothy Maynor?" Stereo Review (January 1969): 69-72.

Soria, D. J. "Artist Life." High Fidelity (August 1967): MA3+.

"Spiritual as Soul Music." Saturday Review (September 4 1976): 38.

Taubman, H. "Million-dollar Voice." Collier's (March 2 1940): 11-12+.

Thomas, P. K. "Temportrait." Musician (May 1940): 87.

"Van McCoy's Music Scene." Sepia (August 1979): 8. Report on the opening of Harlem School of the Arts' new building under the direction of Dorothy Maynor.

Newspaper Articles

Chicago Defender (August 26 1939).

Chicago Defender (October 14 1939).

Christian Science Monitor (August 14 1943): 7.

New York Times (August 13 1939): Sec. IX, p.5. Interview.

New York Times (May 20 1979): 55. Comment on the Harlem School of the Arts.

New York Times (March 9 1980).

Concert Reviews

"Debut." Newsweek (November 27 1939): 25.

"Debut Recital." Etude (February 1940): 75.

"Dorothy Maynor." The Canon (August 1952): 33-34; (September 1952): 68.

"Dorothy Maynor." Music News (December 1949): 33.

"Dorothy Maynor." Musical Courier (November 15 1955): 14-15.

"Dorothy Maynor." Pan Pipes (May 1956): 20.

Dowdy, D., and R. Devries.   "Chicago."   Musical Courier
(April 1955): 27.

"Maynor Makes First Tour of Australia."   Musical America
(June 1952): 20.

Musical America (March 25 1940): 33.

New York Times (November 20 1939): 15.

New York Times (February 25 1940): 8.

New York Times (March 6 1975).

New York Times (May 17 1975).

Thompson, Oscar.   "Exciting Debut Made by Dorothy Maynor."
Musical America (November 25 1939): 15, 27.

"Town Hall Recital."   Musical America (November 15 1955): 22.

ABBIE MITCHELL (1884-1960)

Hare, Maud Cuney.   Negro Musicians and Their Music.
Washington, D.C.: Associated Publishers, 1936, pp. 369-371.

Lemieux, Raymond.   "Mitchell, Abbie."   In Dictionary of
American Negro Biography, eds. Rayford W. Logan and Michael
R. Winston.   New York: W. W. Norton, 1982, pp. 441-443.

Robinson, Wilhelmena S.   Historical Afro-American Biographies
(International Library of Afro-American Life and History).
Washington, D.C.: Associated Publishers, 1976, pp. 229-230.

Ryder, Georgia A.   "Mitchell, Abbie."   In Notable American
Women: The Modern Period, eds. Barbara Sicherman and Carol
Hurd Green.   Cambridge, MA: The Belknap Press, 1980, pp.
317-319.

Southern, Eileen.   Biographical Dictionary of Afro-American
and African Musicians.   Westport, CT: Greenwood Press, 1982,
pp. 275-276.

Articles

Chicago Defender (August 13 1910).

Chicago Defender (February 21 1914).

Indianapolis Freeman (December 31 1898).

Indianapolis Freeman (March 16 1915).

"A Negro Singer Once Had a Ride in Royal Coach."   New York
Herald Tribune (January 5 1936).

New York Age (July 23 1923).

<u>New York Age</u> (April 20 1929).

<u>New York Age</u> (July 21 1934).

<u>New York Age</u> (November 24 1934).

<u>New York Age</u> (November 14 1936).

Obituaries

<u>Jet</u> (April 7 1960): 19.

<u>New York Times</u> (March 20 1960): 86.

<u>Variety</u> (March 23 1960): 63.

LEONA MITCHELL (1949-   )

Southern, Eileen. <u>Biographical Dictionary of Afro-American and African Musicians</u>. Westport, CT: Greenwood Press, 1982, p. 276.

Walsh, Michael. "Mitchell, Leona." In <u>The New Grove Dictionary of American Music</u>, Vol. 3, p. 249.

Articles

Collier, Aldore. "Leona Mitchell: An All-American Opera Star." <u>Ebony</u> (September 1983): 37-38+.

"Destiny Rides Again." <u>Time</u> (October 11 1982): 86.

Opera star Leona Mitchell to have street named for her in home town of Enid, Okla. <u>New York Times</u> (August 21 1981): Sec. III, p. 30.

Wadsworth, Stephen. "Here To Sing: Leona Mitchell's Coming into Her Own." <u>Opera News</u>, Vol. 43, No. 14 (February 10 1979): 10-13.

Waleson, Heidi. "A Lyric Soprano Ventures into Heavier Fare." <u>New York Times</u> (March 20 1983): Sec. II, p. 23.

ANDRE MONTAL (1940-   )

Bloomfield, A. "San Francisco." <u>Opera</u> (August 1964): 545-546.

<u>Kennedy Center Program Notes</u> (September 1973): 19A.

"The Musical Whirl." <u>High Fidelity</u> (July 1966): MA12-13.

OLIVE MOOREFIELD

"New Musical Star in Old Vienna." <u>Ebony</u> (November 1962): 61-62+.

CHARLOTTE WALLACE MURRAY (1885-1982)

Hare, Maud Cuney. Negro Musicians and Their Music.
Washington, D.C.: Associated Publishers, 1936, pp. 378-379.

Obituary. New York Times (March 17 1982): B-8.

JESSYE NORMAN (1945-   )

Abdul, Raoul. "Prelude to Isolde." In Blacks in Classical
Music. New York: Dodd, Mead & Co., 1977, pp. 114-115.

Bernheimer, Martin. "Norman, Jessye." In The New Grove
Dictionary of Music and Musicians, Vol. 13, p. 283.

Ewen, David, ed. Musicians Since 1900: Performers in Concert
and Opera. New York: H.W. Wilson, 1978, pp. 586-587.

Smith, Patrick J. "Norman, Jessye." In The New Grove
Dictionary of American Music, Vol. 3, p. 383.

Southern, Eileen. Biographical Dictionary of Afro-American
and African Musicians. Westport, CT: Greenwood Press, 1982,
p. 291.

Magazine Articles

Clarke, K. "Singers." Music and Musicians, Vol. 27
(September 1978): 44.

"Diva! Jessye Norman is the Toast of the Opera World." Life,
Vol. 8 (March 1985): 99+.

Fleming, S. "Musician of the Month: Jessye Norman." High
Fidelity (July 1973): MA4-5.

Greenhalgh, J. "Jessye Norman." (Interview) Music and
Musicians, Vol. 27 (August 1979): 14-15.

"Here and There." Gramophone, Vol. 53 (August 1976): 271.

"Here and There." Gramophone, Vol. 55 (March 1978): 1540.

"Honoring Jessye Norman." Pan Pipes, Vol. 68, No. 1 (1975):
13.

Hume, P. "A Pride of Sopranos." High Fidelity (June 1984):
61-62+.

"Jessye Norman." Interview, Vol. 14 (April 1984): 96-97.

"Jessye Norman." Music and Musicians, Vol. 20 (November
1971): 16.

"Jessye Norman." Music and Musicians, Vol. 22 (November
1973): 8-9.

"Jessye Norman, La Verite du Chant." (Interview
w/discography) Harmonie, No. 132 (December 1977): 46-53.

"Names, Dates and Places." Opera News (March 9 1974): 6-7.

"Names, Dates and Places." Opera News (August 1977): 12-13.

"Norman, Jessye." Current Biography 1976, pp. 292-295.

Phillips, H. E. "Norman Conquest." Opera News (June 17
1973): 17.

Porter, Joseph. "Jessye Norman: Catch Up America." Encore
(June 7 1976): 31-32.

"SAI's Abroad." Pan Pipes, Vol. 64, No. 3 (1972): 14-15.

Sauerbrei, P. "Augusta to Aida." Fugue, Vol. 3 (October
1978): 32-34. Biographical portrait.

Swan, A. "A Modern Norman Conquest." Newsweek (December 6
1982): 128.

"The Young Professional." Music and Artists, Vol. 5, No. 2
(1972): 13.

Newspaper Articles

Grand Rapids Press (September 3 1972): C-6.

Grand Rapids Press (October 29 1972): H-1.

Gruen, John. "An American Soprano Adds the Met to Her
Roster." New York Times (September 18 1983): Sec. II, p.
17. Profile of J. Norman on the occasion of her Metropolitan
Opera debut.

Guardian (September 15 1972): 9.

Henahan, Donal. Interview with Jessye Norman on the occasion
of her NYC recital debut; discusses difficulties Norman faces
as a black in making a career as classical singer and
operatic performer. New York Times (January 21 1973): Sec.
II, 15+.

Washington Post (August 7 1972): B1+.

Concert Reviews

Chapman, E. "Berlioz's 'The Trojans.'" Musical Events
[London] (November 1972): 4-5.

Dean, W., and B. Millington. "Edinburgh." The Musical Times
(November 1977): 941-942.

New York Times (October 6 1974): D-6.

Stuckenschmidt, H. H. "West Berlin." Opera (UK) (May 1972):
449.

Sutcliffe, J. H. "Berlin." Opera News (March 11 1972): 29.

Weaver, W. "Florence: East Meets West." Opera (UK) (Autumn 1971): 83.

AUBREY PANKEY (1905-1971)

Hare, Maud Cuney. Negro Musicians and Their Music. Washington, D.C.: Associated Publishers, 1936, pp. 382-383.

Southern, Eileen. Biographical Dictionary of Afro-American and African Musicians. Westport, CT: Greenwood Press, 1982, p. 299.

[See also Pankey clippings file in the Music Division of the Performing Arts Research Center at Lincoln Center.]

Articles

Chicago Defender (January 2 1937).

Chicago Defender (February 5 1944).

Chicago Defender (January 7 1956).

New York Age (July 4 1942).

New York Age (August 23 1947).

Concert Reviews

"Aubrey Pankey, Baritone." Musical America (February 10 1944).

"Aubrey Pankey, Baritone." Musical America (January 10 1945).

"Aubrey Pankey in Recital." New York Herald Tribune (April 24 1946).

"Aubrey Pankey Recital." New York Times (April 29 1940). (Debut recital).

F. D. P. "Aubrey Pankey is Heard in Recital at Town Hall." New York Herald Tribune (March 16 1942).

M. A. S. "Aubrey Pankey Recital." New York Times (April 20 1945).

P. B. "Aubrey Pankey is Heard in Recital at Town Hall." New York Herald Tribune (April 20 1945).

"Pankey, Baritone, in Recital." New York Times (March 24 1946).

Obituaries

Music and Artists, Vol. 4, No. 3 (1971): 35.

New York Times (May 11 1971): 42.

Variety, No. 263 (May 1971): 79.

LOUISE PARKER (1925-1986)

Southern, Eileen. Biographical Dictionary of Afro-American and African Musicians. Westport, CT: Greenwood Press, 1982, pp. 300-301.

Articles

Klein, Howard. "Louise Parker Sings Musicianly Recital." New York Times (October 13 1966).

New York Amsterdam News (September 20 1947).

Philadelphia Tribune (November 17 1973).

Robison, Judith. "Louise Parker, Contralto, in Recital Here." New York Herald Tribune (November 31 1961).

Obituaries

The Black Perspective in Music, Vol. 14, No. 3 (Fall 1986): 326.

Variety, No. 324 (September 24 1986): 157.

WILLIS PATTERSON (1930-   )

Southern, Eileen. Biographical Dictionary of Afro-American and African Musicians. Westport, CT: Greenwood Press, 1982, p. 301.

ELWOOD PETERSON (1928-   )

The Oakland Post (May 9 1973).

Southern, Eileen. Biographical Dictionary of Afro-American and African Musicians. Westport, CT: Greenwood Press, 1982, p. 304.

EDWARD PIERSON (1931-   )

Devries, D. "Chicago." Musical Courier (April 1960): 22.

"The Musical Whirl." High Fidelity (October 1970): MA19.

Southern, Eileen. Biographical Dictionary of Afro-American and African Musicians. Westport, CT: Greenwood Press, 1982, p. 307.

ANNIE PAULINE PINDELL (ca.1834-1901)

Hopkins, Pauline E. "Famous Women of the Negro Race." The
Colored American Magazine, Vol. 4 (November 1901).

Southern, Eileen. Biographical Dictionary of Afro-American
and African Musicians. Westport, CT: Greenwood Press, 1982,
pp. 307-308.

DESSERIA PLATO BROADLEY (d.1907)

Southern, Eileen. Biographical Dictionary of Afro-American
and African Musicians. Westport, CT: Greenwood Press, 1982,
p. 309.

Articles

Chicago Defender (July 16 1927).

Indianapolis Freeman (August 19 1893).

Indianapolis Freeman (September 2 1893).

Indianapolis Freeman (August 15 1896).

Indianapolis Freeman (February 16 1907).

New York Age (December 19 1891).

HENRY PRICE (1945-   )

"Names, Dates and Places." Opera News, Vol. 42 (May 1978):
8-9.

LEONTYNE PRICE (1927-   )

Abdul, Raoul. "Debut Recital: Leontyne Price." In Blacks in
Classical Music. New York: Dodd, Mead & Co., 1977, pp.
105-107.

Adams, Russell L. Great Negroes, Past and Present. Chicago:
Afro-Am Publishing Co., 1969, p. 190.

Cherry, Gwendolyn, et al. "Leontyne Price: Mississippi's
Gift to Opera." In Portraits in Color: The Lives of Colorful
Negro Women. New York: Pageant Press, 1962, pp. 83-84.

Chotzinoff, Samuel. A Little Night Music: Intimate
Conversations with [7 artists]... New York: Harper & Row,
1964, pp. 73-96.

Christiansen, Rupert. Prima Donna: A History. New York:
Penguin Books, 1986, pp. 231-233.

Diamonstein, Barbaralee. "Leontyne Price." In Open Secrets:
Ninety-four Women in Touch with Our Time. New York: Viking
Press, 1972, pp. 333-335.

Hemming, Roy. Discovering Music. New York: Four Winds
Press, 1974, pp. 48, 329.

Lyon, Hugh Lee. Leontyne Price: Highlights of a Prima
Donna. New York: Vantage Press, 1973. 218pp.

Rubin, Stephen E. "The Token Black Who Paid Her Dues:
Leontyne Price." In The New Met in Profile. New York:
Macmillan Publishing Co., 1974, pp. 63-72.

Sargeant, Winthrop. "Leontyne Price." Divas. New York:
Coward, McCann, 1973, pp. 135-167.

Smith, Frank E., and Audrey Warren. "Leontyne Price." In
Mississippians All. New Orleans: Pelican Publishing House,
1968, pp. 35-43.

Steane, J. B. The Grand Tradition: Seventy Years of Singing
on Record. New York: Scribners, 1974. Includes a brief
assessment of Price's recorded works.

Biographical Dictionaries

Blyth, Alan. "Price, Leontyne." In The New Grove Dictionary
of Music and Musicians, Vol. 15, pp. 225-226.

_____. "Price, (Mary Violet) Leontyne." In The New Grove
Dictionary of American Music, Vol. 3., p. 629.

Encyclopedia of Opera, 1976.

Ewen, David, ed. Musicians Since 1900: Performers in Concert
and Opera. New York: H.W. Wilson, 1978, pp. 652-656.

International Who's Who, 1977-78.

Robinson, Wilhelmena S. Historical Afro-American Biographies
(International Library of Afro-American Life and History).
Washington, D.C.: Associated Publishers, 1976, p. 239.

Southern, Eileen. Biographical Dictionary of Afro-American
and African Musicians. Westport, CT: Greenwood Press, 1982,
pp. 313-314.

Toppin, Edgar A. A Biographical History of Blacks in America
since 1528. New York: David McKay, 1971, pp. 391-393.

Who's Who, 1977-78.

Who's Who in America, 1960-61.

Who's Who in America, 1976-77.

Who's Who in Opera, 1976.

Who's Who of American Women, 1977-78.

Magazine Articles

"America: to Leontyne Price, Opportunities Are Growing." US News & World Report (March 28 1977): 56.

Barrow, W. "Five Fabulous Females." Negro Digest (July 1963): 78-83.

"The Best of Times: Having Sung the World Over, Leontyne Price's Fondest Memories Are Still of the Met." Horizon, Vol. 26 (October 1983): 42-44.

Blyth, Alan. "Leontyne Price Talks." Gramophone, Vol. 49 (1971): 303.

Burton, M. K. "Best of Times." Horizon (October 1983): 42-43.

Campbell, M. "Lady is a Champ." Biography News (February 1974): 219.

_____. "Leontyne Price: Portrait of a Prima Donna." Music Journal (March 1970): 38-39+.

Chotzinoff, Samuel. "Conversation with Leontyne Price." Holiday (March 1964): 103-104+.

_____. "Little Nightmusic." Harper's Magazine (1964): 73-96.

Cliburn, V., and R. Mohr. "In Praise of Leontyne." Opera News (January 23 1982): 8-11.

Delta (November 1973): 36.

Dennis, P. "Leontyne Price: Praise and Plaudits at the Met." Sepia (February 1962): 46-47.

"Diva Sang for the Old Met Ghosts." Life (September 30 1966): 38-39.

"Diva's Date with Destiny." Ebony (December 1966): 184-192.

Ebert, Alan. "Leontyne - The Price of Being." Essence (February 1975): 64-67.

_____. "The Woman I Thought I'd Be." Essence (August 1975): 44.

"50th Spingarn Medalist (Leontyne Price)." The Crisis (June-July 1965): 378.

"50th Spingarn Medalist." The Crisis (February 1966): 129.

Fitzgerald, C. "Heroine at Home." Opera News (February 4 1961): 14-15.

Garland, Phyl. "Leontyne Price: Getting Out at the Top."
Ebony (June 1985): 31-34+.

Hemming, Roy. "Leontyne Price." Stereo Review, Vol. 36
(January 1976): 62-64.

Hepburn, D. "Leontyne Price: Rare Magic in Opera Roles."
Sepia (July 1961): 42-47.

Hughes, Allen. "Leontyne Price." Musical America (May
1959): 10-11.

"I'm Just A Girl from Laurel Mississippi." Ebony (February
1975): 40-41. Cosmetics ad with biographical information.

"Inimitable Warfields: Loaded with Talent and Blessed with
Some of the Best Breaks, They Make the World Their Oyster."
Our World (April 1955): 31-37.

Jacobson, Robert. "Collard Greens and Caviar." Opera News,
Vol. 50 (August 1985): 28+.

Jenkins, Speight. "Today's Price; Interview." Opera News
(February 12 1972): 15-16.

Jet (December 28 1967): 36.

"A Job Well Done." The Crisis (November 1961): 619.

Kolodin, Irving. "Leontyne Price: I Love Opera, but..."
(Interview) Saturday Review (September 9 1972): 31-34.

_____. "Operatic Career and How It Prospers (Or
Doesn't)." Saturday Review (April 5 1975): 37-38.

Lanier, T. P. "Miss Price on Naxis." Opera News (March 3
1979): 18.

"Leontyne Price Benefit." The Crisis (June-July 1976): 208.

"Leontyne Price Gives Farewell Show at Met." Jet (January 21
1985): 67.

"Leontyne Price: Great Lady of Opera." Negro Digest (August
1962): 3-9. (Reprinted from Show.)

"Leontyne Price--Still the Diva." The Crisis (June-July
1983): 32-33.

"Leontyne Price to Leave the Met After 23 Years." Jet
(December 24 1984): 5.

"Leontyne's Latest." Time (April 7 1961): 83.

"Lovely Leontyne Price." Sepia (December 1966): 81.

McNally, Terrence. "Abdicating the Throne." Horizon (April 1985): 12.

Mayer, G. L. "Prima Donna: Price." American Record Guide (November 1967): 188-189.

"Met Triumph for Leontyne." Life (February 10 1961): 107-110.

"Mistress of Stage and Score." Time (May 30 1960): 35.

Moore, Sally. "Triumphant in a New 'Aida', Leontyne Price says, 'This Season Is a Crossroads for Me.'" People (February 23 1976): 14-16.

Musical America (October 1959): 4. Biography.

"Names, Dates and Places." Opera News (February 13 1971): 5.

"Names, Dates and Places." Opera News (July 1973): 8-9.

"Names, Dates and Places." Opera News (June 1974): 8-9.

"People." Time (March 24 1967): 32.

"People Are Talking About..." Vogue (November 1 1962): 108.

"Porgy Marries Bess." (W. Warfield and L. Price) Our World (December 1952): 41-44.

"Price, Leontyne." Current Biography 1961, pp. 374-375.

"Price, Leontyne." Current Biography 1978, pp. 329-332.

"Prima Donna from Mississippi: Leontyne Price Scales Summitt of Opera with a Dazzling Metropolitan Opera Debut." Ebony (April 1961): 96-98, 100.

"Reflected Glory." Opera News (October 1983): 74.

Rubin, Stephen E. "Price on Price; Interview." Opera News (March 6 1976): 16-20.

Sargent, M. "Leontyne Price Talent, Voice Draws Raves from Country's Top Critics." Down Beat (October 5 1955): 14.

Schickel, Richard. "Leontyne Price: From Mississippi to the Met." Look (January 17 1961): 88-90.

Sheean, V. "Leontyne Price Onstage." Show, Vol. 1 (November 1961): 98-100.

_____. "Spiritual Ground." Opera News (March 28 1964): 23.

"Skylark and Golden Calves." Time (February 3 1961): 45.

"Soprano's Dream." Newsweek (January 31 1955): 81.

"Stars at Home: Leontyne Price." Opera News (February 12 1966): 14-16.

Taubman, H. "12 Most Promising Negro Singers." Ebony (October 1953): 48-52.

Thomas, C. "Three Negroes Receive 1964 Presidential Freedom Medal." Negro History Bulletin (December 1964): 59.

Todd, Arthur. "Leontyne Price - 'Voice of the Century.'" Musical America, Vol. LXXXII, No. 1 (January 1962): 12-15.

"Voice Like a Banner Flying." Time (March 10 1961): 58-60+.

Walsh, M. "What Price Glory, Leontyne! The Prima Donna Assoluta Sings Her Last Operatic Role." Time (January 14 1985): 67.

Newspaper Articles

Anderson, S. H. "Leontyne Price-Still the Diva." New York Times Biography Service (February 1982): 238-239.

Chicago Today (February 27 1972): 62.

Chicago Tribune (July 13 1975): Sec. 1, p. 6.

Chicago Tribune Arts (July 6 1975): Sec. 6, p. 7.

Chicago Tribune Arts and Fun (June 17 1979): 4+.

Coleman, E. "Girl of the Golden Voice." New York Times Magazine (October 15 1961): 37+.

Denver Post Roundup (November 11 1973): 3+.

Detroit Free Press (April 25 1971): B-8.

Hughes, Allen. "Another Major Step for Leontyne Price." New York Times (January 22 1961): Sec. 2, p. 9.

Los Angeles Times (March 5 1961): C5.

New York Herald Tribune (May 3 1953): Sec. IV, p.2.

New York Times (September 11 1966): Sec. II, p. 21.

New York Times (March 20 1981): Sec. III, p. 14. Soprano Leontyne Price reflects on her career.

New York Times (September 13 1981): Sec. XI, p. 4. Interview with Price on her career.

New York Times (February 7 1982): Sec. II, p. 1. Profile of Leontyne Price.

Rubin, Stephen E. "I'm Not Scared Anymore." New York Times (September 16 1973).

Concert Reviews

"Aida." Musical Times (August 1958): 437.

Briggs, E. "Brisbane." The Canon (September 1957): 48.

Brunner, G. "American Artists Score at Berlin Festival."
Musical Courier (December 1960): 31.

"Concert Reviews." The Canon (July 1957): 405, 407.

"Covent Garden." Opera [London] (August 1958): 540.

"Covent Garden." Opera [London] (July 1959): 474.

"Covent Garden Opera." Musical Opinion (August 1958): 697.

"Critics Hail Her Debut at Metropolitan Opera in Verdi's 'Il
Trovatore.'" Jet (February 9 1961): 56.

Dragadze, P. "Price Conquers La Scala." Musical America
(July 1960): 17.

_____. "Verona Arena." Musical America (September 1959):
6.

Gilbert, E. "Detroit." Musical Courier (May 1960): 31.

Hoffer, P. "Welshman at La Scala." Music and Musicians
[London] (July 1960): 26.

Hughes, Allen. "Leontyne Price." Musical America (May
1959): 10-11.

Johnen, L. J. "Cincinnati." Musical Courier (April 1957):
35.

Kolodin, Irving. "Lustrous Leonora." Saturday Review
(October 14 1967): 106.

"Leontyne Price." Musical Courier (November 1 1954): 36.

"Leontyne Price." Musical Courier (December 1 1954): 19-20.

"Leontyne Price." Pan Pipes (January 1959): 39.

"Leontyne Price Engaged for "Met" Next Season." Musical
Courier (February 1960): 19.

"Leontyne Price Soloist in Barber Work." Musical America
(December 1 1959): 37-38.

"Leontyne Price Triumphs in Debut in Trovatore." Musical
America (February 1961): 30-31.

"Leontyne Price Will Make Her Debut at Metropolitan Opera
Company, in January, 1961." Jet (April 28 1960): 60.

"Made Debut at New York Metropolitan Opera, February, 1961; Her Performance Acclaimed." Journal of Negro History (April 1961): 131.

"Makes Triumphant Debut in Title Role of Verdi's "Aida" at La Scala, Milan, Italy. First Negro to Appear in a Major Italian Role at La Scala." Jet (June 9 1960): 62.

Mayer, M. "Price's Ballo. Grist and Lorengar Debuts." High Fidelity (May 1966): 134+.

Mittag, Evon. "Vienna Splendor." Opera News (December 10 1960): 29.

Murphy, R. "On Stage: Leontyne Price." Horizon (March 1961): 72.

"Opens Metropolitan Opera's 1961 Season in Leading Role of Opera 'The Girl of the Golden West.'" Jet (November 9 1961): 60-61.

Rosenfield, J. "A New "Porgy" in Dallas." Saturday Review (June 28 1952): 44.

"Sings "Madame Butterfly" at Metropolitan; also 'Il Trovatore.'" Jet (March 16 1961): 61.

"Tony and Cleo." Newsweek (September 26 1966): 98.

"To Sing "Tosca" at Metropolitan Opera on January 31, 1962; She Sang Same Role on NBC-TV in 1955." Jet (December 28 1961): 62.

"Town Hall Debut." Musical America (December 1 1954): 26.

Wagner, W. "Sydney." The Canon (June 1957): 375.

Wechsberg, J. "The 50th Salzburg Festival." Opera (Autumn 1960): 50.

Wolf, A. W. "Los Angeles." Musical Courier (March 1960): 30.

Television Appearances

"Integrated Love Meets Dixie Test: North Raises Greatest Protest as Leontyne Price Sings Lead Role in TV Opera Tosca." Ebony, Vol. 10 (May 1955): 32-36.

Kolodin, Irving. "'Tosca' on TV, etc." Saturday Review (February 5 1955): 27.

"Leontyne Price: As Donna Anna in Mozart's "Don Giovanni" (NBC-TV). NBC Opera Company Production." Jet (May 19 1960): 62.

"Leontyne Price Has a Leading Role in NBC Opera Company's "Don Giovanni," April 10, 1960 (NBC-TV)." Jet (April 14 1960): 66.

"Leontyne Price Heard in NBC-TV Tosca." Musical America (February 1 1955): 23.

"Leontyne Price's 2-hour "Tosca" Registers a Major First for TV." Variety (January 26 1955): 31.

"Metropolitan Soprano, on Ed Sullivan's Show, April 2, 1961 (CBS-TV)." Jet (April 6 1961): 66.

"TV Tosca." Time (January 31 1955): 68.

FLORENCE QUIVAR

New York Times (August 6 1982): C3.

MURIEL RAHN (1911-1961)

Southern, Eileen. Biographical Dictionary of Afro-American and African Musicians. Westport, CT: Greenwood Press, 1982, p. 316.

Who's Who in Colored America, 1950.

Articles

"Finds Europeans Kind to U.S. Negroes." Variety (January 13 1960): 51.

"Muriel Rahn." Musical America (March 1958): 27.

"New Acts." Variety (July 18 1951): 53.

New York Age (August 3 1935).

New York Age (November 19 1938).

New York Age (February 5 1949).

Rahn, Muriel. "My Most Humiliating Jim Crow Experience." Negro Digest (September 1945): 63-64.

Obituaries

Musical America (September 1961): 74.

New York Amsterdam News (August 12 1961).

New York Times (August 9 1961): 33.

Opera (October 1961): 664.

Opera News (December 30 1961): 36.

Variety (August 9 1961): 63.

LA JULIA RHEA (ca.1908-   )

Southern, Eileen. Biographical Dictionary of Afro-American and African Musicians. Westport, CT: Greenwood Press, 1982, p. 319.

Articles

Chicago Defender (December 28 1935).

Chicago Defender (October 30 1937).

Chicago Defender (September 6 1941).

Chicago Defender (October 25 1941).

Chicago Defender (October 17 1942).

E. C. "La Julia Rhea, Soprano, In Recital at Town Hall." New York Herald Tribune (November 10 1943).

Freedom Journal [Chicago] (May 1974).

New York Age (April 7 1934).

WILLIAM H. RICHARDSON (1869-c1930s)

Hare, Maud Cuney. Negro Musicians and Their Music. Washington, D.C.: Associated Publishers, 1936, pp. 364-367.

Lovingood, Penman. Famous Modern Negro Musicians. 2nd ed. New York: Da Capo Press, 1978. (Reprint of 1921 ed.)

Southern, Eileen. Biographical Dictionary of Afro-American and African Musicians. Westport, CT: Greenwood Press, 1982, p. 320.

PAUL ROBESON (1898-1976)

Davis, Lenwood G. A Paul Robeson Research Guide: A Selected Annotated Bibliography. Westport, CT: Greenwood Press, 1982.

Robeson, Eslanda Goode. Paul Robeson, Negro. New York: Harper, 1930. 153pp.

Robeson, Paul. Here I Stand. Boston: Beacon Press, 1971. (Orig. 1958)

Seton, Marie. Paul Robeson. London: D. Dobson, 1958. 254pp.

FAYE ROBINSON (1943-   )

Forbes, Elizabeth. "Robinson, Faye." In The New Grove Dictionary of American Music, Vol. 4, p. 55.

Southern, Eileen. <u>Biographical Dictionary of Afro-American</u>
<u>and African Musicians</u>. Westport, CT: Greenwood Press, 1982,
p. 324.

Articles

"Names, Dates and Places." <u>Opera News</u>, Vol. 41 (January 29
1977): 8-9.

"Names, Dates and Places." <u>Opera News</u> (June 1980): 6.

JOHN RUSSELL

"Searching for Heroes." <u>Time</u> (February 28 1969): 53.

Ward, H. "Listening In." <u>Music and Artists</u>, Vol. 2, No. 2
(1969): 9.

MARIE SELIKA (ca.1849-1937)

Dannett, Sylvia G. L. <u>Profiles of Negro Womanhood</u>. Yonkers,
NY: Educational Heritage, Inc., 1964. Brief biography.

Hare, Maud Cuney. <u>Negro Musicians and Their Music</u>.
Washington, D.C.: Associated Publishers, 1936, pp. 222-224.

Scruggs, Lawson A. "Madam Selika." In <u>Women of</u>
<u>Distinction</u>. Raleigh, NC: The Author, 1893, pp. 361-363.

Southern, Eileen. <u>Biographical Dictionary of Afro-American</u>
<u>and African Musicians</u>. Westport, CT: Greenwood Press, 1982,
pp. 334-335.

_____. "Selika, Marie." In <u>The New Grove Dictionary of</u>
<u>American Music</u>, Vol. 4, p. 185.

Articles

<u>Cleveland Gazette</u> (March 12 1887).

<u>Cleveland Gazette</u> (April 28 1888).

<u>Indianapolis Freeman</u> (October 10 1886).

<u>Indianapolis Freeman</u> (July 24 1891).

<u>Indianapolis Freeman</u> (December 23 1916).

<u>New York Age</u> (May 24 1919).

<u>New York Age</u> (May 29 1937).

<u>New York Globe</u> (March 3 1883).

<u>New York Globe</u> (May 26 1883).

GEORGE SHIRLEY (1934-   )

Ewen, David, ed. Musicians Since 1900: Performers in Concert and Opera. New York: H.W. Wilson, 1978, pp. 769-771.

Blyth, Alan. "Shirley, George." In The New Grove Dictionary of Music and Musicians, Vol. 17, p. 258.

_____. "Shirley, George." In The New Grove Dictionary of American Music, Vol. 4, p. 219.

Southern, Eileen. Biographical Dictionary of Afro-American and African Musicians. Westport, CT: Greenwood Press, 1982, pp. 337-338.

Articles

Ardoin, J. "George Shirley: 2 Years to the Met." Musical America (December 1961): 48.

"Audition Winners." Musical America (May 1961): 29-30.

"Awards and Honors." Musical Courier (December 1960): 41.

"George Shirley Met Auditions Winner." Musical Courier (May 1961): 8.

"George Shirley, Negro Tenor Sings a Leading Role in Mozart's Opera "Cosi Fan Tutte" in Place of Charles Anthony at Metropolitan Opera House, New York City; Shirley Won the 1960-1961 Metropolitan Opera Auditions." Interracial Review (January 1962): 30.

"George Shirley (Tenor), Shirley Verrett-Carter (Soprano), Billie L. Daniel (Soprano); Among 6 Winners of Opera Auditions Sponsored by Metropolitan Opera in N.Y.C." Jet (April 20 1961): 62.

"George Shirley Winner of Met Opera Audition." Music of the West Magazine (May 1961): 3.

Gould, B. "A Series of Met Firsts." Music Journal (November 1970): 24+.

"Leading Man at the Met." Ebony (January 1966): 84-86+.

Movshon, G. "And We Quote." (Interview) High Fidelity (January 1968): 21.

"The Musical Whirl." High Fidelity (May 1970): 23.

"Names, Dates and Places." Opera News (December 7 1968): 5.

"Names, Dates and Places." Opera News (December 6 1969): 5.

"Names, Dates and Places." Opera News (September 5 1970): 5.

"Names, Dates and Places." Opera News (February 3 1973): 6-7.

"Names, Dates and Places." Opera News (June 1974): 8-9.

"Names, Dates and Places." Opera News (December 18 1976): 6-7.

"Negro Tenor Coming to Glyndebourne." Musical Events (August 1966): 653.

"Pride of Detroit." Opera News (April 14 1962): 15.

Selden-Goth, G. "Young American Singers Bow in Florence Opera." Musical Courier (November 1960): 41-42.

Shirley, George. "The Black Performer: It's Been A Long Hard Road from the Minstrels to the Met." Opera News, Vol. 35, No. 14 (January 30, 1971): 6-13.

"Slated for Success." Musical America (July 1962): 11.

"Spotlight." Music and Artists, Vol. 3, No. 1 (1970): 55.

Stevenson, F. "Pride of Detroit." Opera News (April 14 1962): 15.

Stockholm, G. "Who Ever Heard of a Modest and Likeable Tenor?" Biography News (January 1975): 196.

"Tenor in Whiteface." Time (August 13 1965): 54.

Concert Reviews

Brown, P. "Detached Mourning." Music and Musicians (July 1965): 45.

Chapman, E. "'Pelleas' at Covent Garden." Musical Events [London] (January 1970): 11.

Chiusano, M. "Carnegie Hall." Music and Artists, Vol. 1, No. 1 (1968): 42.

"Don Giovanni." Opera (September 1967): 769.

"Don Giovanni Revived." Musical Events (August 1967): 32.

Greenfield, E. "London Report: Festival in the Ancient City." High Fidelity (October 1966): MA26-27.

Mason, E. "Cool Thinker." Music and Musicians (June 1967): 34-35.

Montagu, G. "Glyndebourne Festival." Musical Opinion (August 1966): 653.

[New York Recital] Musical America (December 1964): 194.

Rosenthal, H. "To Scotland for Operatic Tonic." Opera (July 1967): 594-595.

Syer, W. B. "'Magic Flute', Almost All-American." High
Fidelity (November 1966): MA15.

Ueber, R. "Don Giovanni." Musical America (January 1964):
37.

Ward, H. "Opera/Concert Talk." Music Journal (October
1965): 16.

MARGARET SIMMS

"Two Coloured Prima Donnas." (Trans. from Vore Damer, 1925)
Record Research, No. 65 (1965): 5.

MURIEL SMITH (1923-1985)

Southern, Eileen. Biographical Dictionary of Afro-American
and African Musicians. Westport, CT: Greenwood Press, 1982,
pp. 347-348.

Articles

"Covent Garden." Opera [London] (February 1957): 123.

"Covent Garden Opera." Musical Opinion (February 1957): 266.

Drew, D. "London." Musical Courier (February 1957): 38.

Montagu, G. "Recitals." London Music Events (August 1955):
37.

"Muriel Smith." London Music Events (November 1955): 25.

"Muriel Smith." London Music Events (June 1957): 47.

"Muriel Smith." Musical Opinion (August 1955): 649.

"Muriel Smith." Musical Opinion (May 1957): 457.

"Muriel Smith Sings in England." Musical America (November
15 1956): 11.

"Muriel Smith to Sing at Covent Garden." Musical America
(October 1956): 14.

Obituaries

The Black Perspective in Music, Vol. 13, No. 2 (Fall 1985):
241.

New York Times (September 16 1985): B-18.

RAWN SPEARMAN (1924-   )

Southern, Eileen. Biographical Dictionary of Afro-American and African Musicians. Westport, CT: Greenwood Press, 1982, pp. 355-356.

Spearman, Rawn W. "A Study of Selected Musical Settings for Solo Voice and Piano of the Poetry of Langston Hughes." Dissertation (Ph.D.) Columbia University, 1973.

Articles

"JUGG Award Won by Rawn Spearman." Musical America (April 1 1952): 23.

New York Age-Defender (February 27 1954).

New York Amsterdam News (December 1 1951).

New York Times (October 20 1952).

New York Times (July 26 1954).

"Rawn Spearman." Musical America (June 1951): 18+.

"Rawn Spearman." Musical America (November 1 1952): 22.

"Rawn Spearman." Musical Courier (June 1951): 27-28.

"Rawn Spearman." Musical Courier (November 1 1951): 13.

Silver, E. A. "Porgy and Bess." Musical America (May 1962): 25.

Spearman, Rawn W. "Music and Black Culture." Musart, Vol. 22, No. 1 (1969): 30-31+.

KENNETH SPENCER (1913-1964)

Southern, Eileen. Biographical Dictionary of Afro-American and African Musicians. Westport, CT: Greenwood Press, 1982, p. 356.

Articles

Chicago Defender (January 17 1942).

Chicago Defender (December 5 1944).

Guild, H. "Kenneth Spencer on Concert Life in Alien Lands." Variety (May 14 1958): 57+.

Obituaries

New York Amsterdam News (February 29 1964).

Variety (March 4 1964): 79.

FLORENCE COLE TALBERT (1890-1961)

Beasley, Delilah L.   The Negro Trailblazers of California.
Los Angeles: The Author, 1919.   (See chapter 17)

Hare, Maud Cuney.   Negro Musicians and Their Music.
Washington, D.C.: Associated Publishers, 1936, pp. 368-369.

Lovingood, Penman.   Famous Modern Negro Musicians.   2nd ed.
New York: Da Capo Press, 1978.   (Reprint of 1921 ed.)

Southern, Eileen.   Biographical Dictionary of Afro-American
and African Musicians.   Westport, CT: Greenwood Press, 1982,
pp. 367-368.

Articles

New York Age (July 24 1920).

New York Age (October 29 1927).

New York Age (March 8 1930).

New York Age (November 24 1934).

New York Age (January 15 1936).

New York Amsterdam News (November 2 1927).

Turner, Patricia.   "In Retrospect: Florence Cole Talbert:
"Our Divine Florence."   The Black Perspective in Music
(Spring 1984): 57-79.

FRED THOMAS

Eaton, Q.   "Finals Held in Metropolitan Opera Auditions of
the Air."   Musical America (April 1 1951): 13, 16.

"Fred Thomas."   Music News (April 1952): 12.

"Fred Thomas."   Musical America (March 1952): 18.

"Fred Thomas."   Musical America (December 15 1958): 30.

"Fred Thomas."   Musical Courier (February 1959): 17.

Newspaper Articles

Briggs, John.   "Program is Sung by Fred Thomas."   New York
Times (November 25 1958): 36.

"Fred Thomas at Town Hall."   New York Herald Tribune(?)
(November 28 1958).

"Fred Thomas, Baritone."   New York Times (March 19 1951).

"Fred Thomas Heard in 2d Song Recital."   New York Times
(February 18 1952).

"Fred Thomas Sings." New York Times (October 30 1961).

New York Herald Tribune (October 30 1961).

ARTHUR THOMPSON (1942-   )

Southern, Eileen. Biographical Dictionary of Afro-American and African Musicians. Westport, CT: Greenwood Press, 1982, p. 373.

Articles

Ericson, Raymond. "Thompson Sings in Recital Hall. Young Baritone's Debut Has a Well-Chosen Program." New York Times (October 31 1967).

Metropolitan Opera Stagebill (September 1974).

"New Voices of the Eighties: An Emphasis on Excellence Will Allow Gifted Young Singers to Express Themselves as Individuals." Ebony (March 1983): 58+.

VERONICA TYLER (c.1937-   )

Southern, Eileen. Biographical Dictionary of Afro-American and African Musicians. Westport, CT: Greenwood Press, 1982, p. 380.

Articles

Baltimore Afro-American (September 16 1978).

Carpenter, L. "Yankee Winners of Tchaikovsky Flag Draw a Who's Who at White House Gala." Variety (September 14 1966): 78.

"Collegiate Chorale." Musical America (February 1964): 32.

"Concert Reviews." Variety (January 1 1975): 34+.

Fleming, S. "The New York City Opera." High Fidelity (December 1967): MA9.

Frymire, J. "New York City Opera." Music and Artists, Vol. 1, No. 5 (1968): 29.

"March's Guest Artist." San Francisco Symphony Program Notes (March 1967): 11.

"Marriage of Figaro." Musical America (November 1964): 28.

"Names, Dates and Places." Opera News (September 20 1969): 5.

New York Amsterdam News (October 3 1964).

"New York, N.Y." Music and Artists, Vol. 2, No. 2 (1969): 30.

"Notes on the Program." Philadelphia Orchestra Program Notes (November 3 1967): 18.

Osborne, C. L. "City Opera's "Traviata", "Magic Flute", "Tosca"." High Fidelity (January 1967): MA7-8.

"Porgy and Bess." Musical America (July 1964): 40.

Rich, Alan. "Philharmonic Gives Young People's Concert." Musical America (May 1961): 40.

"Veronica Tyler; Twenty Two Year Old Lyric Soprano to be Guest on N.Y. Philharmonic's Young People's Concert, Sunday, March 19, 1961 on CBS-TV with Leonard Bernstein Conducting and Narrating." Jet (March 23 1961): 66.

"Veronica Tyler, Young Soprano Appears at Monastery Benefit." Biography News (January 1974): 104.

MARGARET TYNES (1929-   )

Southern, Eileen. Biographical Dictionary of Afro-American and African Musicians. Westport, CT: Greenwood Press, 1982, p. 380.

Articles

Ardoin, J. "Spoleto 1961." Musical America (August 1961): 7.

"'Dark Pilgrimage': BBC TV." Opera (September 1962): 636-637.

Frymire, J. "Baltimore Lyric Theatre." Music and Artists, Vol. 1, No. 1 (1968): 49+.

"Girl with Veins of Fire." Time (July 14 1961): 70.

Hepburn, D. "Margaret Tynes: America's Most Underrated Singer." Sepia (August 1959): 36-40.

Kristof, K. "Budapest Conquest." Opera News (March 31 1962): 32.

Lewis, R. "Margaret Tynes." Musical America (December 1960): 81.

McConnell, H. "Spotlight on Spoleto." Opera News (September 30 1961): 29.

Mackinnon, D. A. "Lady Macbeth of Lausanne." Opera News (December 23 1961): 33.

"The Met." Music Journal (January 1975): 45.

"Names, Dates and Places." Opera News (February 24 1968): 4-5.

"Names, Dates and Places." Opera News (Dec. 29-Jan. 5 1973-74): 8-9.

"Names, Dates and Places." Opera News (December 14 1974):
12-13.

New York Age (June 13 1959).

New York Age (August 1 1959).

"Opera on Television." Musical Opinion (August 1962): 650.

Price, G. "Barcelona." Opera (March 1964): 192.

Sandor, F. "Budapest: Excitement at the Opera." Music
Magazine (May 1962): 35.

Schauensee, Max de. "Baltimore." Opera News (April 6 1968):
29.

Ubriaco, R. "The Canadian East." Opera News (November 20
1965): 25-26.

_____. "Toronto." Opera News (November 19 1966): 27.

Weaver, W. "Spoleto." Opera (Autumn 1961): 47.

SHIRLEY VERRETT (1931-   )

Abdul, Raoul. "Miss Verrett as Lady Macbeth." In Blacks in
Classical Music. New York: Dodd, Mead & Co., 1977, pp.
111-113.

Blyth, Alan. "Verrett, Shirley." In The New Grove
Dictionary of Music and Musicians, Vol. 19, p. 678.

_____. "Verrett, Shirley." In The New Grove Dictionary
of American Music, Vol. 4, pp. 457-458.

Ewen, David, ed. Musicians Since 1900: Performers in Concert
and Opera. New York: H.W. Wilson, 1978, pp. 918-922.

Gross, Marthe. "Shirley Verrett." In The Possible Dream:
Ten Who Dared. New York: Chilton Book Co., 1970, pp. 193-204.

Hines, Jerome. "Shirley Verrett." In Great Singers and
Great Singing. New York: Doubleday & Co., 1982, pp. 338-347.

Rubin, Stephen E. "A Met Star at Last: Shirley Verrett." In
The New Met in Profile. New York: Macmillan Publishing Co.,
1974, pp. 63-72.

Southern, Eileen. Biographical Dictionary of Afro-American
and African Musicians. Westport, CT: Greenwood Press, 1982,
p. 383-384.

Steane, J. B. The Grand Tradition: Seventy Years of Singing
on Record. New York: Scribners, 1974. Includes a brief
assessment of Verrett's recorded works.

Who's Who in America, 1966-67.

Articles

"Advent of a Superstar." Newsweek (December 24 1973): 54.

Ardoin, J. "Quote...unquote." Musical America (November 1963): 23.

"Awards and Honors." Musical Courier (December 1960): 41.

Carruthers, B. F. "Shirley Verrett: Singing with the Voice that God Has Given Me." Encore (March 19 1979): 28-30+.

Crowder, C. "Brightness and Starkness." Musical American (March 1962): 17.

Daniels, R. "Romantic at Heart; Interview." Opera News (September 21 1968): 13.

Darden, Norman. "New Empress of Grand Opera." Sepia, Vol. 26, No. 1 (January 1977): 11-21.

"Diva! Shirley Verrett Tells John Gruen What Being an Opera Singer is All About." Opera News, Vol. 40 (January 17 1976): 8-11.

"George Shirley (Tenor), Shirley Verrett-Carter (Soprano), Billie L. Daniel (Soprano); Among 6 Winners of Opera Auditions Sponsored by Metropolitan Opera in N.Y.C." Jet (April 20 1961): 62.

Gruen, J. "Diva!" Opera News (January 17 1976): 9-11.

Harrington, S. "On Target: Shirley Verrett." Vogue (June 1971): 98-99.

Harris, D. "Verrett: Past, Present and Future." Music and Musicians, Vol. 21 (July 1973): 28-31.

Krause, J. "Opera Star Values Home Life." Biography News (January 1975): 214.

Kupferberg, H. "Miss Verrett Joins the Ball Game." Atlantic (January 1969): 113-115.

"Metropolitan Opera's New Star." Ebony (December 1968): 54-56+.

Morsell, F. "Shirley Verrett." The Crisis, Vol. 87 (January 1980): 7-14.

"Names, Dates and Places." Opera News (April 5 1969): 4.

"Names, Dates and Places." Opera News (February 28 1970): 4.

"Names, Dates and Places." Opera News (May 15 1971): 4.

"Names, Dates and Places." Opera News (April 15 1972): 4-5.

"Names, Dates and Places." Opera News (January 26 1974):
10-11.

"Names, Dates and Places." Opera News (December 21 1974):
8-9.

"New Go-Go Girl in Town." Time (October 4 1968): 49.

Porter, Stan. "Shirley Verrett: Profile of Greatness."
Encore, Vol. 5 (May 8 1976): 31-32.

Sargeant, Winthrop. "Profiles: Doing Something." New Yorker
(April 14 1975): 42-46+.

"Shirley Verrett." Opera (UK) (July 1973): 585-589.

"Slated for Success--Nine Young Artists." Musical America
(July 1962): 10.

Smith, P. J. "Musician of the Month." High Fidelity
(November 1968): MA5.

"Verrett, Shirley." Current Biography 1967, pp. 437-440.

Verrett, Shirley. "On a Balanced Repetoire." Music Clubs
Magazine, Vol. 45, No. 4 (1966): 23.

_____. "To Thine Own Voice Be True!" Music Journal (June
1969): 20-21+.

Newspaper Articles

Levine, J. A. "Shirley Verrett Makes History in Opera
Roles." Christian Science Monitor (April 14 1976): 22.

National Observer (June 22 1964): 18.

New York Herald Tribune Magazine (November 3 1963): 35.

New York Herald Tribune (April 14 1966): 16.

New York Post (July 7 1964): 27.

Will, G. "Shirley Verrett Gambles on Superstardom." New
York Times Magazine (January 30 1977): 15-16+.

Concert Reviews

Ardoin, J. "New York Philharmonic." Musical America (April
1962): 52.

Brown, P. "Detached Mourning." Music and Musicians (July
1965): 45.

"Carmen." Musical America (September 1964): 36; (November
1964): 24.

"City Center Firsts." Opera News (September 26 1964): 16-17.

Jacobi, P. "Chicago." Music Magazine (February 1962): 27.

_____. "Spoleto Carmen." Music Magazine (June 1962): 20.

Lewis, R. "Milton Thomas; Shirley Verrett-Carter." Musical America (December 1960): 62.

Mason, E. "First in the Lied." Music and Musicians (July 1965): 36.

"New York Opera and Concert Beat." Musical Courier (December 1960): 34.

[New York Recital] High Fidelity (July 1966): MA21.

"Philadelphia Orchestra." Musical Courier (March 1960): 18.

"Shirley Verrett-Carter." Musical America (December 1 1958): 28.

"Shirley Verrett in the Soviet Union." USSR Illustrated Monthly (February 1964): 36.

Walsh, S. "Kertesz at the Garden." Music and Musicians (July 1966): 39-40.

Weaver, W. "Spoleto." Opera (Autumn 1962): 67.

Wimbush, R. "Shirley Verrett." Gramophone (August 1966): 108-109.

RACHEL WALKER (1873-194?)

Hare, Maud Cuney. Negro Musicians and Their Music. Washington, D.C.: Associated Publishers, 1936, pp. 233-234.

Southern, Eileen. Biographical Dictionary of Afro-American and African Musicians. Westport, CT: Greenwood Press, 1982, pp. 387-388.

Articles

Cleveland Gazette (October 3 1886).

Cleveland Gazette (December 8 1894).

Indianapolis Freeman (February 15 1896).

Indianapolis Freeman (April 17 1897).

Indianapolis Freeman (May 21 1898).

Indianapolis Freeman (March 7 1915).

Indianapolis Freeman (July 22 1916).

WILLIAM WARFIELD (1920-   )

Abdul, Raoul. "Roland Hayes's Children." In Blacks in
Classical Music. New York: Dodd, Mead & Co., 1977, pp. 97-98.

De Lerma, Dominique-Rene. "Warfield, William." In The New
Grove Dictionary of American Music, Vol. 4, p. 477.

Southern, Eileen. Biographical Dictionary of Afro-American
and African Musicians. Westport, CT: Greenwood Press, 1982,
p. 391.

Who's Who in Colored America, 1950.

Articles

Biographical Note. Musical America (July 1953): 13.

Chicago Defender (March 13 1976).

Current, G. B. "An Interview with William Warfield." The
Crisis (January 1985): 32-34.

"Ex-Legiter, N.Y. Negro Concert Find." Variety (May 24
1950): 70.

Fellowes, M. "Building Programs--and Singing Them." Etude
(February 1955): 13+.

"Inimitable Warfields: Loaded with Talent and Blessed with
Some of the Best Breaks, They Make the World Their Oyster."
Our World (April 1955): 31-37.

Kittleson, B. "A Musicians Musician." Billboard (July 13
1963): 16.

Landry, R. J. "Tote That Ballad, Wear Those Tails; William
Warfield Penetrates Darkest Africa for State Dept." Variety
(January 16 1957): 2+.

"Names, Dates and Places." Opera News (March 21 1970): 4.

"Porgy Marries Bess." (W. Warfield and L. Price) Our World
(December 1952): 41-44.

"Rochester Proclaims 'William Warfield Day.'" Musical
Courier (January 15 1952): 18.

"Spotlight." Music and Artists, Vol. 3, No. 2 (1970): 37.

"Spotlight." Music Journal (September 1976): 42.

"'Unirked' Wm. Warfield." Variety (November 14 1956): 76.

Vernon, P. "German Lingo Ban Irks Negro Singer on Israeli
Tour." Variety (October 31 1956): 2+.

Waldrop, G. W. "The Story Behind the Warfield Debut."
Musical Courier (April 1 1954): 23.

_____. "Warfield's Voice is His Visa." _Musical Courier_ (March 15 1957): 2.

"Warfield Comes Home." _Our World_ (June 1952): 52-55.

"Warfield Dropped from Porgy and Bess." _Musical America_ (May 1953): 27.

"Warfield's Career Starts Sensationally." _Musical Leader_ (May 1950): 7.

"William Warfield." _New York Philharmonic Program Notes_ (June 17 1971): 21.

"William Warfield." _Philadelphia Orchestra Program Notes_ (April 17 1954): 696.

"William Warfield." _Variety_ (June 22 1949): 49.

"William Warfield 1st U.S. Negro to Get Bid from La Scala Opera." _Variety_ (July 18 1951): 55.

"William Warfield Tours Africa." _Musical America_ (November 1 1956): 34.

Concert Reviews

"Beethoven in the Bush." _Time_ (July 28 1958): 54.

Blanks, F. R. "Sydney." _The Canon_ (August 1958): 436.

Briggs, E. "Warfield Recital." _The Canon_ (August 1958): 430.

"Copland Conducts Little Orchestra." _Musical America_ (January 15 1959): 16.

"Great New Voice." _Newsweek_ (April 3 1950): 72.

Kammerer, R. "William Warfield." _Musical America_ (December 1 1957): 9-10.

Kolodin, Irving. "Unusual Baritone, Toscanini's Falstaff, etc." _Saturday Review_ (April 1 1950): 30.

_____. "William Warfield's Scarlatti: Motetto da Requiem." _Saturday Review_ (January 24 1953): 30.

Lisac, D. "Foreign Artists Heard During Yugoslavia Season." _Musical America_ (December 15 1956): 12.

[New York Recital]. _High Fidelity_ (June 1970): 24.

"Philadelphia Orchestra." _Musical Courier_ (May 15 1954): 11.

Shayson, R. L. "Two Bravos and One Raspberry." _Saturday Review_ (August 11 1951): 32.

"'Showboat' Star Just Keeps Rollin' Along as Singer, Teacher." _Christian Science Monitor_ (November 15 1984): 1.

"Tours Africa." Musical America (November 1 1956): 34.

"Town Hall Concert." Musical America (February 15 1955): 233.

"Town Hall Recital." Musical America (November 15 1957): 34-35.

Wagner, W. "Goosens and Guest Leaders Bring New Works to Sydney." Musical America (November 15 1950): 35-36.

"W. Warfield." Musical America (November 15 1957): 34-35.

"Warfield Sings Brahms Songs with Philadelphia Orchestra." Musical America (May 1954): 36-37.

"William Warfield." The Canon (August 1950): 27-28; (September 1950): 88.

"William Warfield." Musical America (April 1950): 18.

"William Warfield." Musical America (February 1951): 244.

"William Warfield." Musical America (February 15 1955): 233.

"William Warfield." Musical Courier (April 1 1950): 21.

"William Warfield." Musical Courier (February 15 1951): 57.

"William Warfield." Musical Courier (March 1955): 21-22.

LAURENCE WATSON

"Laurence Watson." Musical America (February 1958): 217.

"Recital is Offered by Watson, Tenor." New York Times (January 26 1958).

"Tenor Sings at Recital Hall." New York Herald Tribune (January 27 1958).

"Town Hall Debut." Musical America (April 1956): 25-26.

FELICIA WEATHERS (1937-   )

Southern, Eileen. Biographical Dictionary of Afro-American and African Musicians. Westport, CT: Greenwood Press, 1982, p. 394.

Articles

Barnes, Clive. "Boris in Caledonia." Music and Musicians (July 1965): 32.

Bims, H. "Felicia Weathers: Dauntless Diva." Ebony (May 1970): 52-56+.

Dettmer, R. "Resumption in Chicago." Opera (December 1968): 966-967.

Eaton, Q. "Winner." Opera News (June 10 1967): 13.

"Felicia Weathers as Producer." Opera (UK), Vol. 31 (April 1980): 339.

Grier, C. "Sore Throat Defeats Aida." Music and Musicians (September 1970): 50.

"Hartford." Opera (U.K.) (March 1970): 219.

"Hartford." Opera News (January 31 1970): 32-33.

Holmes, A. "Houston." Opera News (January 25 1969): 34.

Humphreys, H. S. "Cincinnati: Zoo Opera Going Strong." High Fidelity (October 1970): 22-23.

Jacobson, B. "Lyric Opera-A Happy Return." High Fidelity (January 1969): 20-21.

Koegler, Horst. "Cologne." Opera (November 1965): 826.

Kolodin, Irving. "Music to My Ears." Saturday Review (November 6 1965): 47.

McCredie, A. D. "Hanover." Opera (June 1964): 406.

"Names, Dates and Places." Opera News (November 22 1969): 4.

"Names, Dates and Places." Opera News (September 19 1970): 5.

Osborne, C. "London Opera Diary." Opera (U.K.) (September 1970): 885.

Porter, A. "Glasgow." Musical Times (July 1965): 530.

"Rome." Opera (UK) (September 1977): 892-895.

"Scottish Opera." Opera (July 1965): 538.

Stedman, J., and G. McElroy. "Chicago." Opera News (December 13 1969): 24.

Welsh, C. N. "Graz." Opera (Autumn 1964): 49.

ALAN WENTT - Panama

Frankenstein, A. "San Francisco Report." High Fidelity (January 1968): MA19.

Klein, Howard. "Allan Wentt Gives Debut Recital." New York Times (October 11 1962).

New York Herald Tribune (October 12 1962).

PORTIA WHITE (1917-1968) - Canada

Negro Year Book, 1947.

Southern, Eileen. Biographical Dictionary of Afro-American and African Musicians. Westport, CT: Greenwood Press, 1982, p. 400.

Articles

New York Amsterdam News (March 18 1944).

New York Amsterdam News (March 28 1944).

New York Post Magazine (October 22 1944): 29.

Peck, Seymour. "PM Visits: Singer with a Future." PM [New York] (October 27 1944): 20.

"Portia White, Contralto." Musical America, Vol. 64 (November 25 1944): 12. Concert review.

"White, Portia." Current Biography 1945, pp. 670-671.

CAMILLA WILLIAMS (1922-   )

Cherry, Gwendolyn, et al. "Camilla Williams: Ambassador of Song." In Portraits in Color: The Lives of Colorful Negro Women. New York: Pageant Press, 1962, pp. 79-81.

Jahant, Charles. "Williams, Camilla." In The New Grove Dictionary of American Music, Vol. 4, p. 527.

Southern, Eileen. Biographical Dictionary of Afro-American and African Musicians. Westport, CT: Greenwood Press, 1982, p. 403.

Who is Who in Music, 1951.

Who's Who in Colored America, 1950.

Who's Who in the East, 1951.

Articles

Asklund, G. "Preparing for an Operatic Career." Etude, Vol. 77, No. 2 (February 1954): 15+. Interview.

Bradley, B. "Camilla Williams: Bright Star in Opera's Heaven." Sepia (December 1961): 35-38.

Chicago Defender (August 19 1944).

Editorial. London Musical Events (March 1955): 9.

"Gallery of Concert Artists." Music Journal Annual 1963, p. 112.

New York Amsterdam News (January 20 1962).

New York Herald Tribune (May 15 1946): 19.

New York Post Magazine (October 3 1946): 37.

"U.S. Soprano First Negro to Sing at Vienna Opera." Variety (April 20 1955): 68.

"Williams, Camilla." Current Biography 1952, pp. 632-634.

Williams, Camilla. "Music is Universal." Music Journal (April-May 1960): 28+.

Concert Reviews

"Camilla Williams." London Musical Events (July 1955): 23+.

"Camilla Williams." Music News (February 1952): 13.

"Camilla Williams." Musical Courier (January 15 1952): 16.

"Camilla Williams." Musical Courier (February 1 1952): 23.

"Camilla Williams." Musical Courier (March 1958): 18-19.

"Camilla Williams." Musical Opinion (November 1954): 72.

Campbell, A. "San Francisco." Musical Courier (March 15 1956): 25.

"Debut in the Title Role of Puccini's Madame Butterfly." Opportunity: Journal of Negro Life (January 1947): 42-43.

Ghandi, K. H. "Camilla Williams Sings in Africa." Musical America (March 1959): 38.

Johnen, L. J. "Cincinnati." Musical Courier (February 1956): 88.

Kammerer, R. "Harriman State Park, N.Y." Musical America (September 1960): 10.

Kolodin, Irving. "Camilla Williams." Saturday Review (January 26 1952): 26.

_____. "Modl as Isolde, Copland as Conductor." Saturday Review (February 15 1958): 31.

"Mozart-Mahler List by Philadelphia Orchestra." Musical Courier (December 1960): 17.

"New Butterfly." Newsweek (May 27 1946): 86.

"New Butterfly." Time, Vol. 48 (September 30 1946): 68.

Siegel, L. "Filipino 'Butterfly'." Musical America (April 1962): 31.

Singer, S. L. "Philadelphia." Musical Courier (December 1960): 25.

Stevens, D. "'Traviata', 'Butterfly' at Bear Mountain." Musical Courier (September 1961): 27.

"Sydney." The Canon (May 1962): 23.

Watt, Douglas. "Musical Events." New Yorker (January 19 1952): 68

HARRY WILLIAMS (1850s-1930s/1940s)

Hare, Maud Cuney. Negro Musicians and Their Music. Washington, D.C.: Associated Publishers, 1936, p. 205.

Southern, Eileen. Biographical Dictionary of Afro-American and African Musicians. Westport, CT: Greenwood Press, 1982, pp. 404-405.

Articles

Chicago Defender (February 22 1913).

Chicago Defender (December 22 1917).

Chicago Defender (September 17 1927).

Cleveland Gazette (January 29 1887).

Cleveland Gazette (September 11 1888).

Cleveland Gazette (March 22 1890).

Cleveland Gazette (April 4 1904).

New York Age (June 18 1938).

LAWRENCE WINTERS (1915-1965)

Southern, Eileen. Biographical Dictionary of Afro-American and African Musicians. Westport, CT: Greenwood Press, 1982, p. 411.

Articles

"Black and White Aida." Time (November 8 1948): 82-83.

"Ex-Legiter First Negro in 'Rigoletto'; Goes in with Nine Hours Notice." Variety (October 17 1951): 50.

"Larry Winters: Is He Booked for the Met?" Our World, Vol. 7 (March 1952): 18-21.

Moor, P. "Our Operatic Expatriates." High Fidelity (November 1960): 52.

Musical America (August 1950): 35.

Musical America (April 15 1952): 15. Biographical portrait.

Musical America (May 1952): 15.

New York Age (July 26 1941).

New York Age (January 22 1944).

New York Age (November 14 1959).

Sandberg, I. "Winters Conquers Audiences in Stockholm Opera Debut." Musical America (January 1 1956): 15.

"US Negro Baritone Gets Three German Opera Bids." Variety (August 1 1951): 50.

"Winters Returns from Hamburg Opera." Musical America (January 15 1957): 29.

"Winter's Tale." Newsweek (October 22 1951): 88-89.

Obituaries

New York Herald Tribune (September 28 1965).

Opera (December 1965): 907.

Opera News (February 19 1966): 33.

Variety (September 29 1965): 62.

SIDNEY WOODWARD (1860-1924)

Hare, Maud Cuney. Negro Musicians and Their Music. Washington, D.C.: Associated Publishers, 1936, pp. 231-232.

Southern, Eileen. Biographical Dictionary of Afro-American and African Musicians. Westport, CT: Greenwood Press, 1982, p. 413.

Articles

Cleveland Gazette (October 21 1893).

New York Age (September 28 1916).

New York Age (December 10 1921).

New York Age (February 23 1924).

OPERA COMPANIES

Abdul, Raoul. "Black Opera Companies." In Blacks in Classical Music. New York: Dodd, Mead & Co., 1977, pp. 143-154.

Bronson, A. "Interracial Opera Co., First of Kind, Pays Off in 'Salome' South Tours." Variety (February 16 1955): 1.

Gelb, A. "Outgrowth of 'Porgy': Negro Musical Company Being Planned by Two Sponsors of Current Opera." New York Times (September 6 1953): Sec. 2, p. 1+. R. Breen and B. Davis plan negro repertory Co. (See also response New York Times (September 20 1953): Sec. 2, p.3.)

THE AEOLIAN OPERA ASSOCIATION (New York City/1934)

Afro-American (July 21 1934).

Forbes, Mathew. "Jules Bledsoe, Abbie Mitchell Banish White Superiority Myth." Negro World (July 14 1934): 1.

Sanborn, Pitts. "Negro Cast Sings Opera in Fine Style. Aeolian Troupe Gives Two Illuminating Performances." [New York] World-Telegraph (July 11 1934).

[See also clippings file in the Music Division at the Performing Arts Research Center at Lincoln Center.]

AMERICAN NEGRO OPERA COMPANY (New York City)

Company members, portrait. New York Times (September 10 1944): Sec. 2, p. 4.

Short note on ANOC plans. New York Times (August 7 1944): 9.

COLORED OPERA COMPANY (Washington, D.C./1872-1873)

Hare, Maud Cuney. Negro Musicians and Their Music. Washington, D.C.: Associated Publishers, 1936, pp. 208-209.

Trotter, James M. Music and Some Highly Musical People. Chicago: Afro-Am Press, 1969, pp. 241-252. (Orig. 1878)

Articles

Daily National Republican [Washington, DC] (February ? 1873).

Daily Washington Chronicle [Washington, DC] (February 18 1873).

Philadelphia Evening Bulletin (February 21 1873).

Philadelphia Inquirer (February ? 1873).

DETROIT NEGRO OPERA (Detroit, MI)

Hynson, Mrs. Millie, comp. Scrapbook [record of activities for the Detroit Negro Opera, 1938-1940]. n.p., 1940?. 55pp. [Held by the Detroit Public Library, E. Azalia Hackley Collection]

DRA MU OPERA COMPANY (Philadelphia, PA)

Chicago Defender (September 9 1950).

Southern, Eileen. "Smith, Raymond Lowden." In Biographical Dictionary of Afro-American and African Musicians. Westport, CT: Greenwood Press, 1982, p. 349.

Who's Who in Colored America, 1950.

DRURY OPERA COMPANY (New York City/1900-1930s)

Hare, Maud Cuney. Negro Musicians and Their Music. Washington, D.C.: Associated Publishers, 1936, p. 226.

McGinty, Doris E. "Drury, Theodore." In Dictionary of American Negro Biography, eds. Rayford W. Logan and Michael R. Winston. New York: W. W. Norton, 1982, pp. 192-193.

Southern, Eileen. "Drury, Theodore." In Biographical Dictionary of Afro-American and African Musicians. Westport, CT: Greenwood Press, 1982, p. 115.

Who's Who of the Colored Race, ed. Frank Lincoln Mather. Chicago: n.p., 1915.

Articles

Carter, Robert W.   "The Drury Opera Company in Verdi's 'Aida.'" The Negro Music Journal, Vol. 1, No. 13 (September 1903): 1-4. (Reprinted from the Colored American Magazine.)

Drury, Theodore. "The Negro in Classic Music; or Leading Opera, Oratorio, and Concert Singers." The Colored American (September 5 1902): 324-335.

_____. "The Science of Vocal Culture." The Colored American (January 8 1901): 216-218.

"Tenor and Impresario Drury." Musical Courier, Vol. 44 (April 30 1902): 35.

Newspaper Articles

Chicago Defender (March 30 1918).

Chicago Defender (October 13 1928).

Indianapolis Freeman (October 12 1889).

Indianapolis Freeman (January 11 1890).

Indianapolis Freeman (November 13 1897).

Indianapolis Freeman (May 24 1902).

Indianapolis Freeman (June 4 1904).

New York Age (October 5 1889).

New York Age (January 4 1900).

New York Age (April 6 1905).

New York Age (May 21 1908).

New York Age (May 7 1938).

New York Times (May 29 1906).

Philadelphia Tribune (May 18 1912).

Philadelphia Tribune (June 8 1912).

HARLEM OPERA COMPANY (New York, NY/1950s-)

Southern, Eileen. Biographical Dictionary of Afro-American and African Musicians. Westport, CT: Greenwood Press, 1982, p. 167.

Articles

"Harlem Opera: Al Fresco, but Not in Italian." New York Times (August 11 1977).

Horowitz, Joseph. "Music: 'Solomon and Sheba' by Harlem
Opera Unit." New York Times (May 29 1977).

Shepard, Richard F. "Opera Unit Plans a Birthday Party."
New York Times (February 29 1964).

INDEPENDENT BLACK OPERA SINGERS

Holland, Bernard. "Opera: 10 Black Male Singers." New York
Times (June 8 1982).

Rothstein, Edward. "News of Music: Black Male Singers." New
York Times (March 12 1981): Sec. 3, p. 22.

KARAMU THEATRE - OPERA WING (Cleveland, OH/1949-1967)

Kraus, L. "Karamu: Cleveland Settlement House Promotes All
Opera." Opera News (February 3 1962): 14-15.

Selby, John. Beyond Civil Rights. Cleveland: World
Publishing Co., 1966. History of Karamu House.

NATIONAL NEGRO OPERA COMPANY (Pittsburgh, PA/1941-1962)

Fry, Phyllis. Mary Cardwell Dawson. Washington, D.C.,
1972. Typescript. 10pp. [See Mary Cardwell Dawson
clippings file in the Music Research Division of the
Performing Arts Research Center at Lincoln Center.]

Southern, Eileen. "Dawson, Mary Cardwell." In Biographical
Dictionary of Afro-American and African Musicians. Westport,
CT: Greenwood Press, 1982, p. 98. Biographical sketch of the
NNOC's founder and director.

[See also clippings files for the National Negro Opera
Company and Lillian Evanti in the Music Research Division of
the Performing Arts Research Center at Lincoln Center.]

Articles

Chicago Defender (September 6 1941).

Chicago Defender (October 25 1941).

"Drive to Raise $150,000 for Negro Opera Begins." New York
Herald Tribune (December 11 1944).

Eversman, Alice. "National Negro Opera Company Acclaimed at
Water Gate." Washington Star (August 29 1943).

G. D. G. "National Negro Opera Enchants 12,000 Here."
(Washington, D.C.) Times Herald (August 29 1943?).

Hartzell, Wesley. "City to Hear First Grand Opera by
Negroes; Notable Cast to Present 'Aida' Next Weekend."
Chicago Sunday Herald-American (October 4 1942).

"Negro Opera Company Launched." Musician (November 1941): 176.

"'The Ordering of Moses' Is Sung in Carnegie Hall." New York Herald Tribune (June 16 1951).

"Tea, Music, Dance Commemorate Mary Cardwell Dawson." Staff News/The New York Public Library, Vol. 62, No. 6 (February 8 1973): 29.

Thomson, Virgil. New York Times (March 30 1944): 19. Review of NNOC concert. [Reprinted in Thomson's The Musical Scene, New York, 1945.]

Obituaries

Chicago Defender (March 24 1962).

Music Magazine, Vol. 164 (May 1962): 64.

New York Herald Tribune (March 21 1962).

New York Times (April 21 1962).

Opera News, Vol. 26 (May 5 1962): 31.

Variety (March 28 1962).

OPERA EBONY (Philadelphia, PA/1974-   )

Abdul, Raoul. "Opera Ebony Makes Its Bow." In Blacks in Classical Music. New York: Dodd, Mead & Co., 1977, pp. 155-156.

Southern, Eileen. Biographical Dictionary of Afro-American and African Musicians. Westport, CT: Greenwood Press, 1982, p. 295.

Articles

Gover, R. M. "Opera Ebony's Artistic Landmarks: Their Contribution to History." Opera Quarterly, Vol. 22 (1984): 57-68.

Upstage; news of Opera Ebony, Philadelphia. Cornwell Heights, PA: Opera Ebony, Philadelphia, 1978- .

Williams, H. R. "National Opera Ebony is Alive and Doing Well." The Crisis (April 1983): 25.

Concert Reviews

"Black Opera in Italy." New York Times (April 16 1981): C21.

Davis, Peter G. "Opera Ebony in Debut Work." New York Times (December 5 1977): 50.

Ericson, Raymond. "Double Bill Presented by Opera Ebony."
New York Times (January 28 1979).

_____. "Opera Ebony Troupe Visits Harlem for the First
Time." New York Times (November 14 1980).

"Four Saints in Three Acts." New York Times (April 16 1981):
Sec. 3, p. 21.

Holland, Bernard. "Opera Ebony: Black History." New York
Times (February 15 1983): Sec. 3, p. 11.

Horowitz, Joseph. "Opera: Ebony Company in 'Mariage of
Figaro.'" New York Times (November 17 1980): Sec. 3, p. 20.

Page, Tim. "Frederick Douglass." New York Times (June 30
1985): 46. Review of new opera by Dorothy Rudd Moore.

_____. "Music: Opera Ebony, 2 New Works." New York Times
(February 25 1985): Sec. 3, p. 12. Review of "Journeyin' on
the Underground Railroad" and "Sojourner".

Rothstein, Edward. "Opera: 'Faust.'" New York Times
(December 1 1983): Sec. 3, p. 27; Correction (December 2
1983): Sec. 2, p. 1.

OPERA/SOUTH (Jackson, Miss./1970-   )

Southern, Eileen. Biographical Dictionary of Afro-American
and African Musicians. Westport, CT: Greenwood Press, 1982,
p. 295.

Articles

Ardoyno, Dolores. "Only Black Professional Opera Company."
Sepia (November 1974): 64-66+.

_____. "Opera/South: Opera Company for Blacks." Opera
News (January 6 1973): 10-13.

_____. "Opera/South: Witness for the Defense." Opera
Journal, Vol. 8, No. 4 (1975): 19-26.

Bailey, Ben E. "Opera/South: A Brief History." The Black
Perspective in Music (Spring 1985): 48-78.

Bims, H. "All-Black Opera Raises its Voice." Ebony
(February 1973): 54-56+.

"Divas in Dixie." Newsweek (December 4 1972): 67-68.

Hains, F. "Opera/South: All-Black and Hopeful." High
Fidelity (May 1973): 23+.

New York Times (April 21 1974): 24. Comment on Opera/South.

Concert Reviews

Durrett, C. W. "Carmen in the Jackson Municipal Auditorium."
Opera News (June 1973): 26-27.

_____. "Opera/South Performance of Donizetti's Elixir of
Love in English." Opera News (January 17 1976): 31.

Eggler, B. "Opera/South Company's Otello." Opera News (July
1974): 26.

_____. "Opera/South's Premiere of Ulysses Kay's
Jubilee." Opera News (January 27 1977): 30.

Hains, F. "Opera/South: Bayou Legend." High Fidelity (March
1975): MA25-26.

_____. "Opera/South: Otello." High Fidelity (August
1974): MA29-30.

"Opera in Mississippi: Opera/South Production of W.G. Still's
A Bayou Legend." Time (November 25 1974): 84.

"Opera/South: Elixir of Love First of Two-Year Bicentennial
Season." High Fidelity (March 1976): MA20.

"Opera/South: Flying Dutchman." High Fidelity (August 1975):
MA22.

"Opera/South: Jubilee; Performance in Jackson." High
Fidelity (April 1977): MA19.

"Ulysses Kay's Juggler of Our Lady and William Grant Still's
Highway 1, U.S.A." Opera News (January 13 1973): 23.

5

Reference Works

NEWSPAPER AND PERIODICAL INDEXES

Essay and General Literature Index (1900-1987)
Handbook of Latin American Studies (1935-1985)
Humanities Index (1973-1986)
Index to Periodical Articles by and About Blacks (1950-1983)
International Index (1907-1965)
Magazine Index (May 1982--September 1987)
Music Index (1949-1980)
National Newspaper Index (Sept. 1983--September 1986)
New York Times Index (1930-1986) [All Opera Entries]
Reader's Guide to Periodical Literature (1890-1986)
Social Sciences and Humanities Index (April 1965-1972)
Social Sciences Index (1973-1986)

BIOGRAPHICAL DICTIONARIES

Baker's Biographical Dictionary of Musicians. 6th ed.
Revised edition by Nicolas Slonimsky. New York: Schirmer
Books, 1984.

Berry, Lemuel. Biographical Dictionary of Black Musicians
and Music Educators. Guthrie, OK: Educational Book
Publishers, 1978.

Biography Index (1946-August 1987).

"Black Classical Musicians: Outstanding Artists of the Black
Classical Tradition." In The Negro Almanac: A Reference Work
on the Afro-American, eds. Harry A. Ploski and James
Williams. 4th ed. New York: John Wiley & Sons, 1983, pp.
1127-1147.

Current Biography (1940-1986).

Dictionary of American Biography. New York: Charles
Scribner's Sons, 1943. 20 vols.; and Supplements 1-7.

Ewen, David. Composers Since 1900. New York: H. W. Wilson, 1978.

_____. Musicians Since 1900: Performers in Concert and Opera. New York: H. W. Wilson, 1978. 974pp.

Handy, D. Antoinette. Black Women in American Bands and Orchestras. Metuchen, NJ: Scarecrow Press, 1981. 319pp.

James, Edward T., and Janet Wilson James, eds. Notable American Women, 1609-1950: A Biographical Dictionary. Cambridge, MA: The Belknap Press, 1971. 3 vols.

Layne, Maude Wanzer. The Negro's Contribution to Music. Philadelphia, PA: Theodore Presser, 1942. 88pp. (Now available from Books on Demand, Ann Arbor, MI). Consists of short biographical sketches of 89 musicians, most of whom are classical.

Logan, Rayford W., and Michael R. Winston, eds. Dictionary of American Negro Biography. New York: W.W. Norton, 1982.

Mapp, Edward. Directory of Blacks in the Performing Arts. Metuchen, NJ: Scarecrow Press, 1978.

Negro Year Book, 1952. New York: Wm. H. Wise & Co., 1952, pp. 52-64. Contains biographical material on more than 70 composers, singers and instrumentalists.

The New Grove Dictionary of American Music. Edited by H. Wiley Hitchcock and Stanley Sadie. London: Macmillan, 1986. 4 vols.

The New Grove Dictionary of Music and Musicians. Edited by Stanley Sadie. London: Macmillan Publishing Co., 1980. 20 vols.

The New York Times Obituaries Index 1858-1968. New York: The New York Times/Arno Press, 1970.

The New York Times Obituaries Index 1969-1978. New York: The New York Times, 1980.

Sicherman, Barbara, and Carol Hurd Green, eds. Notable American Women: The Modern Period. Cambridge, MA: The Belknap Press, 1980.

Southern, Eileen. Biographical Dictionary of Afro-American and African Musicians. Westport, CT: Greenwood Press, 1982.

Who's Who in American Music: Classical. Edited by Jacques Cattell Press. 2nd ed. New York: R. R. Bowker, 1985. [Of the more than 9,000 biographies included in this work less than 100 refer to black musicians. The following is a list of those who are included: Elwyn Adams, Leslie Adams, Adele Addison, Betty Allen, Lettie Beckon Alston, T. J. Anderson, Martina Arroyo, David Baker, Kathleen Battle, Gwendolyn Bradley, William Brown, Grace Bumbry, Roque Cordero, Philip

Creech, Arthur Cunningham, Noel Da Costa, James De Preist,
Mattiwilda Dobbs, Simon Estes, Wilhelmena Wiggens Fernandez,
William S. Fischer, James Furman, Reri Grist, Adolphus
Hailstork, Hilda Harris, Barbara Hendricks, Gail Hightower,
Natalie Hinderas, Esther Hinds, Ann Hobson, Isaiah Jackson,
Raymond Jackson, Isola Jones, Ulysses Kay, Sylvia Olden Lee,
Tania Leon, Henry Lewis, Wendell Logan, Seth McCoy, Marvis
Martin, Leona Mitchell, Carman Moore, Dorothy Rudd Moore,
Kermit Moore, John Price, Leontyne Price, Florence Quivar,
William Ray, Faye Robinson, George Shirley, Hale Smith,
Arthur Thompson, Frederick C. Tillis, Shirley Verrett,
Frances Walker, George T. Walker, William Warfield, Andre
Watts, Olly Wilson. All biographies are followed by current
addresses of the artists.]

Who's Who in Opera: An International Biographical Dictionary
of Singers, Conductors, Directors, Designers, and
Administrators. Also Including Profiles of 101 Opera
Companies. Edited by Maria F. Rich. New York: Arno Press,
1976. 684pp.

BIBLIOGRAPHIES

Block, Adrienne F., and Carol Neuls-Bates. Women in American
Music: A Bibliography of Music and Literature. Westport, CT:
Greenwood Press, 1979.

Davis, Lenwood. The Black Woman in American Society: A
Selected Annotated Bibliography. Boston: G.K. Hall, 1975.

De Lerma, Dominique-Rene. Bibliography of Black Music. Vol.
2: Afro-American Idioms. Westport, CT: Greenwood Press,
1981. ["Concert Music", pp. 80-86.]

Floyd, Samuel A., and Marsha J. Reisser. Black Music in the
United States: An Annotated Bibliography of Selected
Reference and Research Materials. New York: Kraus
International, 1983.

Hixon, Don L., and Don Hennessee. Women in Music: A
Biobibliography. Metuchen, NJ: Scarecrow Press, 1975.

Horn, David. The Literature of American Music in Books and
Folk Music Collections: A Fully Annotated Bibliography.
Metuchen, NJ: Scarecrow Press, 1977.

Jackson, Richard. United States Music: Sources of
Bibliography and Collective Biography. New York: Institute
for Studies in American Music/Brooklyn College, 1973.

Joyce, Donald Franklin. Blacks in the Humanities, 1750-1984:
A Selected Annotated Bibliography. Westport, CT: Greenwood
Press, 1986.

Skowronski, Joann. Black Music in America: A Bibliography.
Metuchen, NJ: Scarecrow Press, 1981.

Southern, Eileen. The Music of Black Americans. New York:
Norton, 1983. 2nd ed. Contains an extensive bibliography.

Spradling, Mary Mace, ed. In Black and White: Afro-Americans
in Print: A Guide to Magazine Articles, Newspaper Articles
and Books Concerning More Than 15,000 Black Individuals and
Groups. 3rd ed. Detroit, MI: Gale Research Co., 1980. 2
vols.

Stevenson, Robert. A Guide to Caribbean Music History.
Lima: Ediciones Cultura, 1975.

Tischler, Alice. Fifteen Black American Composers: A
Bibliography of Their Works. Detroit, MI: Information
Coordinators, 1981.

White, Evelyn D., comp. Choral Music by Afro-American
Composers: A Selected Annotated Bibliography. Metuchen, NJ:
Scarecrow Press, 1981. 167pp.

_____. Selected Bibliography of Published Choral Music by
Black Composers. Washington, D.C.: Howard University
Bookstore, 1975.

Williams, Ora. American Black Women in the Arts and Social
Sciences: A Bibliographic Survey. Revised and Expanded
Edition. Metuchen, NJ: Scarecrow Press, 1978, pp. 108-135.
[Lists compositions and recordings for the following artists:
Adele Addison, Martina Arroyo, Margaret Bonds, Grace Bumbry,
Shirley Graham DuBois, E. Azalia Hackley, Helen Hagan, D.
Antoinette Handy, Margaret Harris, Natalie Hinderas, Lena
McLin, Dorothy Rudd Moore, Undine Smith Moore, Julia Perry,
Elaine Pittman, Florence B. Price, Leontyne Price, Philippa
Schuyler, Shirley Verrett.]

Work, Monroe N. "The Negro and Modern Music." In A
Bibliography of the Negro in Africa and America. New York:
Octagon Books, 1965, pp. 440-442. (Reprint of 1928 ed.)

Dissertations

Brown, Ernest J. "An Annotated Bibliography of Selected Solo
Music Written for the Piano by Black Composers."
Dissertation (D.M.A., Performance) University of Maryland,
1976.

George, Zelma Watson. "A Guide to Negro Music: An Annotated
Bibliography of Negro Folk Music, and Art Music by Negro
Composers or Based on Negro Thematic Material." Ann Arbor:
University Microfilms, 1953. 277pp. [New York University,
Ed.D., 1953]

Phillips, Linda. "Piano Music by Black Composers: A
Computer-Based Bibliography." Dissertation (D.M.A.) Ohio
State University, 1977. 305pp.

Articles

De Lerma, Dominique-Rene. "A Concordance of Black Music
Entries in Five Encyclopedias: Baker's, Ewen, Groves, MGG,
and Rich." Black Music Research Journal (1981-1982).

_____. "A Concordance of Scores and Recordings of Music
by Black Composers." Black Music Research Journal (1984):
60-140.

_____. "A Selective List of Choral Music by Black
Composers." Choral Journal, Vol. 12, No. 8 (April 1972): 5-6.

Garcia, William Burres. "Church Music by Black Composers: A
Bibliography of Choral Music." The Black Perspective in
Music, Vol. 2, No. 2 (Fall 1974): 145-157.

Wyatt, Lucius R. "The Present State and Future Needs of
Research in Black Concert and Recital Music." Black Music
Research Journal (1980): 80-94.

DISSERTATIONS AND THESES

Adkins, Cecil, and Alis Dickinson, eds. Doctoral
Dissertations in Musicology. Philadelphia: American
Musicological Society.

Black Perspective in Music (1973-1986). Yearly listings of
new dissertations and books.

Comprehensive Dissertations Index (1861-1985).

De Lerma, Dominique-Rene. Bibliography of Black Music, Vol.
1: Reference Works. Westport, CT: Greenwood Press, 1981.
["Theses" section.]

Dissertation Abstracts International (1986).

Masters Abstracts (1962-1985).

Meadows, Eddie S. Theses and Dissertations on Black American
Music. Beverly Hills, CA: Theodore Front Musical Literature,
1980.

MUSIC COLLECTIONS

Clark, Edgar Rogie, comp. Negro Art Songs. New York: Edward
B. Marks, 1946.

Dett, R. Nathaniel. The Collected Piano Works.
Introductions by Dominique-Rene de Lerma and Vivian McBrier.
Evanston, IL: Summy-Birchard, 1973. 195pp.

Patterson, Willis, comp. Anthology of Art Songs by Black
American Composers. New York: Edward B. Marks, 1977. 148pp.

Trotter, James M. Music and Some Highly Musical People.
Chicago: Afro-Am Press, 1969. (Reprint of 1878 ed.)
Trotter's Appendix contains an extensive collection of works
by 19th century composers: Basil Bares, William Brady, Walter
F. Craig, Edmund Dede, John T. Douglass, Justin Holland,
Sidney and Lucien Lambert, Frederick Elliot Lewis, Jacob
Sawyer, Samuel Snaer, and Henry F. Williams.

Wright, Josephine. Ignatius Sancho (1729-1780): An Early
African Composer in England. The Collected Editions of His
Music in Facsimile. New York: Garland Publishing Co., 1981.
90pp.

DISCOGRAPHIES

De Lerma, Dominique-Rene. Black Concert and Recital Music: A
Selective Discography. Beverly Hills, CA: Theodore Front
Musical Literature, 1976-1982.

_____. The Collector's Guide to Recordings of Music by
Black Composers. Bloomington, IN: Denia Press, 1973. 28pp.

_____. Concert Music and Spirituals: A Selective
Discography. Nashville, TN: Fisk University Institute for
Research in Black American Music, 1981. 43pp. (Occasional
papers, no. 1)

_____. "A Concordance of Scores and Recordings of Music
by Black Composers." Black Music Research Journal (1984):
60-140.

_____. Discography of Concert Music by Black Composers.
Minneapolis, MN: AAMOA Press, 1973. 29pp. (AAMOA Resource
Papers, no. 1.)

_____. "The Teacher's Guide to Recordings of Music by
Black Composers." College Music Symposium, Vol. 8 (Fall
1973): 114-119.

Turner, Patricia. Afro-American Singers: An Index and
Preliminary Discography of Opera, Choral Music and Song.
Minneapolis, MN: Challenge Productions, 1977.

_____. "Afro-American Singers: An Index and Discography
of Opera, Choral Music, and Song." The Black Perspective in
Music, Vol. 9 (Spring 1981): 73-90. An updated supplement to
the above.

_____. Recordings of Afro-American Performers: Opera,
Choral Music and Song, 78 rpm and Cylinder, 1900-1949. New
York: Garland Publishers, 1986.

Record Reviews

Bean, Calvert. "Retrospective: The Black Composers Series."
Black Music Research Newsletter, Vol. 4 (Spring 1981).

"Desto to Release Boxes of Music by Black Composers."
Billboard (August 22 1970): 63.

Duncan, John.   "Art Music by Negro Composers on Record."
Negro History Bulletin, Vol. 31, No. 4 (April 1968): 6-9.

Gerber, L.   "In Two Desto Albums, Music by a Dozen Black
Composers." American Record Guide (April 1971): 476-479.

Henahan, Donal.   "Conductor Brings to Life Blacks' Symphonic
Works." New York Times (May 8 1974): 39.   Discussion of Paul
Freeman's black composers series on Columbia.

Kresh, Paul.   "Art Songs by Black Americans."   Stereo Review
(October 1982): 130.

Moore, Carman.   "The Black Music Aesthetic--Keep It Coming."
New York Times (May 12 1975): 26.   Review of Paul Freeman's 4
lp set "The Black Composers" consisting of works by the
Chevalier de Saint-Georges, Samuel Coleridge-Taylor, William
Grant Still, George Walker, Ulysses Kay, and Roque Cordero.

Southern, Eileen.   "Reviews of Records: Black Composers
Series." Musical Quarterly, Vol. 61, No. 4 (1975): 645-650.

6
Research Centers/ Dictionary Catalogs

As the Black School Sings: Black Music Collections at Black Universities and Colleges with a Union List of Book Holdings. Westport, CT: Greenwood Press, 1987.

Research Centers Directory. 10th ed. Detroit, MI: Gale Research Co., 1986. Vol. 2.

Smith, Jessie Carney. Black Academic Libraries and Research Collections: An Historical Survey. Westport, CT: Greenwood Press, 1977.

Subject Collections: A Guide to Special Book Collections and Subject Emphases as reported by university, college, public, and special libraries and museums in the United States and Canada. Compiled by Lee Ash. 6th ed. New York: R. R. Bowker, 1985. 2 vols.

EAST COAST

NEW YORK

American Music Center. 250 West 54th Street, Room 300, New York, NY 10019. Tel. 212-247-3121/Library - 212-265-8190.

[Catalog of the American Music Center Library. New York: The Center, 1975- . Vol. 1: Choral and Vocal Works; Vol. 2: Chamber Music; Vol. 3: Music for Orchestra, Band, and Large Ensemble; Vol. 4: Opera and Music Theater Works.]

[The National Endowment for the Arts Composer/Librettist Program Collection at the American Music Center. New York: American Music Center, 1979. 304pp.]

Brooklyn College. Institute for Studies in American Music. Bedford Ave. & Avenue H, Brooklyn, NY 11210. Tel. 718/780-5655. Director, H. Wiley Hitchcock.

[Raymond Ericson. "Collection." New York Times (November 21 1971): Sec. 2, p. 20. On the establishing of a collection of over a 100 works by 19th century black composers Joseph White, Lucien and Sydney Lambert, and Edmund Dede at Brooklyn College's Institute for Studies in American Music.]

New York Public Library, Performing Arts Research Center at Lincoln Center. 111 Amsterdam Avenue, New York, NY 10023. Tel. Music-Research Division: 212/870-1650; Recordings-Research Division: 212/870-1663. [See especially the Supplementary Biographical Index, Black Music drawers (behind the Reference Librarian's desk) and Clippings Files for individual artists found in the Music Research Division.]

[Dictionary Catalog of the Music Collection. 2nd edition. Boston: G.K. Hall, 1982. 45 vols.; Dictionary Catalog of the Music Collection Supplement 1974; annual supplements to this catalogue are continued under the title Bibliographic Guide to Music.]

[Dictionary Catalog of the Rodgers and Hammerstein Archives of Recorded Sound. Boston: G.K. Hall, 1981. 15 vols.]

New York Public Library, Schomburg Center for Research in Black Culture. 515 Lenox Ave. (at 135th Street), New York, NY 10037. Tel. 212/862-4000. (See particularly the "Moving Image and Recorded Sound" collection and Vertical Files.)

[Dictionary Catalog of the Schomburg Collection of Negro Literature and History. Boston: G. K. Hall, 1962. 9 vol.; Supplement 1-2. Boston: G. K. Hall, 1962-1972. 6 vol.; annual supplements to this catalog are continued under the title Bibliographic Guide to Black Studies.]

CONNECTICUT

Yale University, New Haven, CT - James Weldon Johnson Memorial Collection of Negro Arts and Letters.

[Brown, Rae Linda. Music, Printed and Manuscript, in the James Weldon Johnson Memorial Collection of Negro Arts and Letters. New York: Garland Publishers, 1982. 322pp. Annotated catalog of this important collection which contains numerous original compositions by composers Leslie Adams, Margaret Bonds, H. T. Burleigh, Melville Charlton, Samuel Coleridge-Taylor, Noel Da Costa, R. Nathaniel Dett, William Levi Dawson, Hall Johnson, Ulysses Kay, Elaine Pittman, Florence B. Price, Hale Smith, William Grant Still, Howard Swanson, and Clarence Cameron White.]

PENNSYLVANIA

Pennsylvania Historical Society, Leon Gardiner Collection. 1300 Locust Street, Philadelphia, Pennsylvania.

Philadelphia Library Company - 1300 Locust Street, Philadelphia, Pennsylvania.

[Afro-Americana, 1553-1906: Author Catalog of the Library Company of Philadelphia and the Historical Society of Pennsylvania. Boston: G .K. Hall, 1973. 714pp.]

MASSACHUSETTS

Boston Public Library, Boston, MA - Music Division.

[Dictionary Catalog of the Music Collection. Boston: G. K. Hall, 1972. 20 vols.; First Supplement (1977), 4 vols.]

Elma Lewis School of Fine Arts, Inc., Dorchester, MA, National Center of Afro-American Artists.

MARYLAND

Morgan State University, Baltimore, MD - Black Music Archives. Director, Dominique-Rene de Lerma.

["Morgan State Opens Black Music Archives." Jet, Vol. 69 (February 10 1986): 25.]

WASHINGTON, D.C.

Howard University. Moorland-Spingarn Research Center. 500 Howard Place, N.W., Washington, D.C. 20059. Tel. 202/636-7239.

[Dictionary Catalog of the Arthur B. Spingarn Collection of Negro Authors. Boston: G.K. Hall, 1970. (Vol. 2 - "Music Catalogue", pp. 657-784.]

[Dictionary Catalog of the Jesse E. Moorland Collection of Negro Life and History. Boston: G.K. Hall, 1970. 9 vol.; First supplement (1976). 3 vols.]

[The Glenn Carrington Collection: A Guide to the Books, Manuscripts, Music, and Recordings. Compiled by Karen L. Jefferson. Washington, D.C.: Howard University, 1977. 119pp.]

[Guide to Processed Collections in the Manuscript Division of the Moorland-Spingarn Research Center. Compiled by Greta S. Wilson. Washington, D.C.: Moorland-Spingarn Research Center, Howard University, 1983. 73pp.]

Library of Congress, Music Division - Washington, D.C.

[Library of Congress Catalogs, Vol. 27: Music and Phonorecords (1953-1957): A Cumulative List of Works Represented by Library of Congress Printed Cards. Ann Arbor, MI: J. W. Edwards, Inc., 1958; Vol. 51: Music and Phonorecords (1958-1962): Author List; Vol. 52: Music and Phonorecords (1958-1962).]

[National Union Catalog (1963-1967): Music and Phonorecords. 3 vols.; Music and Phonorecords (1968-1972). 5 vols.; Music (1973-1977). 8 vols.; continued by annual Library of Congress Catalogs: Music 1978- .]

MIDWEST

ILLINOIS

Chicago Historical Society, Chicago, Illinois - Claude A. Barnett Collection.

Chicago Public Library, Chicago, Illinois - Carter G. Woodson Regional Library, Vivian G. Harsh Collection of Afro-American History and Literature.

[The Dictionary Catalog of the Vivian G. Harsh Collections of Afro-American History and Literature. Boston: G. K. Hall, 1978. 4 vols.

Chicago Public Library, Chicago, Illinois - Cleveland Hall Collection.

Columbia College - Center for Black Music Research. 600 South Michigan Avenue, Chicago, Illinois 60605. Tel. 312/663-9462. Director, Samuel A. Floyd.

INDIANA

Indiana University. Afro-American Arts Institute. 109 North Jordan Avenue, Bloomington, IN 47405. Tel. 812/335-9501. Director, Dr. Herman Hudson.

MICHIGAN

Detroit Public Library, Detroit, Michigan - E. Azalia Hackley Collection.

[Catalog of the E. Azalia Hackley Memorial Collection of Negro Music, Dance, and Drama, Detroit Public Library. Boston: G. K. Hall, 1979. 510pp.]

[Kinney, Esi Sylvia. "The E. Azalia Hackley Collection." Ethnomusicology, Vol. 5, No. 3 (September 1961): 202-203.]

[Lewis, Ellistine Perkins. "The E. Azalia Hackley Memorial Collection of Negro Music, Dance, and Drama: A Catalogue of Selected Afro-American Materials." Dissertation (Ph.D.) University of Michigan, 1978. 194pp.]

SOUTH

TENNESSEEE

Fisk University. Carl Van Vechten Collection. Nashville, Tennessee.

Fisk University. Institute for Research in Black American Music. 17th Avenue North, P.O. Box 3, Nashville, Tennessee 37203. Tel. 615/329-8630.

[Dictionary Catalog of the Negro Collection of the Fisk
University Library, Nashville, Tennessee.   Boston: G. K.
Hall, 1974.   6 vols.]

[Tucker, Veronica E.   An Annotated Bibliography of the Fisk
University Library's Black Oral History Collection.
Nashville, TN: The Library, 1974.   69pp.]

Index
of Artists

Index
of Authors

About the Compiler

JOHN GRAY is a specialist in black culture and tradition, and has contributed articles to *Cadence* and *Coda*.